THRESHOLDS *in* READING

FIRST CANADIAN EDITION

ESL

TAPESTRY

The **Tapestry** program of language materials is based on the concepts presented in ***The Tapestry of Language Learning:*** *The Individual in the Communicative Classroom* by Robin C. Scarcella & Rebecca L. Oxford.

❖

Each title in this program focuses on:

❖

Individual learner strategies and instruction

❖

The relatedness of skills

❖

Ongoing self-assessment

❖

Authentic material as input

❖

Theme-based learning linked to task-based instruction

❖

Attention to all aspects of communicative competence

TAPESTRY

THRESHOLDS *in* READING

FIRST CANADIAN EDITION

Martha Grace Low
University of Oregon

Aïda A. Cunanan
Dawson College

Francis J. Bonkowski
Télé-Université, Université du Québec

HIGH-INTERMEDIATE READING

ITP Nelson
an International Thomson Publishing company

Toronto • Albany • Bonn • Boston • Cincinnati • Detroit • London • Madrid • Melbourne
Mexico City • New York • Pacific Grove • Paris • San Francisco • Singapore • Tokyo • Washington

I(T)P® **International Thomson Publishing**

The ITP logo is a trademark under licence
www.thomson.com

Published in 1998 by
I(T)P® Nelson
A division of Thomson Canada Limited
1120 Birchmount Road
Scarborough, Ontario M1K 5G4
www.nelson.com

Canadian Cataloguing in Publication Data

Low, Martha Grace
Thresholds in reading

(Tapestry series)
ISBN 0-17-605674-2

1. College readers. 2. English language—Textbooks for second language learners. I. Cunanan, Aïda-Alma, 1948- . II. Bonkowski, Francis J. III. Title. IV. Series

PE1128.L68 1997 428.6'4 C97-931021-0

Publisher and Team Leader	Michael Young
Acquisitions Editors	Andrew Livingston and Nicole Gnutzman
Production Editor	Tracy Bordian
Project Editors	Dianne Horton and Mike Thompson
Production Coordinator	Brad Horning
Art Director	Sylvia Vander Schee
Cover Design	Liz Harasymczuk
Cover Tapestry	"Mysteries: Engaged by Secrets"—detail/Jane Kidd; photographed by John Dean
Lead Composition Analyst	Zenaida Diores

Printed and bound in Canada
1 2 3 4 BBM 01 00 99 98

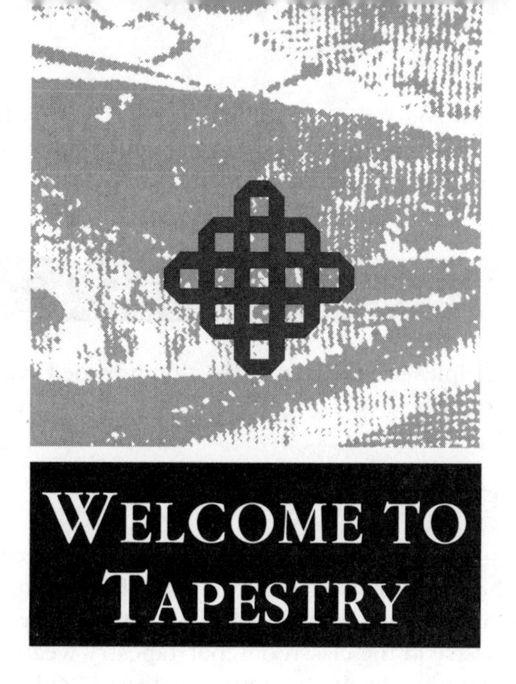

WELCOME TO TAPESTRY

Enter the world of Tapestry! Language learning can be seen as an ever-developing tapestry woven with many threads and colours. The elements of the tapestry are related to different language skills like listening and speaking, reading and writing; the characteristics of the teachers; the desires, needs, and backgrounds of the students; and the general second language development process. When all these elements are working together harmoniously, the result is a colourful, continuously growing tapestry of language competence of which the student and the teacher can be proud.

This volume is part of the Tapestry Program for students of English as a second language (ESL) at levels from beginning to "bridge" (which follows the advanced level and prepares students to enter regular postsecondary programs along with native English speakers). Tapestry levels include:

Beginning
Low Intermediate
High Intermediate
Low Advanced
High Advanced
Bridge

Because the Tapestry Program provides a unified theoretical and pedagogical foundation for all its components, you can optimally use all the Tapestry student books in a coordinated fashion as an entire curriculum of materials. Alternatively, you can decide to use just certain Tapestry volumes, depending on your specific needs.

Tapestry is primarily designed for ESL students at postsecondary institutions in North America. Some want to learn ESL for academic or career-advancement purposes, others for social and personal reasons. Tapestry builds directly on all these motivations. Tapestry stimulates learners to do their best. It enables learners to use English naturally and to develop fluency as well as accuracy.

Tapestry Principles

The following principles underlie the instruction provided in all of the components of the Tapestry Program.

EMPOWERING LEARNERS

Language learners in Tapestry classrooms are active and increasingly responsible for developing their English language skills and related cultural abilities. This self-direction leads to better, more rapid learning. Some cultures virtually train their students to be passive in the classroom, but Tapestry weans them from passivity by providing exceptionally high-interest materials, colourful and motivating activities, personalized self-reflection tasks, peer tutoring and other forms of cooperative learning, and powerful learning strategies to boost self-direction in learning.

The empowerment of learners creates refreshing new roles for teachers, too. The teacher serves as facilitator, co-communicator, diagnostician, guide, and helper. Teachers are free to be more creative at the same time as their students become more autonomous learners.

HELPING STUDENTS IMPROVE THEIR LEARNING STRATEGIES

Learning strategies are the behaviours or steps an individual uses to enhance his or her learning. Examples are taking notes, practising, finding a conversation partner, analyzing words, using background knowledge, and controlling anxiety. Hundreds of such strategies have been identified. Successful language learners use language learning strategies that are most effective for them given their particular learning style, and they put them together smoothly to fit the needs of a given language task. On the other hand, the learning strategies of less successful learners are a desperate grab-bag of ill-matched techniques.

All learners need to know a wide range of learning strategies. All learners need systematic practice in choosing and applying strategies that are relevant for various learning needs. Tapestry is one of the only ESL programs that overtly weaves a comprehensive set of learning strategies into language activities in all its volumes. These learning strategies are arranged in eight broad categories throughout the Tapestry books:

Forming concepts
Personalizing
Remembering new material
Managing your learning

Understanding and using emotions
Overcoming limitations
Testing hypotheses
Learning with others

The most useful strategies are sometimes repeated and flagged with a note, "It works! Learning strategy ..." to remind students to use a learning strategy they have already encountered. This recycling reinforces the value of learning strategies and provides greater practice.

RECOGNIZING AND HANDLING LEARNING STYLES EFFECTIVELY

Learners have different learning styles (for instance: visual, auditory, hands-on; reflective, impulsive; analytic, global; extroverted, introverted; closure-oriented, open). Particularly in an ESL setting, where students come from vastly different cultural backgrounds, learning style differences abound and can cause "style conflicts."

Unlike most language instruction materials, Tapestry provides exciting activities specifically tailored to the needs of students with a large range of learning styles. You can use any Tapestry volume confident that the activities and materials are intentionally geared for many different styles. Insights from the latest educational and psychological research undergird this style-nourishing variety.

OFFERING AUTHENTIC, MEANINGFUL COMMUNICATION

Students need to encounter language that provides authentic, meaningful communication. They must be involved in real-life communication tasks that cause them to *want* and *need* to read, write, speak, and listen to English. Moreover, the tasks—to be most effective—must be arranged around themes relevant to learners.

Themes like family relationships, survival in the educational system, personal health, friendships in a new country, political changes, and protection of the environment are all valuable to ESL learners. Tapestry focuses on topics like these. In every Tapestry volume, you will see specific content drawn from very broad areas such as home life, science and technology, business, humanities, social sciences, global issues, and multiculturalism. All the themes are relevant and important, and they are fashioned into language tasks that students enjoy.

At the advanced level, Tapestry also includes special books, each focused on a single broad theme. For instance, there are two books on business English, two on English for science and technology, and two on academic communication and study skills.

UNDERSTANDING AND VALUING DIFFERENT CULTURES

Many ESL books and programs focus completely on the "new" culture, that is, the culture that the students are entering. The implicit message is that ESL students should just learn about this target culture, and there is no need to understand their own culture better or to find out about the cultures of their international classmates. To some ESL students, this makes them feel their own culture is not valued in the new country.

Tapestry is designed to provide a clear and understandable entry into North American culture. Nevertheless, the Tapestry Program values *all* the cultures found in the ESL classroom. Tapestry students continually have opportunities to become "culturally fluent" in North American culture while they are learning English, but they also have the chance to think about the cultures of their classmates and even understand their home culture from different perspectives.

INTEGRATING THE LANGUAGE SKILLS

Communication in a language is not restricted to one skill or another. ESL students are typically expected to learn (to a greater or lesser degree) all four language skills: reading, writing, speaking, and listening. They are also expected to develop strong grammatical competence, as well as becoming socioculturally sensitive and knowing what to do when they encounter a "language barrier."

Research shows that multi-skill learning is more effective than isolated-skill learning, because related activities in several skills provide reinforcement and refresh the learner's memory. Therefore, Tapestry integrates all the skills. A given Tapestry volume might highlight one skill, such as reading, but all other skills are also included to support and strengthen overall language development.

However, many intensive ESL programs are divided into classes labelled according to one skill (Reading Comprehension Class) or at most two skills (Listening/Speaking Class or Oral Communication Class). The volumes in the Tapestry Program can easily be used to fit this traditional format, because each volume clearly identifies its highlighted or central skill(s).

Grammar is interwoven into all Tapestry volumes. However, a separate reference book for students, *The Tapestry Grammar,* and a Grammar Strand composed of grammar "work-out" books at each of the levels in the Tapestry Program are also available.

AN OVERALL GUIDEBOOK

To offer coherence to the entire Tapestry Program and especially to offer support for teachers who want to understand the principles and practice of Tapestry, we have written a book entitled, *The Tapestry of Language Learning: The Individual in the Communicative Classroom* (Scarcella and Oxford, published in 1992 by Heinle & Heinle).

A Last Word

We are pleased to welcome you to Tapestry! We use the Tapestry principles every day, and we hope these principles—and all the books in the Tapestry Program—provide you the same strength, confidence, and joy that they give us. We look forward to comments from both teachers and students who use any part of the Tapestry Program.

Rebecca L. Oxford
University of Alabama
Tuscaloosa, Alabama

Robin C. Scarcella
University of California at Irvine
Irvine, California

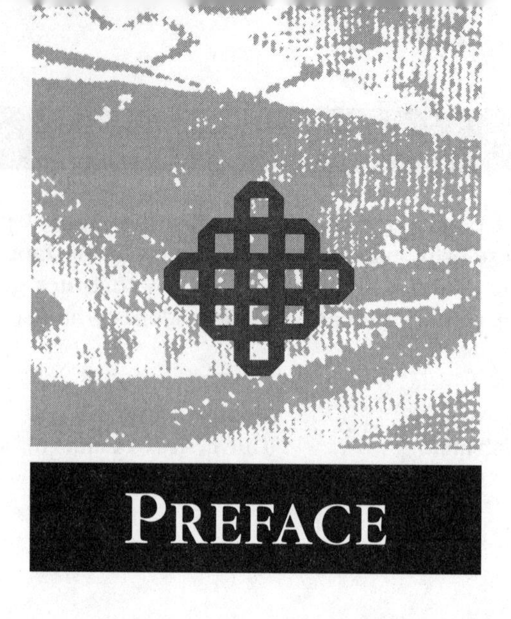

PREFACE

To the Student

A *threshold* is the bottom part of a door frame, the part you step over when you enter a room. We also use the word to describe the beginning of a new experience. This book is entitled *Thresholds* because it may be your first encounter with unsimplified reading in English and with the higher-level academic activities that you will need to do if you enter an English-language college or university.

The focus of the book is reading and vocabulary. The readings are unsimplified and are taken from a variety of sources: books, encyclopedias, newspapers, magazines, and personal journals. The keywords that you will study include some of the most common academic vocabulary in English; these are words that you will encounter again and again in your future reading and that you will want to use in your writing. Whether or not you are planning to use English for higher-level academic study, they are words that every well-educated speaker of English knows and uses, and they will serve you well.

Although you may find the level of some of the readings challenging, don't be discouraged. One purpose of the book is to show you ways, or *strategies,* of approaching unsimplified reading so that you can understand its main ideas. These strategies are keys that can unlock material that you might have thought was unavailable to you.

Finally, each chapter in this book explores several ways of looking at a controversial topic. One of the most important purposes of education is to show students all sides of an issue so they will become well informed. The purpose of these readings is not to lead you in particular directions, but to enable you to reach well-informed opinions.

To the Teacher

Thresholds is a high-intermediate reading text that features unsimplified passages and common academic vocabulary. It serves students training to study at English-language colleges or universities, those studying English out of personal interest, and those who want more English in order to further their career opportunities.

The book was written primarily to meet the needs of a reading course, but it is equally usable in a course that includes a writing component. The Instructor's Manual gives guidelines for use in both kinds of courses.

The First Canadian Edition of *Thresholds in Reading* faithfully adheres to the basic principles and concepts of language learning as outlined by Robin C. Scarcella and Rebecca L. Oxford in their book *The Tapestry of Language Learning: The Individual in the Communication Classroom.* The Canadian edition has kept the basic structure of the original text and retained the activity and exercise types contained in each chapter but has replaced chapters 2 and 7 with relevant Canadian material.

Chapter 2, "Canadian Portraits," profiles several famous Canadians who have made important contributions to Canadian society. Chapter 7, "Beauty," discusses different cultural notions and individuals' perceptions of beauty. Where readings were replaced, great care was taken to choose articles that would be of particular interest to Canadian students and that would reflect the Canadian reality and experience.

Particular skills and tasks are explained in detail when they are introduced. After that, they are recycled in later chapters. If you skip chapters or activities, you may wish to know where these introductory explanations are given.

Chapter 2: Canadian Portraits
- Vocabulary in context
- Making vocabulary cards
- Keyword study and exercises
- Making a chart
- Taking notes from reading

Chapter 3: Native Voices
- Anticipating information in a reading passage
- Developing good habits during reading
- Paraphrasing
- Distinguishing between topic and main idea

Chapter 4: Alternative Education
- Projects
- Summarizing
- Taking notes using graphic formats
- Identifying the topic sentence

Chapter 6: Lies and Truth
- Paraphrasing (in more detail than in Chapter 3)
- Identifying issues and taking positions

Anticipating test questions
Recognizing the structure of a reading passage

Chapter 8: Bigfoot and Company
Analyzing an author's position on a controversy
Arguing both sides of an issue

CHAPTER FEATURES

Chapter 1 is a preliminary unit in which students perform diagnostic tasks, take a reading inventory, and set goals according to their individual academic, career, and personal interests.

Chapters 2 through 8 each centres around a series of readings related to a central topic. Within the chapter, each new passage enlarges upon the previous perspective and provides schema activation for the next, so that by the end, students can synthesize information from several readings in their discussion and writing activities. In addition, certain themes link the content across units: for example, the influence of cultural values on topics such as education, history, and the treatment of endangered species.

Chapters 5 and 7 are consolidation chapters that serve to solidify skills previously presented.

Each chapter opens with schema-activation activities for both vocabulary and content. Reading skill-builders are directly tied to the content of each topic and therefore contribute to comprehension of the whole. Comprehension and skills are developed through interactive activities and through writing assignments that range from personal response and narration to expository and persuasive writing. Reading passages are used as the basis for training in writing from outside sources: e.g., summarizing, paraphrasing, and synthesizing, though not to the extent of writing a full-fledged research paper. You, the teacher, will decide to what extent writing will be emphasized.

Each reading passage is the focus of the following activities:

Identifying the circled reference words
Comprehension questions
Scanning exercises
True–false questions (using paraphrases from the reading)
Identifying the main idea, or taking notes
Vocabulary-in-context exercises
Keyword exercises

If you follow this sequence of activities slavishly, your students will quickly become bored with the repeated format. Pick and choose from what's available in the book in order to vary the way class time is spent. Interspersed in each chapter you'll also find a variety of activities calling for discussion, freewriting, essay writing, cultural surveys, and longer projects. Design your class to stimulate student interest.

ANCILLARY MATERIALS

This book is accompanied by a tape; the selections that it includes are indicated in the text.

The Instructor's Manual includes answers to the exercises, tests with answer keys, and suggestions for facilitating activities. It gives guidelines for picking and choosing if you can't use all of the text in one term, models for adapting the book to semester- or quarter-length terms, and suggestions for integrating a writing component. The manual also includes lists of optional longer readings related to each topic and guidelines for writing sentences with selected keywords.

Martha Grace Low
University of Oregon

Aïda A. Cunanan
Dawson College

Francis J. Bonkowski
Télé-Université, Université du Québec

Acknowledgments

We are most grateful to David Jones and Linda Power of Dawson College and Jacqueline Froidefond of Télé-Université for their invaluable help in suggesting possible reading resources for this edition.

We would also like to thank Andrew Livingston, Executive Editor, for giving us the opportunity to work on this project; Dianne Horton, Project Editor, for her unflagging enthusiasm, encouragement, patience, and support; and Tracy Bordian, Production Editor, for her very able assistance.

ITP Nelson would like to thank the following reviewers for their helpful comments and suggestions: Carolyn Bond, Algonquin College; Joan Kyle-Jones, University of Victoria; and Maureen Sargeant, Saint Mary's University.

Aïda-Alma Cunanan
Francis J. Bonkowski

CONTENTS

Getting Started

1
CHAPTER

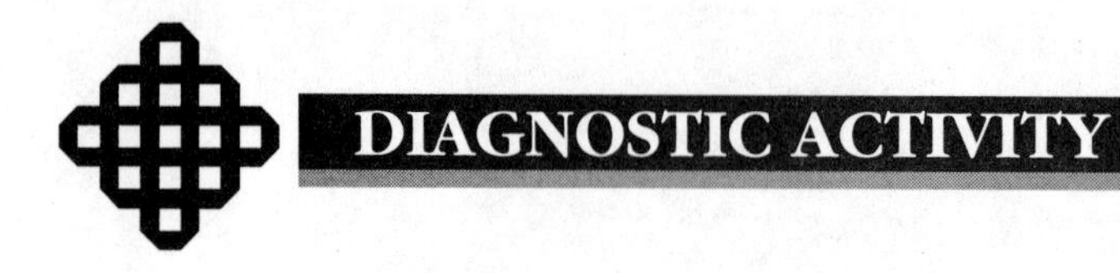

DIAGNOSTIC ACTIVITY

Your teacher will use the following activity to get an idea of your ability in several English skills: listening, reading, speaking, writing, and grammar. Please don't read the story yet. This is what you're going to do:

1. You'll listen as your teacher reads the story aloud. You may ask for a second reading if you wish.
2. You'll read the story silently as many times as you like for about 10 minutes. When you finish, you may ask anything you wish about the events in the story or the vocabulary.
3. Without looking at the story, you'll have about 15 minutes to do a fill-in-the-blank exercise (called a *cloze* exercise).
4. You may study the story again for a few minutes. Then you'll put it aside and you'll work with a partner. Each of you will take turns telling the story to each other. This will give you practice in speaking and will also prepare you for the next step.
5. You may study the story again for a few minutes. Then you'll put it aside and try to write it. You'll have about 15 minutes for this. If you're good at working from memory, feel free to copy any sentences that you can remember; but what's important is that you retell the story so that its meaning, but not its exact wording, is present.

STORY: THE KING'S DECISION

Many years ago there lived a king who was widely known for his wisdom. It was said that he was the wisest man who had ever lived.

One day two women came before him. One of them was carrying a living baby, but the other's baby was dead. The first woman said, "Great king, this woman and I live in the same house. Our babies were born only three days apart. Then one night, she rolled over on her baby in her sleep, and it died. So she exchanged her dead baby for my live one while I was sleeping. When I woke up in the morning, I thought my baby had died! Then I noticed through my tears that it was not my son, but hers."

"Great king, this woman is lying," protested the second woman. "It was her son that died, and now she wants mine. Do not let her take away my only child!"

The king was silent for a moment. Then he spoke. "Each woman claims that the living baby is hers," he said. "Who can decide such a matter when no one else was there to see what really happened?" He turned to one of his guards. "Bring me a sword," he commanded. The sword was brought. "Now," he ordered the guard, "divide the living baby into two parts, and give each woman half."

The guard raised his sword over the screaming baby. "No!" cried the first woman. "Don't do it! Give the baby to her, but don't kill him!"

The other woman said, "No, go ahead and divide him. It's a fair decision."
The guard looked at the king for his orders. The king smiled. "Give the living baby to the first woman," he said. "She is his real mother. She loves her son so much that she would rather give him up than see him harmed."

Cloze Exercise

Instructions: Write only one word in each blank.

Many years ago there lived a ______________ who was widely known for his ______________. It was said that he was ______________ wisest man who had ever lived.

______________ day two women came before him. ______________ of them was carrying a living ______________, but the other's baby was dead. ______________ first woman said, "Great king, this ______________ and I live in the same ______________. Our babies were born only three ______________ apart. Then one night, she rolled ______________ on her baby in her sleep, ______________ it died. So she exchanged her ______________ baby for my live one while ______________ was sleeping. When I woke up ______________ the morning, I thought my baby ______________ died! Then I noticed through my ______________ that it was not my son, ______________ hers."

"Great king, this woman is ______________," protested the second woman. "It was ______________ son that died, and now she ______________ mine. Do not let her take ______________ my only child!"

The king was ______________ for a moment. Then he spoke. "______________ woman claims that the living baby ______________ hers," he said. "Who can decide ______________ a matter when no one else ______________ there to see what really happened?" ______________ turned to one of his guards. "______________ me a sword," he commanded. The ______________ was brought. "Now," he ordered the ______________, "divide the living baby into two ______________, and give each woman half."

The ______________ raised his sword over the screaming ______________. "No!" cried the first woman. "Don't ______________ it! Give the baby to her, ______________ don't kill him!"

The other woman ________________, "No, go ahead and divide him. ________________ a fair decision."

The guard looked ________________ the king for his orders. The ________________ smiled. "Give the living baby to ________________ first woman," he said. "She is ________________ real mother. She loves her son ________________ much that she would rather give ________________ up than see him harmed."

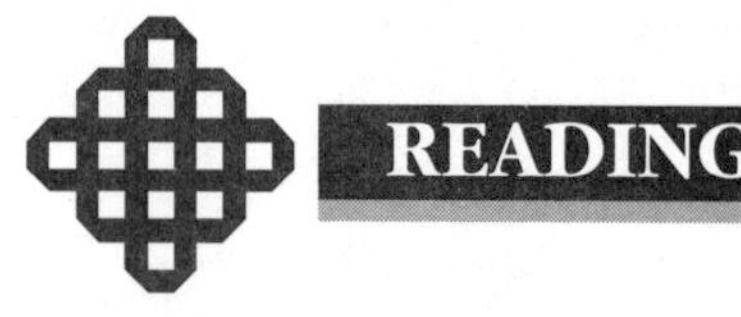

READING INVENTORY

Instructions: Complete the chart and answer the questions below.

GOOD	VERY GOOD		BAD	VERY BAD
		Are these good or bad reading habits?		
____	____	**a.** Read silently, and read every word.	____	____
____	____	**b.** Every time you find a word that you don't know, stop and look it up in your dictionary.	____	____
____	____	**c.** Begin at the beginning and read straight through without stopping.	____	____
____	____	**d.** Use your dictionary only at the end of each section.	____	____
____	____	**e.** Don't use a dictionary.	____	____
____	____	**f.** As you read, try to mentally translate the passage into your native language.	____	____
____	____	**g.** If you find something that you don't understand, stop and think about it. Don't go on to the next part until you understand it.	____	____
____	____	**h.** Say the words in your head as you read them.	____	____
____	____	**i.** Look over the passage briefly from start to finish before you actually read it.	____	____
____	____	**j.** If possible, mark important ideas and words (or unknown words) as you read.	____	____
____	____	**k.** Read a little bit more quickly than is comfortable for you.	____	____
____	____	**l.** Guess what the unknown words mean.	____	____
____	____	**m.** Try to understand the organization of the passage and the relationships among the ideas.	____	____

1. How well do you read in your native language? ______________________

   In English? ______________________

2. Do you enjoy reading in your native language? ______________________

   In English? ______________________

3. What do you find hardest about reading in English? (vocabulary, grammar, speed, concentration, interest, etc.)

   ____

4. What do you like to read for pleasure?

   ____

5. What reading skills would you like to improve in this course?

   ____

SOME SKILLS TO BE ADDRESSED IN THIS COURSE

How much vocabulary do you need?
First of all, how many English words do you think you know now? Think about your reading/listening vocabulary, which is much larger than your writing/speaking vocabulary.

How much vocabulary you need depends on what you want to use English for. If you want to study in a college or university where English is the language of instruction, you'll need a broad vocabulary that includes both everyday and academic words. Most native-speaking undergraduate students have a reading vocabulary of around 20,000 words. Then every year of their studies, they add another one to two thousand words.

Remember this: reading is a process. Vocabulary is a very important part of the process of reading comprehension, probably the most important part. However, if you interrupt your reading to use your dictionary in the middle of a sentence or a paragraph, you may improve your vocabulary a little, but you won't improve your reading at all. Wait to use your dictionary until you come to a good stopping place. Then carefully decide which new words to look up. If you try to look up all of them, you'll still be working when all your friends have closed their books and gone out to enjoy their free time. Worse yet, you'll become discouraged and you may come to hate reading in English. Life is short! Look up only the words that you absolutely need in order to understand the idea of the material. If there are other words that would be useful for you to know, your teacher or this book will point them out to you.

What's the best way to learn new vocabulary?

It's important to understand that you won't remember much new vocabulary unless you find a systematic way of recording it and studying it. There are a number of ways of doing this, including keeping a vocabulary notebook, writing meanings in the margins of a text, or using small vocabulary cards. Different ways work well for different people. You may want to try several in order to find the one that fits your learning style. Or you may have a special way of your own that works for you. If so, tell your teacher and your classmates about it.

How fast should you read?

College students who are native speakers of English generally read at the following speeds:

Very careful study reading	200 words per minute
Normal study reading	300 words per minute
Skimming	450 words per minute
Scanning	600 words per minute

Note two things:

1. The rate of reading depends on what kind of reading you're doing, and that depends on your purpose. "Normal study reading" is the rate used when you're reading a homework assignment in your textbook for the first time. "Very careful study reading" is the rate used when you're reading something very difficult or important or when you're studying for a major examination. Skimming and scanning will be discussed below.
2. These rates are high! If your school has materials to measure your reading speed, your teacher will show you how to use them so that you can find out how fast you can read. If you're planning to attend (or are already attending) a college or university in an English-speaking country, you'll want to build your speed as closely as possible to the rates given above. The amount of reading you'll have to do is very great, and if you are a slow reader, you may fall behind in your work and have trouble catching up.

Skimming and scanning are different from study reading in that they're much faster. When you do them, you don't read everything on the page. They are described below.

What is skimming, and what good is it?

Do you know what skim milk is? In milk production, skimming is the process of taking the cream off the top of the milk. In reading, skimming is similar: you're looking at the top, the surface, but not reading deeply to catch all the information. You just want to know the topic and the main points.

When you skim, do this:

1. Read the title.
2. Read any subheadings.

3. Look at any pictures, charts, graphs, etc., that are included.
4. Read all of the first paragraph.
5. Look for the main points in the paragraphs that follow. They're usually in the first sentence; if not, try the last sentence. If you still haven't found them, look inside the paragraph.
6. Read all of the last paragraph. It will probably contain a summary or some other type of important conclusion.

Here's what skimming looks like: Turn back to page 2 to "The King's Decision." If you were to skim it, here's what you would read:

Skimming: "The King's Decision"

Many years ago there lived a king who was widely known for his wisdom. It was said that he was the wisest man who had ever lived.

One day two women came before him. One of them was carrying a living baby, but the other's baby was dead. . . . .

. . . .

. . . . . . she exchanged her dead baby for my live one . . . . it was not my son, but hers."

"Great king, this woman is lying," . . . .

The king was silent for a moment. . . . .

. . . .

. . . . "Bring me a sword," . . . . "divide the living baby into two parts, and give each woman half."

The guard raised his sword . . . . "No!" . . . . "Give the baby to her . . . ."

The other woman said, "No, go ahead and divide him. . . . . "

The guard looked at the king for his orders. The king smiled. "Give the living baby to the first woman," he said. "She is his real mother. She loves her son so much that she would rather give him up than see him harmed."

Notice that if you read only these parts, you would understand the general idea of the story.

Why skim? Because it's one of the most useful pre-reading skills. Before reading any homework assignment or important material, follow the six steps listed above. Skimming identifies the topic for you and "programs" your brain to know what kind of information it will be receiving. Then when you read, you'll be able to read faster, to understand the material better, and to remember it longer. You'll practise skimming throughout this textbook, and you should make a point of doing it in your outside reading.

What's scanning, and what good is it?

Scanning is looking for specific information in a reading passage. It does not include reading every word, nor even reading for the main idea. Notice that it's the fastest kind of reading on the reading speed table given above. For instance, you might be in the library looking for good materials to use in a research paper. You pick up a book with a title that looks useful. You scan the table of contents to see if your subject is there. You find a chapter title that looks promising. You turn to that chapter and run your eyes quickly down the pages, looking for key words that are related to your topic. That's scanning. If you find what you're looking for, then you might sit down to do some careful study reading. But study reading is different from scanning.

Scanning is a very important reading skill because it saves you time and it directs you to useful information. The secrets to good scanning are:

1. Knowing which *keywords* (useful words to know) to look for. If you can't find the one you're looking for, try another that means the same thing.
2. Not wasting time reading whole sentences. Just look for the key words or phrases.

Scanning is a skill that you'll practise as you use this book, but don't stop here. Use it in your outside reading. It'll save you time and make you a stronger reader.

Build your reading comprehension.
There are many ways to strengthen your reading comprehension. This book will give you practice in identifying the main ideas of reading passages, taking notes from your reading, paraphrasing information in your own words, summarizing passages into a single sentence or a short paragraph, using information from readings in papers of your own, and anticipating test questions.

Outside reading is important.
The materials in this book are designed to interest you, to build your reading skills, and to increase your vocabulary. But a textbook alone isn't enough to make you a strong reader. You should supplement it with outside reading that fits your own interests and needs. It's especially important that you read some longer materials than this book contains. If your school has a reading laboratory, you might find some materials there that interest you. If it doesn't, go to the library and look for books or magazines that are interesting and that don't seem too difficult.

How difficult is "too difficult"? The decision is really yours, but in general, if there's a great deal of new vocabulary and if the grammar of the sentences is very hard for you to follow, you should look for something simpler. That's because very difficult material makes such slow reading that you can't remember what the first part of the sentence was by the time you finish the last part. Or you can't remember what was said in the sentence before, or back at the beginning of the paragraph. If you can read through a paragraph and keep the general ideas in your head from start to finish, that's probably a good level for you, even though there may be new vocabulary and some difficult sentences.

SETTING YOUR OWN GOALS

Your reasons for being in this class might be different from everyone else's. Your strengths and weaknesses in reading and vocabulary are different. So are your interests. That's why it's important for you to set some goals of your own for this course. Consider the following questions.

1. What are you going to use English for after you finish this program?
   What reading and vocabulary abilities will you need in order to do that?
   What kind of materials will you be reading then?
2. In past language courses, what were you good at?
   What ways of studying worked well for you (for example, studying with a partner, studying rules, just reading a lot, asking a teacher to help you, writing notes, writing in your textbook, talking about what you were learning, etc.)?
   Are you good at memorizing vocabulary?
   How do you learn it best?

You'll find it helpful to set short-term objectives for yourself with every chapter in this book. That's because your first objectives may not be very realistic, and you may want to change them. Don't set objectives that you can't possibly achieve, because you'll become discouraged. Take into consideration your interests, your needs, and your abilities.

You should also choose a longer goal for the term, which you can re-evaluate periodically. Take a moment to think about this now, and write it down. Keep it in your notebook or binder. Review it from time to time, and change it as you need or want to.

FREEWRITING: THINKING ABOUT GOALS

Here are some things you'll want to consider in setting goals:

1. How much material you want to read outside of class, and what kind
2. What kind of material you want to learn to read (personal interest, major field, etc.)
3. How fast you want to read by the end of this course
4. What level of comprehension you'd like to reach (for example, 65 percent comprehension of unsimplified reading passages)
5. How many vocabulary words you want to learn each week

6. How much to learn about them: part of speech? pronunciation? example-sentences? how to use them in your writing?

7. What score you'd like to make on the TOEFL or another examination

8. What you especially want to improve in this course

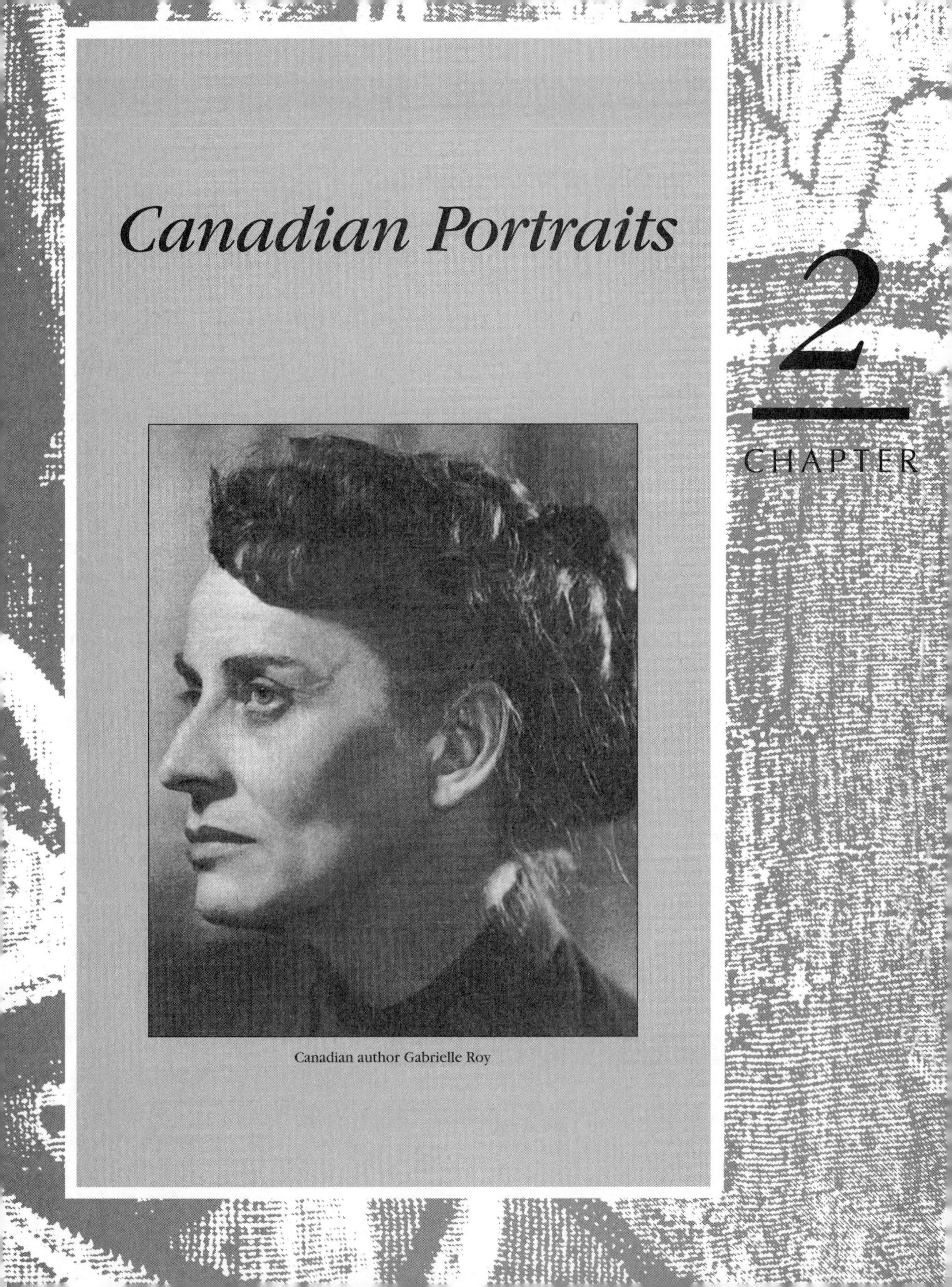

Canadian Portraits

2

CHAPTER

Canadian author Gabrielle Roy

PLANNING YOUR LEARNING

Your teacher will show you the overall goal statement that you wrote at the end of Chapter 1. Review what you wrote and think about how you can work to meet your goal as you study this new chapter.

- How many words do you want to learn? (minimum 66, the number of keywords in the chapter)
- What grade would you like to make on the vocabulary section of the exam at the end of the chapter?
- What grade would you like to make on the reading comprehension section of the exam?
- What are you going to read outside of class?

PREVIEWING THE CHAPTER

- Look at the title of this chapter.
- Look in the Table of Contents at the titles of the six readings in this chapter. Look through the chapter at the pictures and the illustration. What are some things in the pictures and drawings that you are curious about? What do you expect to find out from the readings?
- Which reading do you think you'll be most interested in?

FREEWRITING

Take a few minutes to write everything that you know about a famous Canadian. She or he could be a politician, an actor, or a writer, for example. When you work this way, you're *freewriting.* When you freewrite, you concentrate on content and on expressing yourself so that people can understand you, and you don't spend much time worrying about vocabulary or grammar. Try to write as much as you can in the time you have.

After you finish writing, form a group with two or three classmates and tell each other what you wrote. Did your partners have any information that was different from yours?

LEARNING STRATEGY

Managing Your Learning: Sharing information with partners is a good way to get some idea of what to expect from a reading.

PREPARING TO READ: CONTENT

Many famous Canadians have made their mark in different fields. Working with a couple of partners, make a list of all the famous Canadians you can think of. When you finish, compare your lists.

Now write all the names on the blackboard. Can you identify the field in which each one has made a contribution?

PREPARING TO READ: VOCABULARY

You will encounter the following new words in this chapter's readings. Work with a fellow student. You should use your dictionary if you don't know the answer, or you may skip the question.

1. The giving of money, labour, and goods to charities is called a c_ _ _ _ _ _ _ _ _ _ _.
2. A woman who devotes her life to service, prayer, and worship is a n _ _ .
3. People widely known to the public either during or after their lifetime are said to be f _ _ _ _ s.
4. Well-known painters produce great p _ _ _ _ _ _ _ s.
5. When a person comes up with a new idea or invention, it is called a d _ _ _ _ _ _ _ y.
6. A person who is trained in science is called a s _ _ _ _ _ _ _ t.
7. An i _ _ _ _ _ _ r is a person who thinks up new ways of doing things.
8. The place where people are trained to be doctors is known as a m _ _ _ _ _ l school.
9. A n _ _ _ l is a fictional story with characters and a plot.
10. *Star Trek* is a well-known television s _ _ _.

READING ONE

NOTE: This reading is also on the tape.

Reading process: Very quickly skim the passage by reading the first sentence of every paragraph. Then read more carefully. Mark all the vocabulary items that you don't know, but don't stop to use your dictionary yet.

GABRIELLE ROY: A QUÉBEC WRITER FOR ALL CANADA

1 Gabrielle Roy is undoubtedly the best-known Québec writer in English-speaking Canada. As long ago as 1947 her novel about poor people in Québec, *Bonheur d'Occasion* (1945), was translated into English as *The Tin Flute*, and it was immediately recognized as a major Canadian novel.

2 Since that time Gabrielle Roy has been more successful than any other Québec writer in appealing to people in all parts of Canada. To an extent this is because both her background[1] and her experience have been different from those of most other Québec writers.

Threads

Ideas often last but a day, feelings, dreams almost forever.

Gabrielle Roy

3 Gabrielle Roy was actually born—in 1909—in St. Boniface, Manitoba. Her family had come west from Québec under an abortive scheme to establish French-speaking settlers in the Red River district. She herself went to the Winnipeg Normal School, and then taught for several years in small schools in the rural[2] areas of Manitoba. Not until she was almost thirty did Gabrielle Roy settle[3] in Montréal, after spending[4] two years in France and England studying drama, an interest she had developed while living in Winnipeg.

4 In Montréal, Gabrielle Roy began to write seriously, first stories and articles, and then her novel *Bonheur d'Occasion*, for which she had patiently gathered material and impressions while living close to the people of Québec. For as a Manitoban, Gabrielle Roy regarded Québec at least partly as a strange[5] land.

5 Always in Gabrielle Roy's writing there is the feeling that she looks at what she describes with a kind of detachment; it is a quality that other Québec writers do not possess for they are describing the world in which they were born and bred. This quality gives her books a greater accessibility[6] for readers not familiar with Québec and its way of life; like them, she is an observer, even if a deeply involved one. Indeed books such as *The Tin Flute* and her later novel *The Cashier* (originally published as *Alexandre Chenevert*, 1955) have done a great deal to help English-speaking Canadians understand French-Canadian society and the attitudes of Québec people.

6 But Gabrielle Roy's broad appeal is also related to the fact that she has written more on other parts of Canada than most Québec writers. In fact, most of her books are set[7] in either the Manitoba of her childhood or in the Arctic, which has always fascinated her.

7 Her Manitoba books are not so much novels as groups of interlinked short stories. *La Petite Poule d'Eau* (translated as *Where Nests the Water Hen*, 1950) tells of life in a remote[8] settlement of northern Manitoba. *Rue Deschambault* (translated as *Street of Riches*, 1957) concerns the experiences of a girl growing up among the people of many origins who lived in St. Boniface during the pioneer era. Even if the book is not strictly autobiographical, it obviously embodies many of the experiences and observations of Gabrielle Roy's own childhood,[9] as does its sequel, *La Route d'Altamont* (translated as *The Road Past Altamont*, 1966).

8 In writing of Manitoba Gabrielle Roy was dealing with the familiar terrain of her childhood and her young womanhood as a rural school teacher. In writing of Québec she was dealing with a province whose culture and language she shared and to which she belonged by ancestry. But the Arctic was an unfamiliar[10] world, to which she was not linked either by experience or by ancestry. So she used the Arctic as the setting for novels and stories that had broader themes than the Manitoba fiction (which was so largely dominated by personal memories) and the Québec fiction (in which the frustrations of poor

and narrow lives were seen in the context of Depression-ridden French Canada).

9 For example, *La Montagne Secrète* (*The Hidden Mountain*, 1962) tells of a young artist's discovery, loss and rediscovery of a mountain in the far North, and here Gabrielle Roy is really telling of the struggle all artists undergo to find an authentic[11] way of expressing their subjects once they have decided what they want to paint or write about. And *La Rivière sans Repos* (of which part has been translated as *The Windflower*, 1970) is a group of stories which tells of a society—that of the Inuit—which is in transition and whose people are being forced by circumstances to accept the gifts of the white man's world. These gifts inevitably[12] destroy their traditional cultures, which are based on very specialized hunting techniques. It is a profound and passionate study of the difficulty in the modern world of remaining true to one's self and one's past. And that is a sentiment close to the heart of every French Canadian.

After You Read

Identify the circled reference words.

COMPREHENSION QUESTIONS

1. Why did Gabrielle Roy's family go west to live in Manitoba?

____

2. What quality does Roy possess that makes her different from other Québec writers?

____

3. What geographical regions does Roy write about?

a. ______________ **b.** ______________ **c.** ______________

LEARNING STRATEGY

Personalizing: You can get a better understanding of another person's actions if you try to identify with his or her point of view.

FREEWRITING: VALUES AND POINTS OF VIEW

Gabrielle Roy's *point of view* is the way she felt about what she was doing. In order to understand her point of view, imagine that you are Roy. Why do you want to become a writer? If you succeed, how will you feel? Write an entry about this for your private journal.

Now imagine that you are Roy's sister and you do not agree with her decision to go to Europe to study drama. You want her to stay in Winnipeg and continue teaching school. You are afraid that you will never see her again. Write a letter trying to convince Gabrielle to stay home.

Roy's point of view came partly from her *values*—the ideas and actions that were important to her. One common human value is the desire to experience new ideas. Why was she willing to go off on her own to become a writer?

LEARNING STRATEGY

Managing Your Learning: Find and use the best conditions and time for you to learn new words.

Vocabulary

VOCABULARY STUDY: CHOOSING THE MOST IMPORTANT NEW WORDS

Look at the first paragraph of the above reading. When you were reading, you marked all the vocabulary items that you didn't know; now tell your teacher what those words were in the first paragraph, and she or he will write them on the blackboard. Look at them as a class. Which ones keep you from understanding the general idea of the paragraph? Those are the only ones you should worry about for the sake of comprehension.

Look at the whole reading in this way. Choose not more than ten such words and write them here. You're going to look them up in a moment.

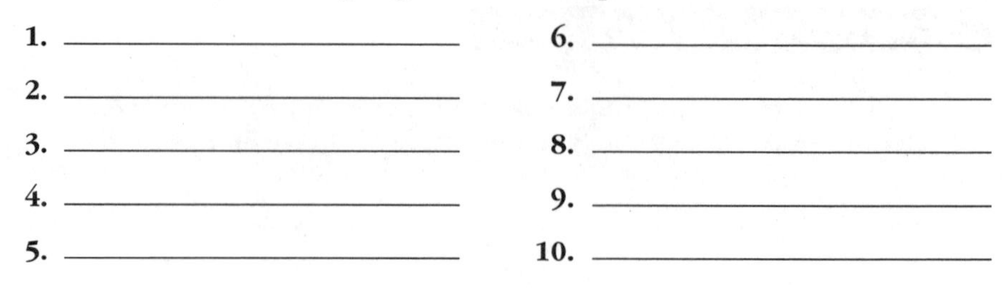

1. ______________ **6.** ______________

2. ______________ **7.** ______________

3. ______________ **8.** ______________

4. ______________ **9.** ______________

5. ______________ **10.** ______________

Now work with a partner and compare your lists. Discuss differences; you can change your list if you think your partner's is better.

LEARNING STRATEGY

Forming Concepts: Use the context to help you understand new vocabulary.

VOCABULARY IN CONTEXT

Some of the unknown words can be understood in a general way because of other information that is provided in the same passage. This surrounding information is called the *context* of the words. In the first paragraph, for instance, the word *novel* may be new to you, but the second sentence contains the title of a novel in both French and English. What are the two titles?

In the fifth paragraph, the context helps you to understand the meaning of *detachment*. What are two other words in the paragraph that give a clue to its meaning?

In the eighth paragraph, the word *terrain* may be new to you. It is a word used in English when talking about places or the physical setting. What was Roy's native province?

You can't always guess the meaning of new words by looking at their context, but often you can learn enough about the word that you can understand the passage in a general way. Usually this kind of understanding is enough. If it's not—if you really can't guess the meaning of the word and you know that it's central to an understanding of the passage—then look it up when you come to a good stopping place, such as at the end of a section or a chapter.

LEARNING STRATEGY

Remembering New Material: Recording new words on cards that you can rearrange makes it easier to remember them.

USING VOCABULARY CARDS

You can buy blank cards ranging in size from very small (like business cards) to much larger. Select the size that's right for the amount of information you want to write on each card. But you should also choose a size that you can handle easily.

Here is some information you may want to write on each card:

- the word on one side and its definition (preferably in English) on the other
- its pronunciation
- its part of speech
- a sample sentence or phrase containing the word

But you may find that recording *all* this information for every word slows you down and discourages you. Find a balance that's helpful but manageable.

Think about how much information you want to record; then go out and buy a stack of cards. Record the ten words that you wrote above. Then add cards for the following words—not because they are necessary in order to understand the general idea of the passage, but because they are useful. These words will be called **keywords** in this book. A list of all the keywords in this chapter is on page 43.

KEYWORDS

NOTE: Following each keyword in the list below is the number of the paragraph (¶) in the reading where the keyword appears.

1. background* ¶2
2. rural ¶3
3. settle ¶3
4. spend ¶3
5. strange* ¶4
6. accessibility ¶5
7. set ¶6
8. remote ¶7
9. childhood* ¶7
10. unfamiliar ¶8
11. authentic* ¶9
12. inevitably ¶9

* Part of your vocabulary study will include making sentences of your own with the keywords marked with an asterisk (*). Study the sentences they appear in, and then imitate the sentence structure when you write your own sentences.

KEYWORD EXERCISE

In this exercise, the keywords are printed in italics.

1. *Meanings:*
   - The *background* part of a picture is farthest from the viewer.

     QUESTION: What do you think is the opposite of *background?*
   - One's *background*, including experience, knowledge, and training, strongly influences how one thinks and feels.

     QUESTION: To what extent does your *background* influence the kinds of foods you eat today?
   - The music and sound effects are part of the *background* in a play or motion picture.

     QUESTION: Which movie has the best *background* sound effects you have ever heard?
   - Explain the similarity among the three meanings.
2. *EXAMPLE:* Gabrielle Roy taught for several years in small schools in *rural* Manitoba.

Name two things that you like and two things that you dislike about *rural* life.

Like	*Dislike*
a. ____________________	**a.** ____________________
b. ____________________	**b.** ____________________

If you don't know anything about *rural* life, what do you imagine it to be like?

3. *EXAMPLE:* Gabrielle Roy *settled* in Québec in her late twenties.

You'll notice in the dictionary that *settle* has several meanings. Which of the sentences below contains the same meaning as the sentence in the reading?
- The young couple has finally *settled* in their new home.
- It is not easy to *settle* in a new country.
- He has to *settle* his affairs before moving abroad.

4. *Meanings:*
- Someone who *spends* all his money will never be rich.
- If you *spend* the day in the sun, you'll probably get a sunburn.
- He *spent* his entire inheritance at the casino.

QUESTION: Where would you like to *spend* your next vacation?

5. Which of the following words mean the same thing as *strange*?
peculiar unusual odd quiet unfamiliar

EXAMPLE: Gabrielle Roy regarded Québec at least partly as a strange land.

6. Look at the parts of the word *accessibility*. What's the connection between the meanings of the parts and the meaning of the word?

____

7. *EXAMPLE:* Most of Gabrielle Roy's books are *set* in either Manitoba or the Arctic.

If you were going to write a story or book, where would you *set* the events?

____

8. *EXAMPLE:* Some of Roy's stories tell of life in *remote* places.

Finish the sentences:

One *remote* place ________________________________.

The Inuit ________________________________.

9. Which of the following are elements of the word *childhood?*
youth baby parent pregnant aunt

EXAMPLE: We don't know very much about Gabrielle Roy's *childhood*.

10. Rank the following hobbies from least to most *unfamiliar* to you.

_______ **a.** Photography

_______ **b.** Horseback riding

_______ **c.** Stamp collecting

_______ **d.** Swimming

EXAMPLE: The Arctic was an *unfamiliar* world to Gabrielle Roy.

11. Which of the following words are not synonyms for the word *authentic?*
consistent genuine true veritable faithful

EXAMPLE: Writers need to find an *authentic* voice once they decide what they want to write about.

12. *EXAMPLE:* Fast-moving changes in today's world *inevitably* cause a certain amount of stress.

What will *inevitably* happen if you ...

a. eat too much food? ____________________

b. don't take care of your health? ____________________

c. stop seeing your friends? ____________________

REVIEW

Now that you have studied the vocabulary, reread or reskim the passage.

NOTE: This reading is also on the tape.

QUÉBEC JE T'AIME / I LOVE YOU

1 A blanket of heavy snow covered the roofs in my village the day I arrived in this world. My father welcomed me with joy even though he would have preferred a boy. That night, he was particularly moved by the gnarled branches of the pine trees, so typical to Japan, as they bent under the weight of the snow—just as in a print of the famous artist Hiroshige. He decided then and there to call me Miyuki: *yuki* means snow in Japanese and *mi* means deep. I was the second daughter, and the child born after me was another sister.

2 I think often about my birth when winter holds sway over the fields and rivers of Québec and decorates[1] the cities with icicles from the roof edges. All those silent touches are familiar to me. One could say that I was predestined to live in a snow-filled country, even though the road that led me to Québec was long and full of unexpected detours.[2]

"Première Communion." Reprinted from Miyuki Tanobe, *Québec, Je T'Aime/I Love You.* Montreal: Tundra Books of Montreal, 1976. Reprinted with permission of the author.

3 Kamakura, the city where I passed my childhood, is 45 miles [72 km] from Tokyo. It has a magnificent huge bronze statue of Buddha that dates from 1257, and people like to walk its pretty streets that tell of its artistic and literary past. My family was interested in the arts. My father, an eye doctor, still has two great passions: the violin and old Japanese prints. My mother sang and played the *koto*, a kind of zither with thirteen strings. My two sisters also have a talent for music: one is a violinist in New York City, and the other intends to teach piano in Japan.

4 I decided to become a painter. After I finished my art studies, I left Japan for Paris. That was during the winter of 1963–1964. I spent three years there but I never allowed a single human being to appear in my paintings. Even though the atmosphere of the Boul'Mich where I lived throbbed with life because of the students, I painted only streets, lanes and houses. It wasn't until I discovered Greece, its sun and its islands, that I started to take an interest in people.

5 I remember very clearly the first person I painted. In an old quarter of Athens, near a tavern, I met a huge man with a moustache and a stomach that hung out. He sold chewing gum. Every time I came to that district to sketch, he greeted me with mocking eyes. One day he offered me some gum. It had no flavour whatever but it did give me an excuse to ask if I might sketch him, and he agreed. I was to learn later, much to my surprise, that he was a drug pusher.[3]

6 At least I had overcome my inhibition[4] against putting people in my paintings and I began to understand the importance of the human warmth around me: the *bouzouki* players on the terraces of the cafés, the singers and dancers in the street, the people who stopped to take a glass of wine, the crowd in shirtsleeves, the lovers who embraced in the laneways and even the children wetting beside the tables in the restaurant. From then on I never stopped putting this daily life, so rich in humanity, into my paintings.

7 I returned to Paris, my head full of these new riches. There, in one of those shaky little elevators that look like birdcages, I met a French Canadian, who, a few years later, would become my husband. On his return to Canada he sent me piles of books on Québec, its geography and history, and its artists. I longed[5] to go there right away, but I felt I had to return to Japan. Then I went back to Greece and also visited Africa, before that lovely afternoon in June 1971 when I got off the plane at Dorval Airport in Montréal.

8 I rented a flat on Sherbrooke Street facing Lafontaine Park and immediately started on my discovery of Québec. With the help of my French-Canadian friend, I went to libraries to study the stories and legends of Québec, I visited art galleries, I explored the length and breadth of Montréal like an unhurried tourist: Place d'Armes, and Notre Dame Church; the Old City—Bonsecours Church and Market, Chateau de Ramezay where the last governor of New France and even Benjamin Franklin lived. I also travelled up to Lac Saint-Jean where I saw the phantom village of Val-Jalbert and I wound[6] my way through Gaspé and the North Shore. How many memories I brought back!

9 But I was most fascinated by the houses in the working-class districts of Montréal with walls of red brick, their green roofs, their balconies and outside staircases of all shapes: Saint-Henri, Little Burgundy, the district near Lafontaine Park known as the "molasses quarter," the Main or St. Lawrence Boulevard with its little groceries and corner restaurants, the backlanes[7] with the lively shouts of children, the clothes lines on the back balconies, the mothers working as they kept an eye on their children, and children skating, tobogganing, building snowmen. In Québec City I made the same discoveries in Lower Town, which is particularly splendid during the winter carnival because of its extraordinary exhibition of ice sculptures.

10 I often ask myself where I get this insatiable[8] interest in the daily lives of people. It's something I was never taught, but I feel an inner need to get to know them, to talk to them, to listen to them and to understand them. At night before I go to sleep, I still think about them. I have been very saddened to see houses that have inspired so many of my paintings being demolished. At one of my exhibitions in a Montréal art gallery, a man came up to speak to me; I noticed he was hiding[9] something behind his back.

11 "Without knowing it, you have given life back to me," he said. "I am a doctor and I was born on Robin Street, near Amherst, right in the centre of the molasses quarter. You painted the house where I was born just before it was demolished." He pointed a finger at one of my paintings where the *nihonga* technique had captured the texture of the bricks. "Nothing of (it) remains," he went on, "but I kept a souvenir that is very precious to me. I have it here."

12 With tears in his eyes, the doctor brought out an old brick, all chipped and spotted with cement which he placed beside my painting. "(This) is all that remains of my childhood," he said.

13 My, but I felt proud[10] of myself that day.

Threads

Creating art is "fresh seeing."

Emily Carr, artist

After You Read

Identify the circled reference words.

COMPREHENSION QUESTIONS

1. When did Tanobe decide to incorporate human figures in her paintings?

____

____

2. What fascinated Tanobe most about Montréal?

____

____

3. How did Tanobe touch the life of a doctor from Montréal?

____

____

TRUE–FALSE QUESTIONS

Circle "True" or "False" and tell the number of the paragraph where you found your answer.

			¶ number
1. While in Paris, Tanobe met someone who changed the direction of her life.	T	F	_____
2. Many of the houses that appear in Tanobe's paintings are still standing.	T	F	_____

Vocabulary

KEYWORDS

1. decorate* ¶2
2. detour ¶2
3. drug pusher ¶5
4. inhibition ¶6
5. long* ¶7
6. wind ¶8
7. backlane ¶9
8. insatiable* ¶10
9. hide ¶10
10. proud* ¶13

KEYWORD EXERCISE

1. ***EXAMPLE:*** "Winter holds sway over the fields and rivers of Québec and *decorates* the cities with icicles from the roof edges."
   How do people *decorate* their homes for Christmas in your country?

   ____

2. What *detours* did Tanobe take before moving to Québec?

____

EXAMPLE: Life is full of unexpected *detours.*

3. *Matching:*

_____	1. *insatiable*	a.	being satisfied with oneself
_____	2. *backlane*	b.	idea or emotion preventing you from doing something
_____	3. *wind*	c.	person who sells things illegally
_____	4. *hide*	d.	synonym: unquenchable
_____	5. *proud*	e.	narrow road between a row of houses
_____	6. *long*	f.	move in a crooked way
_____	7. *inhibition*	g.	antonym: show
_____	8. *drug pusher*	h.	desire to do something

REVIEW

Now that you have studied the vocabulary, reread or reskim the passage.

LEARNING STRATEGY

Understanding and Using Emotions: Focusing on what you *can* understand in a reading helps you develop a positive attitude and increases your comprehension.

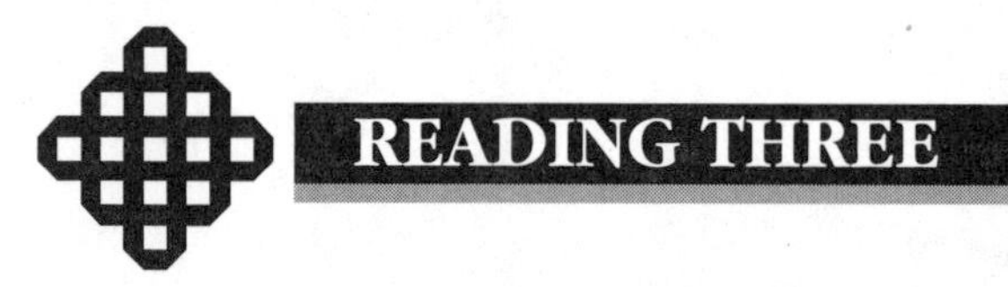

READING THREE

Reading process: Your teacher will give you a minute and a half to skim each of the parts in this reading. After you've skimmed everything, read each part at your own speed, marking vocabulary as usual. When you come to the end of each part, review it and think about its main points.

COMPREHENSION: NAMING THE PARTS OF THE READING

Look at Parts Two and Three. For each one, write a title that gives a good idea of its content.

CANADA'S EARLIEST WOMEN SETTLERS

Part One: Introduction

1 In the drama of Canada's history, women have generally been credited with minor roles or behind-the-scenes chores.[1] Most historians have concentrated on the hero, showing how the "great man" has always been at centre stage, shaped by his times and yet influencing them; history = biography = history. This historical approach is not so satisfactory with women, for although there were certainly outstanding women in our past, their greatest contributions have been made collectively. In some instances, the women belonged to[2] a formal organization with explicit aims, such as the *Ursuline Order*[a]. In other cases, a number of women worked separately but to a common end, as the writers on early English Canada have added greatly to our understanding of that era. Finally, there were women who fought their individual battles for entry into the various professions; their individual successes eventually combined to effect a change in the nature of Canadian society.

2 Recently, Canadian historians have turned to writing "social history," which focuses on the daily struggles[3] of ordinary men, women and children. Perhaps now women will receive more attention—and perhaps people will discover that many of these "ordinary women" were in fact quite extraordinary and deserving of acclaim.

3 This neglect of the woman's role has been partially due to the fact that many of the earliest women arriving in Canada, women quite worthy[4] to be called heroic, were associated with religious orders. To become a nun is to become virtually anonymous; one working for the glory of God does not seek recognition from mankind. And so these women, humble and self-effacing, were accepted at their own valuation and remained in history, as they did in the society of early Québec, in the background. It is surely time to lift the veil.

Part Two

4 Prominent among these women was Madame de la Peltrie, a wealthy[5] widow who, despite family objections, came to Québec in 1639. She brought with her Mère Marie de l'Incarnation and two other nuns, and established a branch of the Ursuline Order in New France. Together, these indomitable[6] women founded a convent for Indian children, whom they loved dearly. They lived in wretched surroundings, worked to exhaustion and struggled in any spare moments to learn the Indian language. The letters of Mère Marie tell a great deal about these early days. Many of her letters were to wealthy women in France. Although some responded, there was never enough money for the nuns to live at more than a bare subsistence level.

5 But Madame de la Peltrie yearned for[7] even greater hardships than these. She appealed to go into the Huron mission field, perhaps to seek the martyrdom that came to Pères Lalement, Jogues and several others, but the Jesuits refused her services. So Madame de la Peltrie was at Québec to meet Jeanne Mance when she arrived. This beautiful young woman had been determined from an early age to become a missionary in Canada, and she eagerly[8] joined Maisonneuve's expedition to found a *mission*[b] at Montréal. The project was strongly opposed by the governor of Québec because the site for the new mission was deep in Iroquois territory. However, the small group containing a handful of women, could not be deterred—nor could Madame de la Peltrie, who was determined to join in this adventure. Despite the governor's

forebodings, they arrived safely at Montréal. The women immediately raised an altar and a Mass of thanksgiving was celebrated.

6 A habitation, including a chapel, was built before winter. The next year Jeanne Mance's hospital was built—outside the walls of the fort, for lack of space within. It was, of course, vulnerable to attacks, which came often and supplied her with patients.

7 In 1660, despite poor health, Jeanne Mance undertook[9] the onerous trip back to France to seek badly needed funds. She went to the rich widow who had subsidized her first journey to Québec, spoke movingly of the needs of the colony and received another substantial donation. She left most of the money to be invested by a French nobleman of her acquaintance, keeping only enough for the most pressing needs at Montréal. She spent some time gathering[10] new recruits, then met with her "banker" just before her ship sailed. When he was questioned about his investment plans, the gentleman assured her, "My daughter, God will provide for you." In fact, he had applied the money to his own debts and never repaid it.

Part Three

8 Another of the nuns was Marguerite Bourgeoys, who came to establish the first girls' school in Montréal. All four of these women—Jeanne Mance, Madame de la Peltrie, Mère Marie and Marguerite Bourgeoys—seemed to thrive on hardship and deprivation. The "delicate" Jeanne Mance died first, at age 67, and Marguerite Bourgeoys lived to be 80. During her long life she also founded a religious order, The Sisters of the Congregation, and acted as chaperone[11] to the King's Daughters.

9 The King's Daughters—these women played a more traditional role. In pioneering times there is always a shortage of marriageable women, and the gap is filled in various ways. The early fur traders, both French and Scottish, often took Indian wives. The women served the men faithfully, showing them how to live off the land, acting as their translators, bearing their children, but were frequently abandoned. *Intendant*[c] Jean Talon wanted French brides[12] for the colonists establishing their seigneuries along the St. Lawrence in the 1660s. The parish priests in France found these brides, who were sent off to the New World in several shiploads, carefully supervised at all times. Many were wards of the state, and all were given the customary dowry by the King when they were married; hence, the name of King's Daughters. Naturally, most of these girls found husbands almost immediately and received their dowry, generally consisting of an ox, a cow, two chickens, two barrels of salt meat, two pigs and eleven *crowns.*[d] The few girls who went unclaimed usually chose to enter a convent rather than return, humiliated, to their home parish.

10 Life for those who married may well have been better than what they left behind, but it was far from easy. Buxom, healthy-looking women were the first to be chosen, for they were expected to bear numerous children (the first "family allowance" went to parents who reared ten or more children!) and put in a hard day's work. A Swedish traveller of about this time wrote that the woman of New France "has a hard life full of suffering, especially among the working classes. She is always to be seen in the fields, the meadows or in the stables, there is no form of work to which she does not turn her hand." In addition to all this, a woman with any education was expected to teach both her children and her husband how to read and write. This situation continued far into the future; more than a century later, Governor Simcoe's wife noted in her diary that, "The Canadian women are better educated than the men, who

take care of their horses and attend little to anything else, leaving the management of their affairs to the women."

11 It is interesting to note that there were "brideships" in English Canada as well. There was a dearth of women in early British Columbia about the time of the Gold Rush, and the Columbia Emigration Society of London came to the rescue. Groups of prospective brides were sent on at least three ships arriving in Victoria in the 1860s. It appears that these women had their pick of suitors—though, regrettably, a few discovered that the miners would pay handsomely for their favours and simply couldn't resist this more lucrative way of life.

SPECIALIZED VOCABULARY

[a]*Ursuline Order:* a group of women banded together for a common purpose.

[b]*mission:* the headquarters of a religious group.

[c]*intendant:* an administrative officer responsible for finance, justice and the police.

[d]*crowns:* silver coins.

After You Read

Identify the circled reference words.

COMPREHENSION QUESTIONS

1. Why has the history of the earliest women arriving in Québec been neglected?

____

2. What happened to the donation that Jeanne Mance received in France?

____

3. What was the traditional role of the King's Daughters?

____

LEARNING STRATEGY

Remembering New Material: You can remember information better if you think of new ways to organize and present it.

Vocabulary

VOCABULARY IN CONTEXT

1. Find the word *order* in ¶1. What do you think it means?
2. Find the word *dowry* in ¶9. What does it mean?

KEYWORDS

1. chores* ¶1
2. belong to ¶1
3. struggle* ¶2
4. worthy ¶3
5. wealthy ¶4
6. indomitable ¶4
7. yearn for* ¶5
8. eagerly ¶5
9. undertake ¶7
10. gather ¶7
11. chaperone* ¶8
12. bride ¶9

KEYWORD EXERCISE

1. Which house *chore* do you like the least? ____________________

   EXAMPLE: Washing the dishes was Jill's main chore around the house.

2. Did you *belong to* any student clubs when you were in high school? Can you name them?

   ____

3. Which of these words could be substituted for *struggle* in the following phrase from the reading?

   ... the daily *struggles* of ordinary men, women and children ...

   conflicts fights violence battles encounters

4. ***EXAMPLE:*** Many of the earliest women arriving in Canada, women quite *worthy* to be called heroic, were associated with religious orders.

   Think of a well-known woman from your own nation or culture. What did this person do to be *worthy* of her reputation?

5. Which of the following is an antonym for *wealthy*?

   miserable unknown sick poor

   If you were *wealthy*, name three things that you would own.

   ______________ ______________ ______________

6. Madame de la Peltrie and Mère Marie de l'Incarnation were *indomitable* women who loved the Indian children they met in the New World.

Name two qualities of these *indomitable* women.

a. ______________________ **b.** ______________________

7. ***EXAMPLE:*** After travelling in South America for a month, Sylvie *yearned for* home.

Finish the sentences:

After completing his master's degree, Raymond yearned for ___________.

Emily ____.

8. Which one of the following words does not mean the same thing as the others?

suddenly keenly eagerly anxiously

9. ***EXAMPLE:*** Despite not having a lot of money, Nicolas decided to *undertake* a trip to Hong Kong.

Name something you would like to *undertake* before you are too old.

10. *Gather* can be a transitive verb (with a direct object) ...

EXAMPLE: Jeanne Mance *gathered* many new recruits in Montréal.

... or an intransitive verb (with no direct object) ...

EXAMPLE: Many people *gathered* on the corner.

NOTE: Don't confuse *gather* with *collect*. People *gather* things that they want to use; they *collect* things that they want to have and to show to people. *Collecting* things can be a hobby, but not *gathering* things.

Finish the sentences:

If you were in the forest and you wanted to build a fire, you would gather ____.

Collecting ____________________________ is a popular hobby.

11. Have you ever acted as *chaperone* at a party or dance?

EXAMPLE: *Chaperones* have lots of responsibilities.

12. Which of the following words are connected with the idea of a *bride*?

woman marriage wedding convent husband

EXAMPLE: Jean Talon wanted French *brides* for the colonists.

LEARNING STRATEGY

Managing Your Learning: After you try out new learning strategies, evaluate them and find ways to keep using the ones that match your needs and your learning style.

REVIEW

Now that you've studied the vocabulary, reread or reskim the passage.

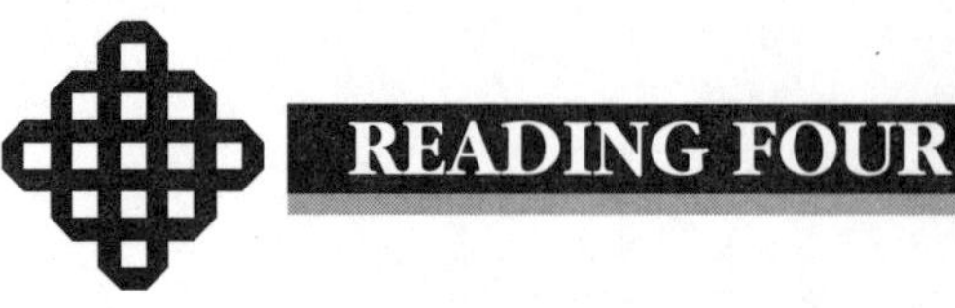

READING FOUR

Reading process: Let's work on speed. Your teacher will give you two minutes to read as far as you can in the following passage. Mark where you stop. Then you'll start at the beginning again and be given another two minutes. See how much farther you can go this time. Then do it a third time. Finally, just read straight through without any time limit.

NORMAN BETHUNE: DOCTOR UNDER FIRE

1 When we think of famous Canadian doctors, the name of Norman Bethune is always on our list. Bethune served as a doctor in three wars and gave his life in a war in China. Even today, more than fifty years after he died, the Chinese people still think of him as a great hero. Though Bethune was not afraid of danger,[1] he was much more than a brave adventurer. He overcame[2] great personal difficulties in his short life. And he was very well known as a scientist and inventor.

2 Norman Bethune was born in Gravenhurst, Ontario, on March 3, 1890. In 1909, at the University of Toronto, Norman began to study science to get into medical school. Before entering medical school, however, he worked as a lumberjack. When World War I began, in August 1914, Norman had completed only two years of medical school, but he decided to join the army. In 1915, he served as a *stretcher-bearer*[a] in France. He was not there to fight, but he had one of the most dangerous jobs in the army. He rescued wounded[3] soldiers by giving (them) first aid and helping to carry them away from the battle on stretchers.

Threads

Be a leader yourself, though you only lead yourself, for every leader starts by first leading himself.

Norman Bethune

3 In 1916 he graduated from medical school, in the same class as that of Frederick Banting, who would later discover a drug called *insulin.*[b] Instead of returning to the army, young Dr. Bethune joined the British Royal Navy, serving as a surgeon on a ship. Afterwards, he worked for a short time as a family doctor, then spent six months as a medical officer with the Canadian Air Force.

4 In 1926, he was diagnosed as having tuberculosis, a common cause of death around the world at that time. The disease was sometimes called "the white plague" or "consumption," and its symptoms[4] included a bad cough, fever, and loss of weight. The usual treatment was rest, sometimes for years, in special hospitals called sanatoriums. Bethune was not a good patient and often stayed up late to party with friends at the sanatorium. And he would not stop smoking cigarettes, though he knew (they) were bad for his lungs. After a year of rest, he was not cured.[5] Then doctors tried a new operation on Bethune called "artificial pneumothorax" (AP). The operation and the two months of rest that followed cured Bethune of this dreaded disease.

5 At the age of 37, he decided to become a chest surgeon and help people with tuberculosis. His first job was at the Royal Victoria Hospital in Montréal with Dr. Edward Archibald, one of the world's best chest surgeons. Bethune taught at McGill University, learned chest surgery from an expert, and did his own research. But after a while, the two men did not get along very well. Bethune found Archibald too slow and too careful. Archibald thought that Bethune rushed through operations and risked the lives of his patients. In 1933, Bethune took charge of chest surgery[6] at Sacré Coeur Hospital in Cartierville, Québec, and continued to live in Montréal.

Norman Bethune

6 Though Bethune did a lot of research, he was more successful as an inventor. He was often unhappy with surgical instruments and wrote that many were "out-worn and clumsy." He was even known to throw[7] instruments across the operating room! Bethune invented dozens of instruments himself. One of his inventions was a machine to perform AP. But his most popular invention was called the "Bethune rib shears." He got the idea from a pair of shoemaker's shears, used to cut leather. The rib shears are still made and sold today, more than sixty years after Bethune invented them.

7 Though he was successful, Bethune was troubled by the effects of the Great *Depression.*[c] There was no *medicare*[d] in Canada, and many poor people could not afford[8] to visit a doctor. In the summer of 1935, Bethune visited Russia, which was then part of the Soviet Union, a communist country. Though Bethune did not like everything he saw in Russia, he did like their medicare system. So he decided to become a communist and crusaded[9] for medicare in Canada. He was not successful during his lifetime; the Canadian government did not introduce medicare until thirty years later.

8 In 1936 Bethune left Canada to serve as a doctor in the Spanish Civil War. He supported the Spanish government in its fight against the fascist leader, General Francisco Franco, who was trying to take control of Spain by force. After less than two months in Spain, Bethune set up a *blood transfusion service*[e] to help the wounded. It was the first mobile[10] blood transfusion service in the world. Bethune gave many transfusions himself and was often in danger of being killed or wounded. A year later he left Spain, never to return.

9 In 1938, China was at war with the Japanese forces that had invaded its country. Bethune volunteered to serve in northern China with the communist army, led by Mao Tse-tung. For the next year and a half, Bethune worked flat out,[11] bringing medical treatment to wounded soldiers, wherever they were, using mobile medical teams.

10 Bethune faced terrible challenges. There were very few trained doctors or nurses, so he set up training courses and wrote medical textbooks himself. Surgical instruments were in short supply, so Bethune again started to make his own. He needed a way of carrying his supplies to the battles, so he invented a box that fitted over the back of a mule.

11 On October 28, 1939, Bethune cut his finger during an operation. He kept on working, but the finger became infected.[12] His body was too weak to resist the spread of the infection, and he died of blood poisoning at the age of 49. He did not live to see the defeat of the Japanese in World War II or to see Mao Tse-tung become the leader of China.

12 Even to this day the Chinese learn about Bethune in school and see many pictures of him in books and on posters and stamps. However, it wasn't until

1972, thirty-three years after his death, that the Canadian government finally announced that Bethune was "a Canadian of national historic significance."

SPECIALIZED VOCABULARY

[a] *stretcher-bearer:* a person who carries the sick, wounded, or dead on a type of portable bed.

[b] *insulin:* a hormone secreted by the pancreas that enables the body to use sugar and other carbohydrates.

[c] *Great Depression:* the period of time beginning in the late 1920s and lasting through the 1930s when the economy was very bad in many parts of the world.

[d] *medicare:* the system of public health care in a country.

[e] *blood transfusion service:* the act of transferring blood to a person.

After You Read

Identify the circled reference words.

COMPREHENSION QUESTIONS

1. How did Bethune deal with his illness?

   ____

   ____

2. What contributions did Bethune make in Spain and China?

   ____

   ____

3. What was one of Bethune's most popular inventions?

   ____

   ____

TRUE–FALSE QUESTIONS

			¶ number
1. Bethune was not the easiest person to get along with.	T	F	______
2. An unintentional mistake cost Bethune his life.	T	F	______

Vocabulary

KEYWORDS

1. danger ¶1
2. overcome* ¶1
3. wounded ¶2
4. symptoms ¶4
5. cure* ¶4
6. surgery ¶5
7. throw ¶6
8. afford* ¶7
9. crusade ¶7
10. mobile ¶8
11. flat out ¶9
12. infected ¶11

KEYWORD EXERCISE

1. Which of the following words are related to *danger?*
   threat peril coincidence harm unlucky

   EXAMPLE: The mountain climber's life was in *danger* because of the great cold.

2. ***EXAMPLE:*** Norman Bethune *overcame* great personal difficulties in his short life.

   Describe one event in your life in which you *overcame* great odds to achieve something.

3. ***EXAMPLE:*** Bethune rescued *wounded* soldiers by giving them first aid.

   List three ways you can get *wounded* on a camping trip.

   a. ________________ **b.** ________________ **c.** ________________

4. ***EXAMPLE:*** The patient was allowed to go home because he didn't have any more *symptoms* of the illness.

   What are some *symptoms* of the common head cold?

   ____

5. ***EXAMPLE:*** It took Bethune several years to be *cured* of his illness.

   Finish the sentences:

   It is not easy to ______________________________.

   The sick child ______________________________.

6. Look for the word in ¶5 that means the person who performs *surgery.* What is it? ______________________

   Which of the following is *surgery?*
   an operation diet exercise medicine chemotherapy radiation therapy

   EXAMPLE: Sometimes it takes a long time to recover after *surgery.*

7. *Meanings:*
   - If you *throw away* your money on foolish things, you'll soon be broke.
   - If you *throw cold water on* the idea, your friend will be discouraged.
   - If you *throw up* after eating, the food was probably not fresh.

   QUESTION: Why do you think Bethune would sometimes *throw* his instruments across the operating room?

8. *EXAMPLE:* Most young people cannot *afford* a new car.

   Finish the sentences:

   A busy person ______________________________.

   I can't __________________________________.

9. *EXAMPLE:* Bethune believed so strongly in medicare in Canada that he *crusaded* for it.

   What did Terry Fox *crusade* for? ____________________

10. *EXAMPLE:* The couple vacation every winter in their *mobile* home in the south.

    What is an antonym of *mobile?* ____________________

    What is the noun form of this word? ____________________

11. Have you ever worked *flat out* on a project or activity? What was it?

    ____

    EXAMPLE: Bethune worked *flat out* during the war in China.

12. What is one way to fight serious *infections?*____________________

    EXAMPLE: The wound became *infected* because of the dirty bandage.

REVIEW

Now that you have studied the vocabulary, reread or reskim the passage.

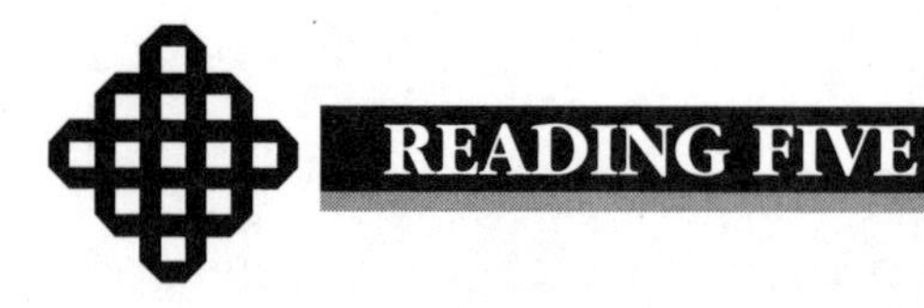

READING FIVE

FREDERICK BANTING: DISCOVERER OF INSULIN

1 The career of Frederick Grant Banting, the discoverer of insulin, demonstrated that extensive scholarship and a wide background in research are not needed to conceive[1] a brilliant idea that may be of great scientific and practical value. Banting thought of insulin—which has saved[2] the lives of many thousands of *diabetics*[a]—before he became a research professor; after

becoming a research professor he made no other great discovery.

Frederick Grant Banting

2 Banting was an Ontario farmer's son, born at Alliston in 1891. When he was a schoolboy he saw a scaffolding collapse and watched the doctor giving first aid to two badly injured masons. He was so impressed by the idea of giving immediate help to human suffering that he decided on the spot[3] to become a doctor, and when he went to the University of Toronto he entered the medical school and graduated in 1917.

3 It was the middle of World War I and Banting enrolled in the Medical Corps. In the battle of Cambrai, he was tending casualties under fire when he himself was badly wounded; for that day's action he won the Military Cross. On returning to Canada after the war he started a practice in London, Ontario. It was not a very busy one and he had time to think about medical problems, particularly the problem of diabetes. He had the idea that if a *pancreatic hormone*[b] in a pure form could be injected into the blood stream, this might enable the body to use up the blood sugar, and so the notorious[4] "wasting" effects of the disease could be controlled. How to do it was the problem. On the night of October 30, 1920, he woke up with the basic idea in his mind and wrote in his notebook: "Tie off pancreas ducts of dogs. Wait six or eight weeks. Remove[5] and extract."

4 Banting immediately went with his idea to Professor J.R.R. Macleod, head of the department of physiology at the University of Toronto, and Macleod was sufficiently interested to give him laboratory facilities and the assistance of a graduate student, Charles H. Best. In the summer of 1921 Banting and Best isolated insulin and purified it with the assistance of J.B. Collip so that it could be experimentally tested on human patients. It proved an immediate and dramatic success and in 1923 the Nobel Prize was awarded jointly to Banting and Macleod, who in fact had nothing directly to do with the research though he was nominally in charge of the project because of his professorial status. Banting was at first inclined to refuse the award because Best was not honoured. But in the end he shared[6] his half of the $40,000 award with Best, while Macleod shared his with Collip, for whom Banting had conceived a rooted dislike during their period of working together.

> It was the miracle we had been hoping for but there was nothing accidental involved. We had simply found what we had been looking for.
>
> *Charles H. Best, co-discoverer of insulin*

5 On the strength of his achievement and his celebrity,[7] Banting was appointed the University of Toronto's first professor of medical research in 1923. He was knighted and elected to the Royal Society of Canada and to the much more prestigious[8] Royal Society in London. But though he later suggested some interesting directions of research which other men followed up, Banting remained essentially a man of one great insight[9]—the midnight hunch that led

him, even before he had the means of research, in the direction of discovering insulin. He made no other discovery of major medical or scientific importance.

6 When World War II began in 1939, Banting enlisted again in the Canadian Army Medical Corps, with the rank of captain. In February 1941, he was sent on a scientific mission to Britain, but the plane crashed while attempting a forced landing on a frozen lake in eastern Newfoundland. Banting's lung was pierced[10] by the wreckage and he died long before help could reach him.

SPECIALIZED VOCABULARY

[a] *diabetics:* people who suffer from *diabetes,* a disease in which the body is unable to absorb normal amounts of sugar and starch.

[b] *pancreatic hormone:* insulin produced by the body's pancreas gland.

After You Read

Identify the circled reference word.

COMPREHENSION QUESTIONS

1. Where did Dr. Banting get the insulin for his experiments?

 ____

2. Name the people who shared in the Nobel Prize.

 ____

3. What boyhood incident made Banting want to become a doctor?

 ____

TRUE–FALSE QUESTIONS

			¶ number
1. Banting made only one important discovery in his lifetime.	T	F	_____
2. Banting served his country in both world wars.	T	F	_____

Vocabulary

KEYWORDS

1. conceive* ¶1
2. save ¶1
3. on the spot ¶2
4. notorious ¶3
5. remove* ¶3
6. share* ¶4
7. celebrity ¶5
8. prestigious ¶5
9. insight* ¶5
10. pierce ¶6

KEYWORD EXERCISE

1. *Meanings:*
   - To *conceive* of something is to think up an idea.

   QUESTION: Name one invention that Michelangelo *conceived* of.
   - To *conceive* a child is to become pregnant.

   QUESTION: How many children did your mother *conceive*?
   - Explain the similarities between the two meanings.

2. *Meanings:*
   - If you rescue a drowning person, you *save* his or her life.
   - If you *save* a little money from each paycheque, you may become wealthy.
   - You can *save* your eyes by reading large-print books.

   QUESTION: How does insulin *save* people's lives?

3. ***EXAMPLE:*** As a youngster, Banting saw a doctor treat two injured men and decided *on the spot* to become a doctor.

   When you go shopping for expensive items, are you able to make a decision *on the spot?*

4. ***EXAMPLE:*** Jack the Ripper was a *notorious* criminal.

   Who is the most *notorious* person you can think of?

5. ***EXAMPLE:*** Banting had the idea of *removing* the pancreas from dogs.

   Finish the sentences:

   The doctors wanted to remove ________________________________.

   When entering a Japanese house, people should ________________.

6. ***EXAMPLES:*** Banting *shared* the Nobel Prize with several other people.

   I *shared* my lunch with my roommate.

Finish the sentences:

Children have to be taught to share ______________________________.

Rich nations should ______________________________.

7. *Meanings:*

A *celebrity* is a well-known person.

EXAMPLE: She met lots of *celebrities* at the party.

If you discover a cure for cancer, you will attain worldwide *celebrity.*

EXAMPLE: Banting attained *celebrity* for discovering insulin.

Explain the similarities between the two meanings.

EXAMPLE: The Royal Society in London is a *prestigious* association.

Have you or anyone in your family ever received a *prestigious* award?

8. Which of the following words are related to *insight?*

wisdom luck understanding penetration discovery

EXAMPLE: Sigmund Freud had great *insight* into human nature.

9. *EXAMPLE:* Banting's lung was *pierced* in a plane crash.

Finish the sentences:

A nail pierced ______________________________.

The little girl wanted ______________________________.

REVIEW

Now that you've studied the vocabulary, reread or reskim the passage.

LEARNING STRATEGY

Remembering New Material: Making up paragraphs that contain new words helps you remember them more easily.

NOTE: This reading is also on the tape.

DAVID SUZUKI: CANADA'S POPULARIZER OF SCIENCE

David Suzuki

1 Canadian broadcast journalist and writer David Suzuki has appeared on television for the past sixteen years as the enthusiastic, engaging, and knowledgeable host[1] of the celebrated *CBC*[a] series *The Nature of Things.* He has been recognized along with such figures as Jacques Cousteau and Carl Sagan as one of the world's most effective[2] popularizers of science.

2 A prize-winning *geneticist*[b] and university teacher, Suzuki launched his first career, in zoological research, in the United States in 1961, after completing his undergraduate and graduate studies at American institutions. He returned to Canada a year later and, in 1963, set up a laboratory at the University of British Columbia, where he became a full professor at the age of 33. His pathbreaking discoveries regarding temperature-sensitive genetic mutations in fruit flies earned him, in 1969, 1970, and 1971, the E.W.R. Steacie award, given annually to the most outstanding Canadian research scientist under the age of 33.

3 In the 1970s Suzuki withdrew from active research to devote himself primarily to broadcast journalism. In the past quarter century, he has anchored dozens of popular and critically acclaimed radio or television series, miniseries, and specials. His radio credits include such shows as *Quirks and Quarks* (1974–79) and *It's a Matter of Survival* (1989); he both originated and hosted the two shows. His television shows include *Science Magazine* (1974–79), *A Planet for the Taking* (1985), and *The Secret of Life* (1993) as well as *The Nature of Things*, which currently[3] airs in more than fifty countries.

Threads

Education has failed in a very serious way to convey the most important lesson science can teach: Scepticism.

David Suzuki

4 David Suzuki is Canada's best-known environmental crusader and a dedicated civil rights[4] activist. In addition to demystifying science for nonscientists, he frequently addresses controversial issues in his broadcasts and other public forums. These include the social responsibility of scientists, the social implications of gene therapy and other scientific innovations, and the dangers posed by the economic and political pressures of scientists. He is also concerned[5] with the deficiencies in science education, the consequences of underfunding basic research, and the unwitting or intentional misuses of scientific data and statistics.

5 Suzuki has also strived to alert people to the threats[6] to the biosphere that have resulted from humankind's attempts to dominate the planet. "As a scientist, I know how ignorant we are of the biological and physical world," he wrote in *Metamorphosis* (1987), his autobiography, "yet we continue to cling to the lie that we *know* what we're doing. The truth is that we have no idea." He is convinced that "the ecological crisis[7] that afflicts the world is, at its base,

a result of the tremendous alienation that we feel from the natural world." He has endeavoured to foster, particularly in children, a "spiritual connection with nature," so that people will "consider the water and the air and the soil their home."

6 In 1990 he and Dr. Tara Cullis, his wife, founded the David Suzuki *Foundation.*[c] According to Suzuki, (it) is dedicated to developing "a vision of sustainable communities living within the planets' carrying capacity ... a strategy[8] for communities to work toward that vision, and a communications plan to help work through the strategy."

7 According to Clyde H. Farnsworth, Suzuki's "forest of graying tresses, laser-like gaze, and goatee" have become instantly recognizable[9] throughout Canada. In a profile of him for *International Wildlife* (September/October 1988), Jerry Buckley wrote that Suzuki is "passionate, driven, irreverent, brilliant, charismatic, and controversial,[10] usually all in the same sentence."

SPECIALIZED VOCABULARY

[a] *CBC:* Canadian Broadcasting Corporation, the English-Canadian public broadcasting network.

[b] *geneticist:* a scientist trained in the biological area dealing with the principles of heredity and variation in animals and plants.

[c] *foundation:* an institution that has its own source of money.

After You Read

Identify the circled reference words.

COMPREHENSION QUESTIONS

1. What are some of Suzuki's main interests?

____

____

2. What is Suzuki best known for?

____

____

3. What message does Suzuki try to give children?

____

____

TRUE–FALSE QUESTIONS

				¶ number
1.	Suzuki did most of his studies in Canada.	T	F	_____
2.	Suzuki thinks that science holds the answer to most of humanity's problems.	T	F	_____

Vocabulary

KEYWORDS

1. host ¶1
2. effective* ¶1
3. currently ¶3
4. rights ¶4
5. concerned* ¶4
6. threat* ¶5
7. crisis ¶5
8. strategy ¶6
9. recognizable* ¶7
10. controversial ¶7

KEYWORD EXERCISE

1. As you'll notice in your dictionary, the word *host* has several meanings.

Choose the sentence below with the same meaning as the sentence in ¶1.

- David Suzuki is an engaging and knowledgeable *host.*

a. A *host* of soldiers appeared in the distance.

b. She is always such a gracious *host.*

c. Barbara Frum *hosted* a very popular radio show for many years.

2. In your opinion, which of the following would be the most *effective* way to reduce unemployment?

a. lower taxes

b. spend more on government programs

c. lend money to small businesses

3. Look at ¶3 and find the word *currently.* What part of speech is it?

____

EXAMPLE: His music is *currently* very popular.

Finish the sentences:

The prime minister is *currently* ______________________________.

The hockey team ______________________________________.

4. If you have a *right* to do or have something, it means no one should stop you from doing it or having it. *Rights* are things that people want to do or have, not things that they have to do but don't want to.

   Name an activity that only citizens of a country have the *right* to do.

5. What part of speech is *concerned* in this sentence: He is *concerned* with the inadequacies in science education.

   Which of the following sentences contains the same use and meaning?

   a. There's great *concern* in Canada about the high level of unemployment.

   b. The public is also *concerned* about the problem of homelessness.

6. *Matching:*

_____	**1.** *threat*	**a.**	synonym: visible
_____	**2.** *crisis*	**b.**	a skillful plan
_____	**3.** *strategy*	**c.**	debatable
_____	**4.** *recognizable*	**d.**	sign of possible harm
_____	**5.** *controversial*	**e.**	state of danger

REVIEW

Now that you've studied the vocabulary, reread or reskim the passage.

Writing a Biography

Choose a person whom you admire and who serves as a role model for you. Briefly describe this person's background and personal accomplishments. Explain why she or he is so important in your life.

Evaluating Learning Strategies

In this chapter you have been presented with several learning strategies. Think for a moment about the strategy of making vocabulary cards. Was this helpful for you? Do you think that you will want to keep using it? If not, can you revise or simplify it to make it more useful?

Look back over the chapter at the other learning strategies that were presented. Were there any that weren't very helpful to you? What wasn't helpful about them? Which ones did you find helpful? Think about times and ways that you can keep them in your future reading. If you know of other strategies that were not suggested in this chapter, tell your classmates about them.

Evaluating Your Learning

	Very little	*Quite a bit*	*A lot*
You know some new vocabulary.	________	________	________
Your comprehension is stronger.	________	________	________
You can pick out the most important words in a passage.	________	________	________
Your writing has improved.	________	________	________
You learned something about famous Canadians.	________	________	________

KEYWORDS FOR CHAPTER 2: CANADIAN PORTRAITS

Verbs
afford
belong
conceive
concern
crusade
cure
decorate
gather
hide
long
overcome
pierce
remove
save
set
settle
share
spend
throw
undertake
wind
yearn for

Nouns
accessibility
background
backlane
bride
celebrity
chaperone
childhood
chores
crisis
danger
detour
drug pusher
host
inhibition
insight
right
strategy
struggle
symptom
surgery
threat

Adjectives
authentic
controversial
effective
indomitable
infected
insatiable
mobile
notorious
prestigious
proud
recognizable
remote
rural
strange
unfamiliar
wealthy
worthy
wounded

Adverbs
currently
eagerly
flat out
inevitably
on the spot

Native Voices

3

CHAPTER

INTRODUCTION

PLANNING YOUR LEARNING

Review your overall goal statement. How much progress did you make toward it in the last chapter? Do you want to change it? Think about how you can work to meet your goal as you study this new chapter.

- How many words do you want to learn? (minimum 68, the number of keywords in the chapter)
- What grade would you like to make on the vocabulary section of the exam at the end of the chapter?
- What grade would you like to make on the reading comprehension section of the exam?
- What are you going to read outside of class?

PREVIEWING THE CHAPTER

- Think about the title of this chapter. What do you think the term "Native Voices" means?
- Look in the Table of Contents at the titles of the seven readings in this chapter. Look through the chapter at the pictures and the maps. What are some things that you would like to learn about?
- Which reading looks the most interesting?

FREEWRITING: NORTH AMERICAN INDIANS

- What do you know about North American Indians? Take a few minutes to make a list. If you're unsure about something, write it down and put a question mark after it. Make your list as long as you can in the time your teacher gives you.
- After you finish writing, show your list to two or three of your classmates. Do you and your partners have any differences of information or opinion? Where did you get your information? How could you find out if it's accurate?

LEARNING STRATEGY

Managing Your Learning: As you skim, forming questions that you expect a reading to answer will improve your learning.

PREPARING TO READ: CONTENT

Look at the title, subheadings, box, and map in the following reading. What kinds of information do you expect to read in it? Make a list of at least five items.

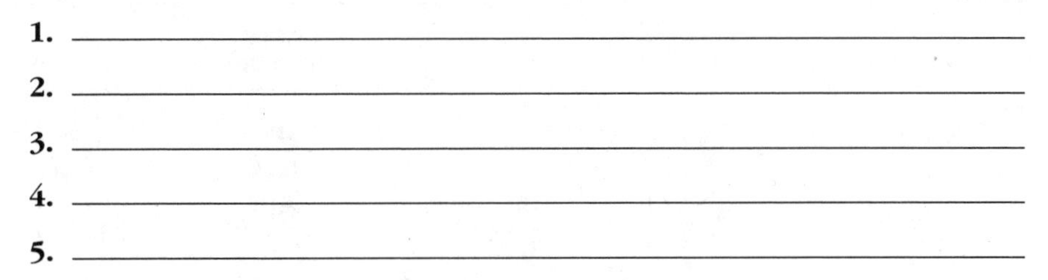

PREPARING TO READ: VOCABULARY

Working alone, list ten vocabulary items that you might expect to find when reading about North American Indians. If you know some words in your native language but not in English, look them up in your bilingual dictionary and write the English equivalents. This "vocabulary preview" will make your reading easier when you encounter these words and concepts.

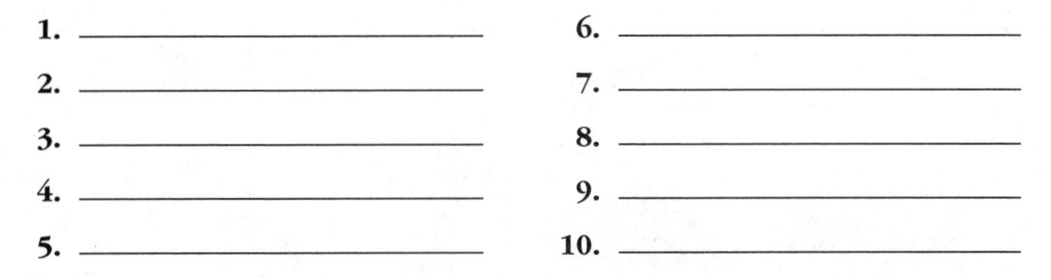

As you read the following article, look for information that tells more about what you already knew, or that differs from what you had heard.

Reading process: You have already done the first step in skimming, which is to look at the title and the subheadings. Now skim each section quickly. Then as you read it more carefully, highlight whatever new vocabulary you wish. As you finish reading each section, skim it again for review.

An Introduction to North American Indian Cultures

STEREOTYPES AND DIVERSITY[3]

Threads

A stereotype is a generalized belief that all members of a group are the same in some way.

1 American Indians are one of the most famous ethnic groups in the world, yet people have usually gotten their impressions of them from comic books, television, and cowboy films. Such sources may lead people to believe that all Indians were bloodthirsty savages, or on the other hand that they were "children of nature" who never did anything wrong. Some believe that Indians never lied, that their languages were very simple and had limited vocabularies, that they were lazy, or that they couldn't adapt to modern life. All these views are what we call *stereotypes* of Indians.

2 The problem with stereotypes is that they are either untrue or only partly true. The members of any group may be similar in some ways, but they are never all the same. Some Indians were/are cruel, some kind; some warlike, some peaceful; some quiet, some talkative; some lazy, some hardworking; some today prefer traditional life, while others have left traditions behind. Believing stereotypes about American Indians keeps us from appreciating the richness and complexities[1] of their cultures.

3 In fact it's difficult to talk about "Indians" because it is a mistake to view American Indians as one large culture. That's because there are hundreds of tribal cultures in the western hemisphere, and the Native population of North America alone stands at about three million today. Before Europeans settled in the Americas, members of the Native populations thought of themselves as Iroquois or Navajo or Comanche—never as members of a larger group that included the entire population of the two continents. Remember, it was Columbus who gave the one name *Indians* to all the Natives he found; and later European settlers followed his example with all the ethnic groups from the northernmost part of Canada to the southern tip of South America. In reality there are countless variations[2] in values, religious beliefs, customs, and life styles among such diverse[3] peoples as the Apache of the Southwestern United States, the Sioux of the Great Plains, the Seminole of the Southeast, the Huron of the Eastern Woodlands, the Ute of the Great Basin, the Nez Percé of the Northwest Plateau, the Kwakiutl of the Northwest Coast, the Yurok of California, the Cree of the Subarctic. Before white settlement changed the face of the land, there were specialized hunting-gathering cultures, farming cultures, fishing cultures. Different economies influenced the development of different social systems, housing styles, religious beliefs.

4 Why, then, should we study such diverse cultures in one chapter called "Native Voices"? The answer is that once Columbus had opened the door to the millions of Europeans who would come to the Americas over the next 500 years, suddenly the Native peoples all had something in common for the first time: they were more like each other than they were like the Europeans (or the Africans or the Asians who followed). The various tribes or bands also experienced similar treatment at the hands of these newcomers. This encounter between the European newcomers and the first Americans led—on both sides—to great misunderstanding and mistrust and to the shedding of rivers of blood.

5 So it is possible to generalize[4] about Indians, as long as we keep in mind that generalizations[4] don't cover all members of all groups. Please remember this as you continue to read in this chapter. Note also that the terms *Indian, Native American* (used in the United States), and *Native peoples* (used in Canada) will be used interchangeably. Other interchangeable terms will be *tribe* (United States), *band* (Canada), *nation,* and *ethnic group* to refer to various groups of Native Americans.

6 The map on page 50 groups North American Native cultures into ten regions. Within each region, despite many variations, we find certain similarities due to common climate,[5] vegetation, and game; due to common ancestors and intermarriage in some cases; and due to trade among the tribes in that particular area. For example, the peoples who inhabited the western part of the Great Plains centred their culture on the most important game[6] animal there: the American bison or buffalo. Because the buffalo moved from place to place, so did they; consequently, they needed housing that could be carried with them. All of the cultures that inhabited this region used the

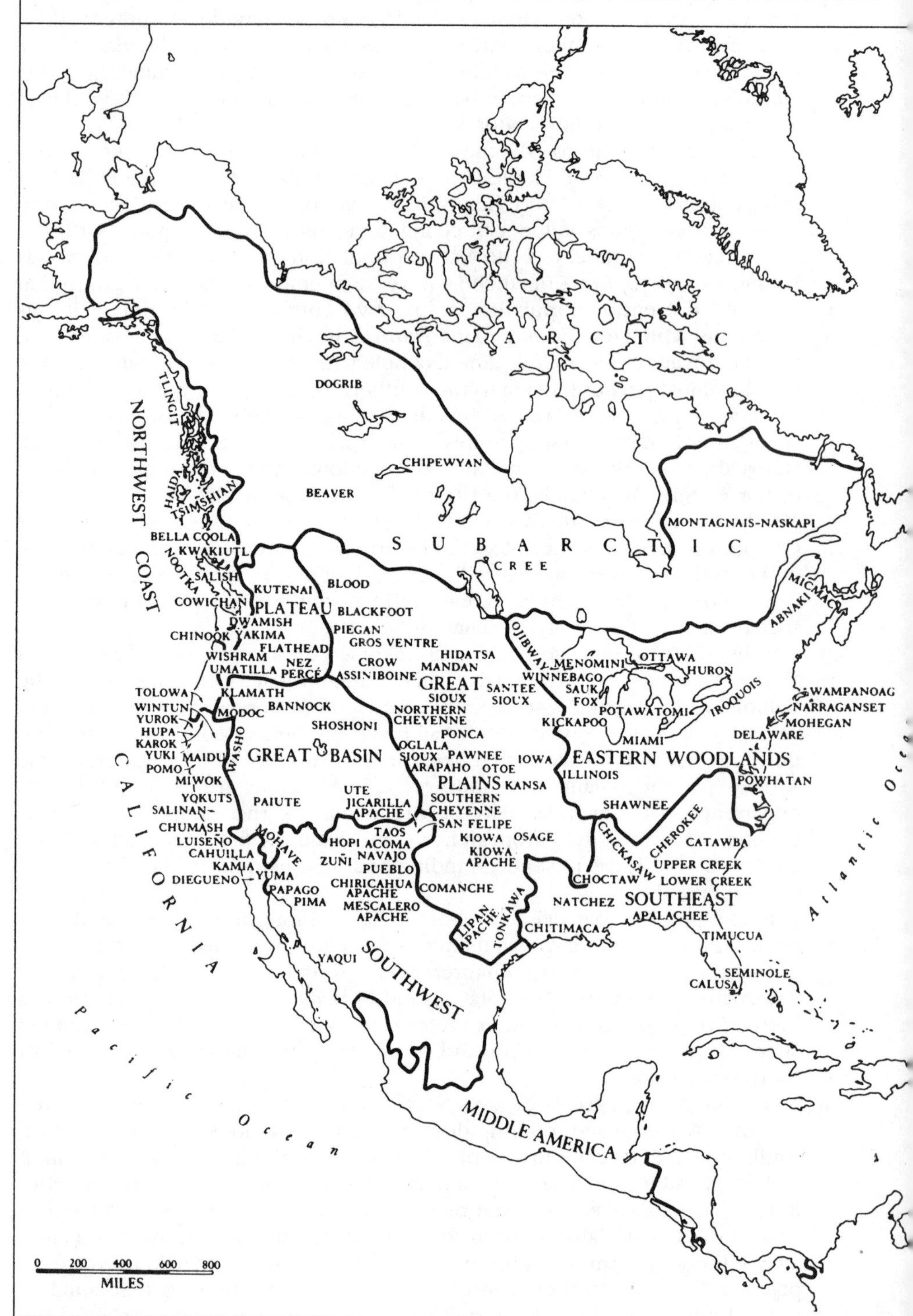
NATIVE AMERICAN TRIBES AND CULTURE AREAS, CIRCA 1650
ARCTIC
SUBARCTIC
NORTHWEST COAST
PLATEAU
GREAT BASIN
CALIFORNIA
GREAT PLAINS
EASTERN WOODLANDS
SOUTHEAST
SOUTHWEST
MIDDLE AMERICA
Pacific Ocean
Atlantic Ocean
DOGRIB
CHIPEWYAN
BEAVER
CREE
MONTAGNAIS-NASKAPI
MICMAC
ABNAKI
TLINGIT
HAIDA
TSIMSHIAN
BELLA COOLA
KWAKIUTL
NOOTKA
SALISH
COWICHAN
KUTENAI
BLOOD
BLACKFOOT
PIEGAN
GROS VENTRE
DWAMISH
YAKIMA
CHINOOK
FLATHEAD
WISHRAM
UMATILLA
NEZ PERCÉ
CROW
ASSINIBOINE
HIDATSA
MANDAN
SANTEE SIOUX
SIOUX
NORTHERN CHEYENNE
PONCA
OGLALA SIOUX
PAWNEE
ARAPAHO
OTOE
IOWA
KANSA
SOUTHERN CHEYENNE
KIOWA
KIOWA APACHE
OSAGE
COMANCHE
LIPAN APACHE
TONKAWA
TOLOWA
WINTUN
YUROK
HUPA
KAROK
YUKI
POMO
MAIDU
MIWOK
WASHO
KLAMATH
MODOC
BANNOCK
SHOSHONI
UTE
PAIUTE
YOKUTS
SALINAN
CHUMASH
LUISEÑO
CAHUILLA
KAMIA
DIEGUENO
MOHAVE
YUMA
PAPAGO
PIMA
JICARILLA APACHE
TAOS
SAN FELIPE
HOPI
ACOMA
ZUÑI
NAVAJO
PUEBLO
CHIRICAHUA APACHE
MESCALERO APACHE
YAQUI
OJIBWA
MENOMINI
OTTAWA
HURON
WINNEBAGO
SAUK
FOX
POTAWATOMI
IROQUOIS
KICKAPOO
MIAMI
ILLINOIS
SHAWNEE
WAMPANOAG
NARRAGANSET
MOHEGAN
DELAWARE
POWHATAN
CHEROKEE
CHICKASAW
CATAWBA
UPPER CREEK
LOWER CREEK
CHOCTAW
NATCHEZ
APALACHEE
CHITIMACA
TIMUCUA
SEMINOLE
CALUSA
0 200 400 600 800
MILES

teepee, a house made from buffalo hides and long poles; it could easily be taken down, carried by horses, and set up again in another place. The different Plains tribes shared a number of other features[7] also. But we must keep in mind that there were also many differences among these groups, and the existence of some similarities does not mean that they were similar in everything.

NATIVE AMERICAN TRADITIONAL CULTURES

7 American Indian tribes depended on nature, whether they were farming or hunting or fishing communities. As a result they believed in the importance of living in harmony with nature and with all its parts. They saw all nature as interconnected: its life forms, both animals and plants; geological features such as mountains, rocks, and rivers; and weather—the four winds, rain, snow. Nature for them was filled with spiritual forces[8] that affected their lives. People were not the most important beings, but only one part of the larger network, neither more nor less important than the other parts. Destroying[9] the balance of nature would bring misfortune, illness, and death to the tribe.

The earth is your mother,
she holds you.
The sky is your father,
he protects you.
Sleep,
sleep.
Rainbow is your sister,
she loves you.
The winds are your brothers,
they sing to you.
Sleep,
sleep.
We are together always
We are together always
There never was a time
when this
was not so.

—*Traditional lullaby, Laguna Pueblo*

8 Religious ceremonies[10] were performed to mark important stages of life (births, marriages, deaths) and to ask the spirits[8] for help or to thank them. It was common for individual people to believe that they each had one particular spirit that helped them personally; often this spirit was associated with a particular type of animal such as the bear or the wolf.

9 In family life, men and women generally performed separate tasks. In most nations the men did the hunting or farming; the women prepared food, tanned the animal hides, and made clothing. Marriage came early; in some tribes it might be arranged by the families, in others the couple might choose for themselves. Usually an extended family (several generations, including aunts and uncles) lived together or near each other, and everyone helped with work and with children. There was much variation in childrearing. In some tribes

children were never punished; in others they were controlled very strictly. Children played games and imitated the adult roles that they would take for themselves when they grew up. Special ceremonies marked a young person's passage from childhood into adulthood.

10 The food they ate depended on the climate, the customs, and what could be found. Many tribes gathered wild nuts, berries, roots, seeds, and herbs for teas and for medicines. Hunters brought home deer, antelope, buffalo, rabbits, birds, seals, turtles, or other game that might exist in their region. Farming communities lived on whatever their mixture of soil and climate allowed—mainly beans, corn, and squash in the dry Southwest. Fishing tribes caught and smoked fish and ate shellfish.

11 Before the Europeans arrived, most Native Americans wore clothing made from animal hides. Some wove cotton and woolen cloth, and along the Northwest Coast, they wove cloth made from strips of tree bark. The amount of clothing worn depended largely on the climate. For shoes some wore sandals, some soft leather moccasins.

12 Housing varied greatly, depending on climate, available materials, and customs. Nomads[11]—people who move from place to place—used housing that could be broken down and carried with them. Peoples who stayed in one place might build from stone, wood, earth, or brick, whichever was common in their area. In some tribes many families lived together in large houses; in others, each family had its own dwelling place.

> May it be beautiful, my house;
> From my head may it be beautiful;
> To my feet, may it be beautiful;
> All above me, may it be beautiful;
> All around me, may it be beautiful.
> —*Traditional Navajo prayer*

NOMADS OF THE GREAT PLAINS REGION

13 Let's look more closely at the inhabitants of one particular area: the nomadic tribes of the western and central Great Plains area, which included the Blackfeet, Crow, Sioux, Kiowa, and some smaller nations. These peoples lived a simple and rather poor life until around 1740, when two European introductions came their way: the horse and the gun. These made their traditional way of life much easier and permitted their cultures to grow strong for the next 150 years, until the disappearance of the buffalo around 1890.

14 For these cultures were totally dependent on the buffalo. They did not farm and did little fishing or gathering. The buffalo provided them with meat for food, hides for clothing and for their teepees, and bones and horns to make into tools. They burned dried buffalo dung for fuel. The people followed the great herds[12] on foot and hunted them in very simple ways until the horse and the gun suddenly made life richer and easier. More meat could be killed with a gun from the back of a horse than on foot with a spear or bow and arrow, and more of it could be carried home. Teepees could be larger with horses to carry the hides and poles that they were made from. Hunters, warriors, and villages could move farther than they had been able to move before.

15 These nations were warlike, and their warfare was also greatly changed by the horse and the gun. They raided villages of other tribes to steal horses, which were a measure of wealth. In addition to the number of horses he had, a man's importance in his tribe was measured by his bravery in war and by the number of enemies he had killed, though also by his wisdom or his abilities at healing and communicating with the spirits.

16 The spiritual life was very important to the Plains tribes. People took dreams and visions[13] very seriously and believed that these could predict the future and should guide their actions. Young men left the village and went alone into the wilderness for a time, during which they fasted and prayed in hopes that a personal spirit would visit them in a dream. This spirit would advise and teach them and would become their protector for the rest of their lives. It often took the form of an animal, and the young man might then think of the bear, or the mountain lion, or the eagle as his own special guide. The belief in visions was so strong that young men might go without food for days and might actually cut their bodies in hopes that doing so would bring them into communication with the spirit world. In the Sun Dance, young Blackfeet men sometimes pushed sharpened sticks through the skin of their chests. These sticks were tied to a tall pole with leather thongs. Then the young men sang, prayed, and danced until their movements tore the sticks out of their bodies. This ceremony was believed to lead to visions and to spiritual guidance.

17 The tribes travelled in small bands, coming together in larger groups once a year to exchange news, have games and competitions, and hold important ceremonies. Important decisions were made by councils of the men during these yearly gatherings. Because survival[14] in hunting, warfare, and village life depended on people's cooperating[15] with each other, decisions were generally made by discussion and group agreement. Public shame and disapproval were very strong methods of controlling people's behaviour. The most serious punishment that a person could receive was exile from the tribe, because a lone Indian would readily be killed by enemy tribes. When possible, exiled men

banded together in small groups of outlaws and they no longer followed the rules or advice of the other members of the tribe.

18 But this way of life did not last forever. With the destruction[9] of the buffalo herds by white hunters around 1890, the tribes lost their source of food and the central feature of their culture. Nothing was the same after (that.)

After You Read

Identify the circled reference words.

COMPREHENSION QUESTIONS

1. In the first section of the reading, which paragraphs talk about stereotypes?

   ____

   Which paragraphs talk about diversity? ______________________________

2. Give an example of a stereotype of North American Indians. ______________

   How could you find out if it were true or not? ______________________________

   ____

3. Who gave the name "Indians" to Native Americans? ______________________________

   ____

4. Look at the map on page 50. Name one tribe or nation from any four of the regions:

   Subarctic: ______________________________

   Northwest Coast: ______________________________

   Plateau: ______________________________

   California: ______________________________

   Great Basin: ______________________________

   Southwest: ______________________________

   Great Plains: ______________________________

   Eastern Woodlands: ______________________________

   Southeast: ______________________________

   - Which of the tribes on the map had you heard of before? Highlight or underline them on the map.
   - Are you living in one of these regions now? If so, which one?

     ____

   - Study the names of the tribes in your region. Remember them and try to learn something about them.

5. In the second section of the reading, identify the topic of each paragraph.

¶7 ______

¶8 ______

¶9 ______

¶10 ______

¶11 ______

¶12 ______

6. What did the white people bring to the Plains Indians that greatly changed their way of life?

a. ______ b. ______

7. What was the most important feature of Plains Indian life? ______

______

8. Why did the Plains cultures grow weaker around the end of the nineteenth century? ______

______

TRUE–FALSE QUESTIONS

			¶ number
1. People were more important than nature to Native peoples.	T	F	______
2. Indians never punished their children.	T	F	______
3. Ceremonies were very important in Native cultures.	T	F	______
4. Food was variable, depending on the climate and customs.	T	F	______
5. Most Indians were vegetarians.	T	F	______
6. Cloth was unknown to Native North Americans until the arrival of Europeans.	T	F	______
7. Each Indian family lived in a separate tent made from animal skins.	T	F	______

LEARNING STRATEGY

Remembering New Material: Thinking about what you have learned from a reading makes you remember it better and longer.

FREEWRITING: REVIEWING WHAT YOU HAVE READ

What did you learn from this reading passage that you didn't already know? List one or two things and comment on them. Did you find anything that contradicted information you had heard? Did anything surprise you? What interested you most?

LEARNING STRATEGY

Overcoming Limitations: Knowing good readers' habits and practising them helps you become a stronger reader.

Developing Good Habits During Reading

What goes through a good reader's mind as she or he reads? In addition to thinking about the content, a good reader thinks about the reading process in the following ways:

1. Good readers make predictions about what's coming next.
2. Good readers form pictures in their heads as they read.
3. Good readers make connections between the content and their own experience, or with things that they already knew.
4. Good readers recognize problems that they are having and they think about them as they read.
5. Good readers know some strategies for solving their reading problems.

Your own reading will become stronger if you use these thought processes as you read. Your teacher will demonstrate each one, using material from another chapter as examples. Listen carefully to what she or he says: she or he is thinking aloud, showing you what your own thoughts can be as you read. Imitate these ways of thinking as you look back on the passage that you just read in this chapter. Then in future readings, practise them until they have become habitual to you too.

Vocabulary

VOCABULARY IN CONTEXT

1. Look at ¶s 11 and 14. What do you suppose *hides* and *poles* are? What clues make you think so?

2. Look at ¶8. What do you suppose it means by *stages* of life?

   What makes you think so?

3. Look at ¶9. What do you think *extended family* might mean?
   What makes you think so?

VOCABULARY STUDY: CHOOSING THE MOST IMPORTANT NEW WORDS

As you learned in the previous chapter, good readers don't look up every new word in the dictionary. They select only those which (1) are most important and which (2) they can't figure out from the context.

Look at the new words that you highlighted as you read. Decide carefully which ones you want to look up. Choose no more than fifteen.

KEYWORDS

1. complexities ¶2
2. variation ¶3
3. diverse,* diversity ¶3, title
4. generalize, generalization ¶5
5. climate ¶6
6. game ¶6
7. feature* ¶6
8. spiritual force, spirit ¶s7, 8
9. destroy,* destruction ¶s7, 18
10. ceremony ¶8
11. nomad ¶12
12. herd ¶14
13. vision ¶16
14. survival ¶17
15. cooperate* ¶17

KEYWORD EXERCISE

1. *Complexities* are the interconnected parts that make something *complex,* which is an antonym for *simple.* We can use the word to talk about physical objects, ideas, or relationships between people. For example, human relationships—even good ones—are very *complex.*
   Name a *complex* machine.

   EXAMPLE: Believing stereotypes about North American Indians keeps us from appreciating the richness and *complexities* of their cultures.

2. If you wanted to eat soup for dinner, you could choose from many *variations* of it. What are some of them?

   EXAMPLE: There are countless *variations* in values and customs among North American Indian tribes.

3. The population of North America is very *diverse.* Can you name four of the largest ethnic groups that live there?

   a. ______________________ **c.** ______________________

   b. ______________________ **d.** ______________________

   EXAMPLE: *Diverse* ethnic groups populated North America before the arrival of the Europeans.

4. The following statement is a *generalization:*

   Chinese people never let their feelings show.

   - What's dangerous about *generalizations* in general?
   - About this one in particular?

   EXAMPLE: *Generalizations* don't cover all members of all groups.

5. Which of the following are elements of the *climate* of a country?

   population total square kilometres wind
   temperature yearly rainfall

   EXAMPLE: Some flowers grow well in cold, wet *climates,* while others prefer hot, dry ones.

6. Which of the following are examples of *game?*

   horses buffalo deer sheep ducks

   EXAMPLE: Native North Americans hunted *game* for food, skins, and feathers.

7. Are there some *features* of homes in your culture that are different from most homes that you have seen in North America?

   EXAMPLE: Certain tribes shared *features* with other tribes.

8. Does your culture believe in *spirits?* If so, what do you call them, and what can they do?

   EXAMPLE: They each had one particular *spirit* that helped them personally.

9. Which of the following can cause the most *destruction?*

   floods earthquakes hurricanes (= typhoons)
   tsunamis wars

   EXAMPLE: White hunters *destroyed* the buffalo herds that the tribes depended upon.

10. What *ceremony* have you attended most recently, either in your own country or in another?

    EXAMPLE: Religious *ceremonies* were an important part of the life of each tribe.

11. You have read that the *nomadic* tribes of the Great Plains lived in teepees. What are some other kinds of housing that other *nomads* live in, and why?

    EXAMPLE: *Nomads* are people who move from place to place.

12. The word *herd* generally applies to a group of animals that have feet (called "hooves") like buffaloes' feet. Which of the following groups of animals would not be called a *herd?*

    dogs horses sheep snakes cattle goats

    EXAMPLE: The people followed the great buffalo *herds* on foot.

13. *Meanings:*

    - A *vision* is like a dream that you have, only you're awake, not asleep.

      EXAMPLE: Religious leaders may have *visions* in which they can see the future.

• Your *vision* is the quality of your eyesight.

EXAMPLE: She has better *vision* in her right eye than in her left.

• What's the similarity between the two meanings?

14. If you got lost in the forest, what are some things that you could do to help yourself *survive?*

EXAMPLE: People had to cooperate in order to *survive.*

15. Which of the following activities requires the most *cooperation?*
building a house   earning a university degree   raising a child

REVIEW

Now that you have studied the vocabulary, reread or reskim the passage.

READING TWO

NOTE: This reading is also on the tape.

Storytelling was one of the most common ways of passing along the history, values, and traditions of many Native North American ethnic groups. Folk stories were often told around the evening fire. Some people knew hundreds of stories, and they were considered important historians and guardians of the tribal way of life. They usually chose one or two younger people as students and taught them the stories so that they could continue to be passed down from generation to generation.

In the following Mohawk story, look for the answers to these two questions:

• What were the old women doing in the Longhouse?
• What were three magic things brought out by the women?

Reading process: Skim the story before you read it carefully. After you read it, skim it again and mark where the answers to the two questions above appear.

NATIVE ORIGIN

1 The old women are gathered in the *Longhouse.*[a] First, the ritual[1] kissing on the cheeks, the eyes, the lips, the top of the head; that spot where the hair parts in the middle like a wild river through a canyon.

2 A Grandmother sets the pot over the fire that has never gone out. To let the flames die is taboo, a break of trust. The acorn shells have been roasted the night before. Grandmother pours the boiling water over the shells. An aroma

rises and combines with the smell of wood smoke, sweat, and the sharp-sweet odour of blood.

3 The acorn coffee steeps and grows strong and dark. The old women sit patiently in a circle, not speaking. Each set of eyes stares sharply into the air or fire. Occasionally, a sigh is let loose from an open mouth. A Grandmother has a twitch in the corner of her eye. She rubs her nose, then smooths her hair.

4 The coffee is ready. Cups are brought from a wooden cupboard. Each woman is given the steaming brew. They blow on the swirling liquid, then slurp the drink into hungry mouths. It tastes good. Hot, dark, strong. A little bitter, but that is all to the good.

5 The women begin talking among themselves. They are together to perform a ceremony. Rituals of old women take time. There is no hurry.

6 The magic things are brought out from pockets and pouches.

7 A turtle rattle made from a she-turtle who was a companion of the woman's mother. It died the night she died, both of them ancient and tough. Now, the daughter shakes the rattle, and mother and she-turtle live again.

8 A bundle containing a feather from a hermit thrush. This is a holy feather. Of all the birds in the sky, hermit thrush is the one who flew to the Spirit World. It was there she learned her beautiful song. She is clever[2] and hides from sight. To have her feather is great magic. The women pass the feather. They tickle each other's chins and ears. Giggles and laughter erupt in the dwelling.

9 Bundles of corn, kernels of red, yellow, black. These also are passed from wrinkled hand to dry palm. Each woman holds the corn in her hand for a while before giving it to her sister.

10 Leaves of Witch Hazel and Jewelweed. Dandelion roots for chewing. Pearly Everlasting for smoking. These things are given careful attention. Much talk is generated over the old ways of preparing these gifts.

11 A woman gives a smile and brings a cradleboard from behind her back. There is nodding of heads and laughter and long drawn-out "ahhhhhs." The cradleboard has a beaded back that a mother made in her ninth month. An old woman starts a song; the others join her:

Little baby
Little baby
Ride on Mother's back
Laugh, laugh
Life is good
Mother shields[3] *you*
Mother shields you.

12 A Grandmother wipes her eyes, another holds her hand and kisses the lifelines.

13 Inside the cradleboard are bunches of moss taken from a *menstrual house.*[b] This moss has staunched lakes of blood that generations of women have squeezed from their wombs.

14 The acorn drink is reheated and passed once more. A woman adds wood to the fire. She holds her arms out to the flames. Another woman comes behind her with a warm blanket. She wraps it around her friend and hugs her shoulders. They stand before the fire.

15 A pelt of fur is brought forth. It once belonged to a beaver. She was found one morning, frozen in the ice, her lodge unfinished. The beaver was thawed and skinned. The women worked the hide until it was soft and pliant. It was the right size to wrap a newborn in, or to comfort old women on cold nights.

16 A piece of flint. An eagle bone whistle. A hank of black hair, cut in mourning. These are examined with reverence.

17 The oldest Grandmother removes a pouch from around her neck. She opens it with rusty fingers. She spreads the contents in her lap. A fistful of dark earth.

18 It smells clean, fecund. The women inhale the odour. The metallic taste of iron is on their tongues, like a sting.

19 The oldest Grandmother scoops the earth back into her pouch. She tugs at the string. It closes. The pouch lies between her breasts, warming her skin. Her breasts are supple and soft for one so old. Not long ago, she nursed a sister back to health. A child drank from her and was healed[4] of evil spirits that entered her as she lay innocent and dreaming.

20 The ceremony is over. The magic things are put in their places. The women kiss and touch each other's faces. They go out into the night. The moon and stars are parts of *Sky Woman.* She glows—never dimming, never retreating.[5]

21 The Grandmothers gather inside the Longhouse. They tend the fire.

SPECIALIZED VOCABULARY

[a] *Longhouse:* a communal dwelling.

[b] *menstrual house:* the place where women retired when they had their menstrual period.

[c] *Sky Woman:* a mythological figure.

After You Read

COMPREHENSION QUESTIONS

1. What were the old women doing in the Longhouse?

___

2. Name three of the magic things brought out by the women.

___

3. In ¶12, why does the Grandmother "wipe" her eyes?

___

4. Why is fire an important element in this story?

___

Charting Cultural Values

What information does the story give about Mohawk values? Take a piece of paper and divide it in half vertically. Write two titles: Native Values on one side, and

Euro-Canadian Values on the other. List the Mohawk values that you just noted, and write "(Mohawk)" after them. You'll add more to this list later, and you'll use the information in a paper that you're going to write.

Vocabulary

VOCABULARY IN CONTEXT

In ¶10, what do you think the word *generated* means? What context clues make you think so?

VOCABULARY STUDY

Look at the new vocabulary that you marked.

KEYWORDS

1. ritual ¶1
2. clever ¶8
3. shield ¶11
4. heal ¶19
5. retreat ¶20

KEYWORD EXERCISE

1. ***EXAMPLE:*** The women performed many *rituals* such as kissing each other on the cheek.

   Name one important *ritual* in your family.

2. ***EXAMPLE:*** The *clever* hermit thrush hid from sight as she flew to the spirit world.

   Name some *clever* people that you know and give an example of their cleverness.

3. ***EXAMPLE:*** A good water-repellent coat can *shield* your clothes from the rain and snow.

   What are some other elements you might want to *shield* yourself from?

4. What are some injuries that take a short time to *heal*?

   EXAMPLE: The baby's cut finger *healed* in a few days.

5. Which of the following words are synonyms of the verb *retreat*?

   reduce go back run away hesitate withdraw

   EXAMPLE: The letter carrier *retreated* quickly when he saw the huge dog.

REVIEW

Now that you have studied the vocabulary, reread or reskim the passage.

READING THREE

Chief Dan George was a hereditary chief of the Coast Salish tribe and an honorary chief of the Squamish tribe. He appeared in numerous television shows and films, including National Film Board productions. In 1971 he received the New York Film Critics Award for Best Supporting Actor for his role in "Little Big Man," which starred Dustin Hoffman. In the following emotional speech he talks of the challenges facing Native peoples.

MY VERY GOOD FRIENDS ...

1 Was it only yesterday that men sailed around the moon ... And can they now stand up on its barren surface? You and I marvel that man should travel so far and so fast ... Yet, if they have travelled far then I have travelled farther ... and if they have travelled fast, then I faster ... for I was born a thousand years ago ... born in a culture of bows and arrows. But within the span of half a lifetime I was flung across the ages to the culture of the atom bomb ... And from bows and arrows to atom bombs is a distance far beyond a flight to the moon.

2 I was born in an age that loved the things of nature and gave them beautiful names like Tes-wall-u-wit instead of[1] dried-up names like Stanley Park.

3 I was born in an age that loved all nature and spoke to it as though it had a soul ... I can remember going up Indian River with my father when I was very young ... I can remember him watching the sun light fires on Mount Pay-nay-nay as it rose above its peak. I can remember him singing his thanks to it as he often did ... singing the Indian word "thanks ... " so very, very softly.

4 And then the people came ... more and more people came ... like a crushing rushing wave they came ... hurling the years aside!! ... and suddenly I found myself a young man in the midst of the twentieth century.

5 I found myself and my people adrift[2] in this new age ... but not part of it.

6 Engulfed by its rushing tide, but only as a captive eddy ... going round and round ... On little reserves, on plots of land we floated in a kind of grey unreality ... ashamed[3] of our culture which you ridiculed ... unsure of who we were or where we were going ... uncertain of our grip on the present ... weak in our hope of the future ... And that is pretty well where we stand today.

7 I had a glimpse of something better than this. For a few brief years I knew my people when we lived the old life ... I knew them when there was still a dignity in our lives and feeling of worth in our outlook. I knew them when there was unspoken confidence in the home and a certain knowledge of the path we walked upon. But we were living on the dying energy of a dying culture ... a culture that was slowly losing its forward thrust ...

8 What is it like to be without pride[4] in your race, pride in your family, pride and confidence in yourself? What is it like? You don't know for you never tasted its bitterness.

9 I shall tell you what it is like. It is like not caring about tomorrow for what does tomorrow matter. It is like having a reserve that looks like a junk yard because the beauty in the soul is dead and why should the soul express an external beauty that does not match it? It is like getting drunk for a few brief moments, an escape from ugly reality and feeling a sense of importance. It is most of all like awaking next morning to the guilt of betrayal. For the alcohol did not fill the emptiness[5] but only dug it deeper.

After You Read

COMPREHENSION QUESTIONS

1. What does the writer mean when he says he "was born a thousand years ago"?

____

2. List some of the writer's fondest memories as a child.

____

3. Why do the writer's people no longer care how their environment looks?

____

CONTINUING YOUR CHART OF CULTURAL VALUES

Can you find anything in this reading to add to your list of Native values? (Look in (¶2-3.)

Vocabulary

KEYWORDS

1. instead of ¶2
2. adrift ¶5
3. ashamed ¶6
4. pride ¶8
5. emptiness ¶9

KEYWORD EXERCISE

1. ***EXAMPLE:*** She decided to read a book *instead of* going to the movies.

   Finish the sentences:

They wanted to name their daughter Catherine ______________________.

The Indians preferred their own place names ______________________.

2. ***EXAMPLE:*** Chief Dan George and his people were *adrift* in the modern world.

   Finish the sentences:

   The fishermen found themselves adrift in the middle of the lake because ___.

   In a new country it is easy to ______________________.

3. Why do you think the Indians became *ashamed* of their Native culture?

   EXAMPLE: He was so *ashamed* of failing the exam he didn't tell his parents.

4. What do you take a great deal of *pride* in?

   EXAMPLE: The young woman took *pride* in a job well done.

5. When one loses a friend or a loved one dies, there is a tremendous feeling of *emptiness.* Is there an occasion or event that gave you a sense of *emptiness?*

REVIEW

Now that you have studied the vocabulary, reread or reskim the passage.

READING FOUR

Reading process: As usual, begin by reading the title, reading the first paragraph, skimming the rest, and then reading the last paragraph. Then read everything carefully. When you finish, follow the instructions given at the end of the reading.

Contact and Beyond

Part One

Notes

1 The history of Indian-white relations[1] is a bloody one. The problems that arose were a result of misunderstanding, mistrust, and—most important—great differences in values between the European and the Native cultures. Conflict[2] began as soon as Columbus landed in the New World. In most cases the Indians were friendly and helpful to the strangers at first, giving them food and showing them how to make a living off lands that were new to them. But relations turned ugly as the whites began cutting down the forest, plowing up the land to make farms, putting up fences. Perhaps most of all, the whites claimed

personal possession of land and believed that they had the right to keep other people off of it. This was a complete contradiction[3] of the Native attitude[4] toward land, which was that it belonged to all the forms of life that lived on it. No one had the right to claim it for their own.

> Our land is more valuable than your money. It will last forever ... It was put here for us by the Great Spirit and we cannot sell it because it does not belong to us.
> —*A Blackfeet chief, northern Great Plains*

Treaties

Whites agreed to

____

Indians agreed to

____

2 As more and more settlers arrived needing more and more land, relations between the two groups worsened. The United States and Canadian governments' solution for this conflict was to make treaties with the Natives, just as they would with any other foreign government. These treaties were agreements, signed by both sides, that met the white people's interests and that made certain promises to the Indians. In most of them, the whites claimed the right to use particular areas of land and the Indians agreed to give them up and to move away, sometimes to other land that the whites agreed to give them in exchange. This other land was not their ancestral[5] homeland and was generally land that neither they nor the whites wanted to live on. In addition, the Indians were usually required to agree to keep peace with the whites and to recognize[6] the power of the white government. In return, the whites usually agreed to pay money and goods to the Indians and to protect them.

Problems

1.

2.

3.

3 The Indians' problem with the treaties was that their attitude toward land ownership and use was totally different from the whites'. They often did not realize that in giving the white people the rights to the land, they were giving up[7] their own rights to use it. In the eyes of the whites, they were buying the land from the Indians, but the very idea of buying and selling land was foreign to Indian cultures. But if they didn't sign, it soon became clear that the whites would take the land anyway and might make war on them.

4 A third problem was that the whites broke most of the treaties. As the years passed and the white population grew, more and more settlers moved onto Indian lands, pushing the Indians further and further west. A tribe might sign a treaty and move onto less desirable land, only to be forced to sign another treaty and move again several years later. The Cherokee people of the eastern United States were moved to 36 different locations by treaties signed between 1721 and 1835. This or that tribe often went to war with the settlers, but the population of any one tribe was small and their weapons were no match for the guns of the white men.

Part Two

History

1.

2.

5 By 1830 the whites had settled much of the land east of the Mississippi River, which runs north and south and divides the eastern third of the United States from the western two-thirds. In that year the government decided that they would simply remove most of the Indians from the eastern part of the country and force them to live west of the river, where few whites wanted to live at that time. By 1840 more than 70,000 Indians had been torn from their homelands and forcibly moved. Many of them died on the journey. The Indian name for this removal is the Trail of Tears.

> The whites were always trying to make the Indians give up their life and live like white men—go to farming, work hard and do as they did—and the Indians did not know how to do that, and did not want to anyway ... If the Indians had tried to make the whites live like them, the whites would have resisted, and it was the same way with many Indians.
>
> *—Wamditanka (Big Eagle), Santee Sioux, northern Great Plains*

6 But that wasn't the end of the story. In 1848 gold was discovered in California, attracting[8] a movement of whites all the way across the continent. Once in California, they killed the game and pushed the Indians off their homelands there. A few years later, after the United States Civil War ended in 1864, thousands of white families began to make their way across the Mississippi River north and west along the Oregon Trail to "new" lands. Meanwhile in Canada, whites were attracted by the trade in furs and by the availability of lands for farming and ranching in the western territories. Of course, these lands were already occupied by Indian tribes. Of course, the Indians resisted.[9] And as before, they were eventually defeated and new treaties were signed—most of which were broken, as before.

3.

4.

5.

7 Some of the Indian nations were traditionally warlike; others were peaceful by nature. Either way, they lost. But in the meantime thousands of people were killed on both sides, and many of them were not soldiers or warriors, but innocent men, women, and children who were in the wrong place at the wrong time, or whose only offence was that they were white, or were Indian. Each case of bloodshed became a reason for revenge[10] in some people's minds, continuing the cycle on and on.

Part Three

8 The reason that it finally stopped was not because the two groups were finally wise enough to sit down, talk, and develop respect for each other—it was because the whites had better weapons, more power, and greater numbers. Furthermore, they acted as one large group against small Native bands that were divided, not united. The Indians' food source had lessened as the whites cleared the land, destroying the homes of the game that they depended on. Within a ten-year period white hunters had killed off the millions of buffalo on the Great Plains, partly because buffalo hides had become popular among white people, but partly just because they knew that the destruction of the herds would destroy the power of the Plains Indians. The Europeans also brought with them diseases that were new to the Indians and that took many lives. When Columbus arrived in 1492, the Indian population of the present United States was somewhere between one and two and a half million people, in present Canada about 350,000; by 1900 it had been reduced to less than a quarter of a million in the U.S. and to under 100,000 in Canada.

Reasons for

1.

2.

3.

> I have heard that you intend to settle us on a reservation near the mountains. I don't want to settle. I love to roam over the prairies. There I feel free and happy, but when we settle down we grow pale and die.
>
> *—Satanta, Chief of the Kiowas, southern Great Plains*

The Trail of Tears

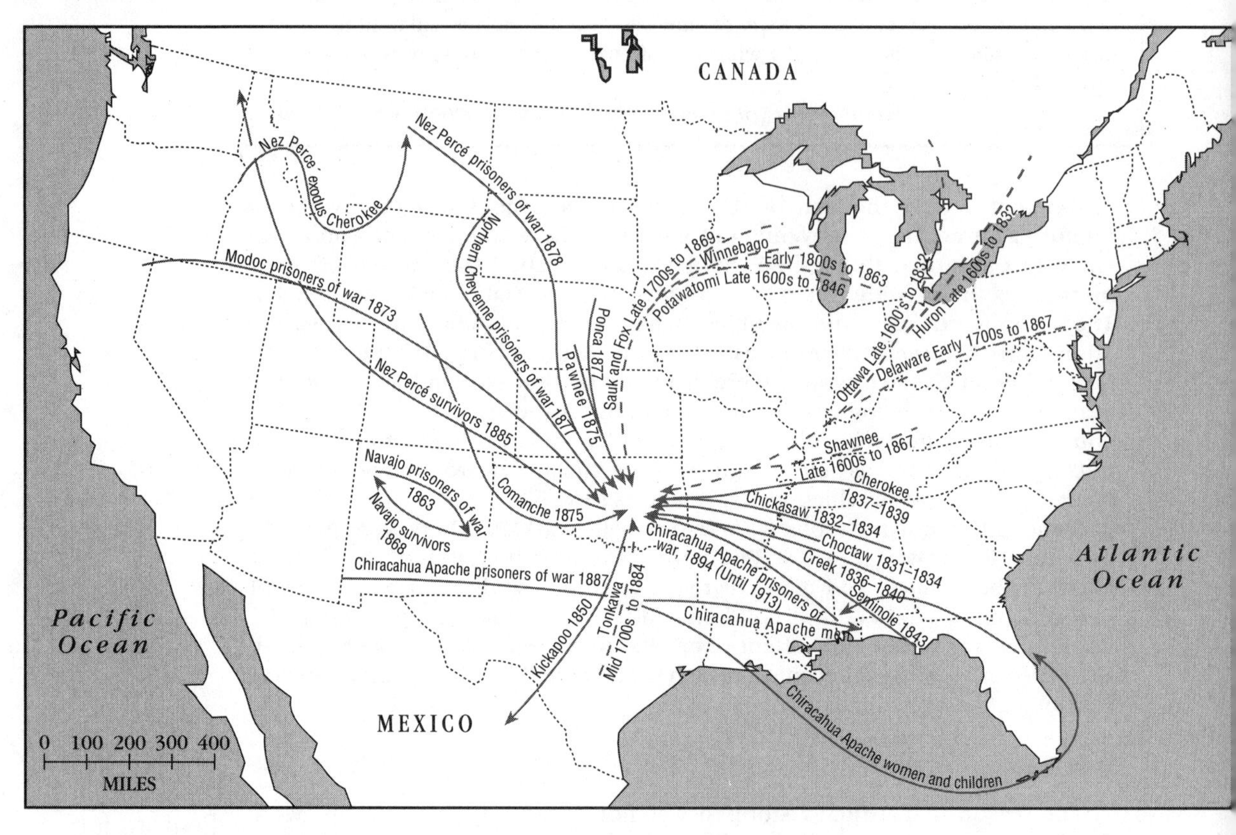

Problems of reservation life

1.

2.

3.

9 Most of the remaining Indians were herded onto *reservations* (United States) or *reserves* (Canada), land set aside for their use by the government. Most of these areas are not on the tribes' ancestral homelands, though some are. But life on the reservations was not at all like life had been before. The traditional way of life no longer seemed possible and continued to be attacked[11] in reserve schools, which attempted[12] to replace Indian customs, values, and languages with white customs, values, and English. The Indians were caught between the old way of life and a new one that they did not want. For many years the only power was held by white government agents, leaving the Natives no real power in their communities or in their own personal lives. Not surprisingly, alcohol and depression[13] became serious problems on the reservations, as well as unemployment,[14] poverty,[15] and poor health. The future looked unpromising for Native Americans as recently as the middle of the twentieth century.

10 Today there are about 285 Indian reservations in the United States. They range in size and population from less than one acre (0.4 hectares) and fewer than ten Indians to about 14 million acres (six million hectares) and about 150,000 Indians. The land they occupy may be desert, forested, mountainous, or plains. Just under half of the Indian population lives on them, while in

Canada, about 59 percent of the Native peoples live on reserves. The most common jobs on the reservations are in farming, ranching, and manufacturing. Some reservation Indians live well, but on the whole they have high unemployment rates, low incomes, little education, and poor health.

After You Read

Identify the circled reference words.

COMPREHENSION: NAMING THE PARTS OF THE READING

For each part of the reading, write a heading that tells what it is about.

LEARNING STRATEGY

Forming Concepts: Writing brief notes of the most important ideas in a reading helps you review and remember the material.

TAKING NOTES AS YOU READ

Now review the reading passage, focusing on comprehension. In the right-hand margin you'll notice some incomplete lists and diagrams; once you have completed these, they will serve you as good notes of the most important information and as a study guide. This is a model of a useful way to take marginal notes in your textbooks.

In order to take good notes, you have to understand not only the content, but also how it's organized. Turn to the Appendix on page 250. This lists some of the most common ways to organize written material, and it also tells you some common *markers* or *signals* that help you recognize the organization. What are the organizational patterns that are mentioned in this Appendix?

1. Look at ¶s 3 and 4. Find the words in each paragraph that tell you they're organized around a description of problems. Circle these markers. Then complete the notes.
2. Look at ¶s 5 and 6. Find the markers that tell you the organization is chronological. Circle them. Then complete the notes.
3. Complete the rest of the marginal notes. When you finish, compare your work with a partner.

Useful tips for notetaking:

- Don't use complete sentences
- Abbreviate and use symbols

What do you think these abbreviations and symbols mean? Inds & whs signed trts

Can you read this sentence? Gold disc in CA; attracted whs to Ind lands

TRUE–FALSE QUESTIONS

			¶ number
1. Native Americans believed that land could not be bought or sold because it did not belong to people.	T	F	________
2. The white people honoured most of the treaties.	T	F	________
3. The United States government asked the Native peoples if they would like to move west across the Mississippi River.	T	F	________
4. Whites and Indians wanted the same land, though often for different purposes.	T	F	________
5. Native North Americans have to live on reserves or reservations today.	T	F	________

DISCUSSION AND WRITING: REWRITING HISTORY

Working in groups, discuss why there was so much conflict and bloodshed between the European-Americans and the Native North Americans. Make suggestions as to how this conflict could have been avoided.

Then choose one of the following writing assignments:

1. If you could rewrite history, tell the story of how the Native North Americans and the European newcomers learned to live peacefully.
2. Where did these problems begin? What could have been done to prevent them?

Vocabulary

KEYWORDS

1. relations ¶1
2. conflict ¶1
3. contradiction ¶1
4. attitude* ¶1

9. resist* ¶6
10. revenge ¶7
11. attack ¶9
12. attempt* ¶9

5. ancestral ¶2
6. recognize ¶2
7. give up* ¶3
8. attract* ¶6
13. depression ¶9
14. unemployment ¶9
15. poverty ¶9

KEYWORD EXERCISE

1. *Meanings:*
   - *Relations* between people are the ways in which they behave toward each other.

     EXAMPLE: *Relations* between Indians and whites soon turned ugly.
   - Your *relations* are your family, both immediate (parents, children) and extended (uncles, aunts).

     EXAMPLE: Most of her *relations* live in Winnipeg.
   - Explain the similarities between the two meanings.
2. Think of a *conflict* that is happening somewhere in the world today. Who are the groups of people who are having the conflict? What is it about? How could it be solved?
3. What was the *contradiction* between the white and the Native attitudes toward ownership of land?

   EXAMPLE: The white attitude was a complete *contradiction* of the Native attitude toward land.
4. What was the difference between the white and the Native North American *attitudes* toward land? Toward nature?
5. *Ancestral* is the adjective form of the noun *ancestors.* Which of the following are not your *ancestors?*

   cousins parents aunts grandparents great-grandparents

   EXAMPLE: Indians generally preferred to live on their *ancestral* homelands.
6. *Meanings:*
   - When you *recognize* someone, you know who they are because you have seen them before.

     EXAMPLE: I didn't *recognize* you in those dark glasses.
   - When you *recognize* the power of a government, you accept its power over you and you agree to let it have that power.

     EXAMPLE: The treaties said that the Indians had to *recognize* the white government.
   - Explain the similarities between the two meanings.
7. ***EXAMPLES:*** The treaties required the Indians to *give up* their lands.
   I've just *given up* smoking.

Finish the sentences:
When he became a Muslim, he had to give up ______________________.

My husband lost his job, so we had to ______________________.

8. ***EXAMPLE:*** The discovery of gold *attracted* settlers to the Yukon.

   Finish the sentences:
   Magnets attract ______________________.

   If you put a lamp outside, it will attract ______________________.

   The good-looking ______________________.

9. In many parts of the world, individuals or groups of people *resist* what their governments want them to do. Name some of those countries.
   How many different forms of *resistance* can you think of?

   EXAMPLE: When white people moved onto their lands, the Indians generally *resisted.*

10. An English proverb says, "Living well is the best *revenge.*" What do you think that means?

    EXAMPLE: Each case of bloodshed became a reason for *revenge* in some people's minds.

11. ***EXAMPLE:*** In the discussion that followed, the manager *attacked* my suggestion.

    Finish the sentences:
    The soldiers attacked ______________________.
    The mountain lion ______________________.

12. ***EXAMPLE:*** The settlers *attempted* to make a new life in the strange land.

    Finish the sentences:
    For the first time, I attempted to ______________ recently.
    When she got lost in the woods, she ______________________.

13. Which of the following are elements of *depression?*

    supplies surprise force sadness disappointment

    EXAMPLE: His *depression* led to alcoholism, which only made the *depression* worse.

14. Which of the following problems can be connected with *unemployment?*

    homelessness divorce pollution overpopulation crime

    EXAMPLE: *Unemployment* is a serious problem in towns where large factories have had to shut down.

15. List three common causes of *poverty.*

REVIEW

Now that you have studied the vocabulary, reread or reskim the passage.

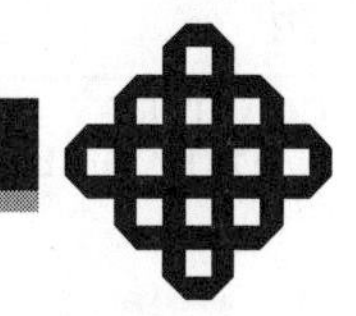

READING FIVE

NEVER SELL THE BONES OF YOUR FATHER AND YOUR MOTHER

1 Soon after this my father sent for me. I saw he was dying. I took his hand in mine. He said: "My son, my body is returning to my mother earth, and my spirit is going very soon to see the Great Spirit Chief. When I am gone, think of your country. You are the chief of these people. They look to you to guide them. Always remember that your father never sold this country. You must stop your ears whenever you are asked to sign a treaty selling your home. A few years more, and white men will be all around you. They have their eyes on this land. My son, never forget my dying words. This country holds your father's body. Never sell the bones of your father and your mother." I pressed my father's hand and told him I would protect his grave with my life. My father smiled and passed away to the spirit land.

2 I buried him in that beautiful valley of winding waters. I love that land more than all the rest of the world. A man who would not love his father's grave is worse than a wild animal.

—Heinmot Tooyalaket (Chief Joseph), Nez Percé, Northwest Plateau

Threads

One does not sell the earth upon which the people walk.

Tashunka Witko (Crazy Horse), Oglala Sioux, western Great Plains

> The earth was created by the assistance of the sun, and it should be left as it was ... The country was made without lines of demarcation, and it is no man's business to divide it.
>
> *—Heinmot Tooyalaket (Chief Joseph), Nez Percé, Northwest Plateau*

After You Read

COMPLETING YOUR CHART

Using information from Reading Five, complete your chart of cultural values. Then compare your chart with a small group of classmates.

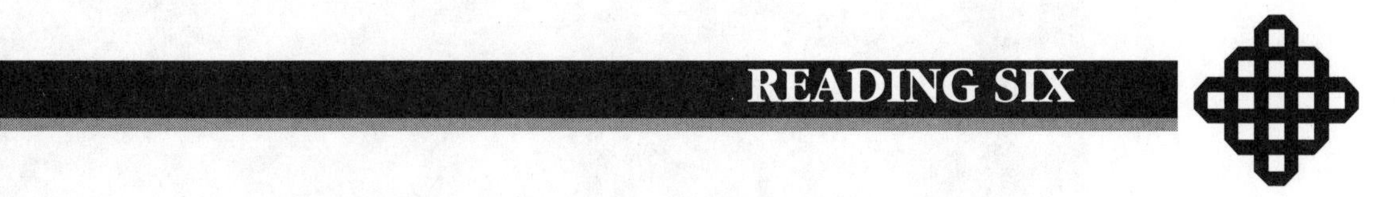

READING SIX

Carol Geddes is an Indian from the Tlingit Nation in the Yukon.

GROWING UP NATIVE

1 I remember it was cold. We were walking through a swamp near our home in the Yukon bush. Maybe it was fall and moose-hunting season. I don't know. I think I was about four years old at the time. The muskeg was too springy to walk on, so people were taking turns carrying me—passing me from one set of arms to another. The details about where we were are vague, but the memory of those arms and the feeling of acceptance I had is one of the most vivid of my childhood. It didn't matter who was carrying me—there was security in every pair of arms. That response to children is typical of the Native community. It's the first thing I think of when I cast my mind back to the Yukon bush, where I was born and lived with my family.

2 I was six years old when we moved out of the bush, first to Teslin, where I had a hint of the problems Native people face, then to Whitehorse, where there was unimaginable racism. Eventually I moved to Ottawa and Montréal, where I further discovered that to grow up Native in Canada is to feel the sting of humiliation and the boot of discrimination.[1] But it is also to experience the enviable security of an extended family and to learn to appreciate the richness of the heritage and traditions of a culture most North Americans have never been lucky enough to know. As a filmmaker, I have tried to explore these contradictions, and our triumph over them, for the half-million Aboriginals who are part of the tide of swelling independence of the First Nations today.

3 But I'm getting ahead of[2] myself. If I'm to tell the story of what it's like to grow up Native in northern Canada, I have to go back to the bush where I was born, because there's more to my story than the hurtful stereotyping that depicts Indian people as drunken welfare cases. Our area was known as 12-mile (it was 12 miles from another tiny village). There were about 40 people living there—including 25 kids, eight of them my brothers and sisters—in a sort of family compound. Each family had its own timber plank house for sleeping, and there was one large common kitchen area with gravel on the ground and a tent

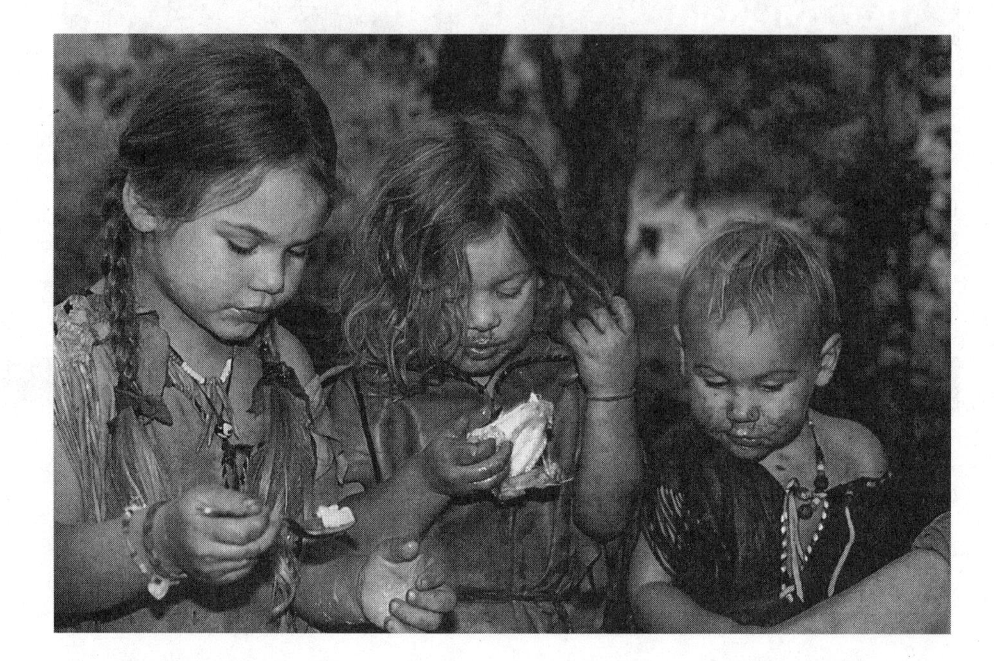

frame over it. Everybody would go there and cook meals together. In summer, my grandmother always had a smudge fire going to smoke fish and tan moose hides. I can remember the cosy[3] warmth of the fire, the smell of the good food, and always having someone to talk to. We kids had built-in playmates and would spend hours running in the bush, picking berries, building rafts on the lake and playing in abandoned mink cages ...

4 There's a very strong sense of family in the Native community, and a fondness[4] for children, especially young children. Even today, it's like a special form of entertainment if someone brings a baby to visit. That sense of family is the one thing that has survived all the incredible difficulties Native people have had. Throughout a time of tremendous problems, the extended family system has somehow lasted, providing a strong circle for people to survive in. When parents were struggling with alcoholism or had to go away to find work, when one of the many epidemics swept through the community, or when a marriage broke up and one parent left, aunts, uncles, and grandparents would try to fill those roles. It's been very important to me in terms of emotional support to be able to rely on[5] my extended family. There are still times when such support keeps me going.

5 Life was much simpler when we lived in the bush. Although we were poor and wore the same clothes all year, we were warm enough and had plenty to eat. But even as a youngster, I began to be aware of some of the problems we would face later on. Travelling missionaries would come and impose themselves on us, for example. They'd sit at our campfire and read the Bible to us and lecture us about how we had to live a Christian life. I remember being very frightened by stories we heard about parents sending their kids away to live with white people who didn't have any children. We thought those people were mean and that if we were bad, we'd be sent away, too ...

6 The residential schools were another source of misery for the kids. Although I didn't have to go, my brothers and sisters were there. They told stories about having their hair cut off in case they were carrying head lice, and of being forced to do hard chores without enough food to eat. They were told that the Indian culture was evil, that Indian people were bad, that their only hope was to be Christian. They had to stand up and say things like "I've found the Lord," when a teacher told them to speak. Sexual abuse was rampant[6] in the residential school system.

7 By the time we moved to Whitehorse, I was excited about the idea of living in what I thought of as a big town. I'd had a taste of the outside world from books at school in Teslin (a town of 250 people), and I was tremendously curious about what life was like. I was hungry for experiences such as going to the circus. In fact, for a while, I was obsessed with stories and pictures about the circus, but then when I was 12 and saw my first one, I was put off by the condition and treatment of the animals.

8 Going to school in Whitehorse was a shock. The clash[7] of Native and white values was confusing and frightening ... We were always told the white teachers knew best, and so we had to do whatever they said at school. And yet I had a really strong sense of receiving mixed messages about what I was supposed to do in the community and what I was supposed to do at school.

9 Pretty soon I hated school. Moving to a predominantly white high school was even worse. We weren't allowed to join anything the white kids started. We were the butt of jokes because of our secondhand clothes and moose meat sandwiches. We were constantly being rejected. The prevailing attitude was that Indians were stupid. When it was time to make course choices in class—

between typing and science, for example, they didn't even ask the Native kids, they just put us all in typing. You get a really bad image of yourself in a situation like that. I bought into[8] it. I thought we were awful. The whole experience was terribly undermining ... With a Grade 9 education, I started to work at a series of menial[9] jobs.

10 Seven years later something happened to me that would change my life forever.[10] I had moved to Ottawa with a man and was working as a waitress in a restaurant. One day, a friend invited me to her place for coffee. While I was there, she told me she was going to university in the fall and showed me her reading list ... My eyes moved down the list, and my heart started beating faster and faster as I suddenly realized I could go to university, too! ... I graduated five years later, earning a bachelor of arts in English and philosophy (with distinction) ...

11 Today, there's a glimmer of hope that more of us Native people will overcome the obstacles that have tripped us up ever since we began sharing this land. Some say our cultures are going through a renaissance.[11] Maybe that's true. Certainly there's a renewed interest in Native dancing, acting and singing, and in other cultural traditions. Even indigenous[12] forms of government are becoming strong again. But we can't forget that the majority of Native people live in urban areas and continue to suffer from alcohol and drug abuse and the plagues of a people who have lost their culture and have become lost themselves. And the welfare system is the insidious glue that holds together the machine of oppression of Native people ...

12 The wheels are in motion for a revival, for change in the way Native people are taking their place in Canada. I can see that we're equipped, we have the tools to do the work. We have an enormous number of smart, talented, moral Indian people. It's thrilling to be part of this movement.

13 Someday, when I'm an elder, I'll tell the children the stories: about the bush, about the hard times, about the renaissance, and especially about the importance of knowing your place in your nation.

After You Read

Identify the circled reference words.

COMPREHENSION QUESTIONS

1. What does the author remember first about her childhood in the bush?

____

2. What was the author's opinion of the missionaries who came to live with her and her extended family?

____

CONTINUING YOUR CHART OF CULTURAL VALUES

Can you find anything in this reading to add to your list of Native values?

LEARNING STRATEGY

Forming Concepts: *Paraphrasing*, or rewriting information in your own words, makes you think carefully about the information and helps you master it.

PARAPHRASING

Paraphrase:

1. During early childhood: ______________________________
2. At residential school: ______________________________
3. At the age of six: ______________________________
4. In high school: ______________________________
5. Seven years later: ______________________________

TRUE–FALSE QUESTIONS

			¶ number
1. The extended family provided the author with a great deal of emotional support.	T	F	______
2. The author was tremendously impressed when she saw her first circus.	T	F	______
3. The author's classmates in high school were interested in learning about her Native customs.	T	F	______
4. The author heard about university from a friend.	T	F	______
5. The author is optimistic about the future of the native people.	T	F	______

Vocabulary

KEYWORDS

1. discrimination ¶2
2. get ahead of ¶3
3. cosy ¶3
7. clash ¶8
8. buy into ¶9
9. menial ¶9

4. fondness ¶4
5. rely on ¶4
6. rampant ¶6
10. forever ¶10
11. renaissance ¶11
12. indigenous ¶11

KEYWORD EXERCISE

1. Give an example of one form of *discrimination* that Native kids experienced in school.
2. Which of the following verbs means the same thing as *get ahead of?*

   succeed   leave   move forward too quickly   find out about   go away

   EXAMPLE: I don't want to *get ahead of* myself, so I'll start at the beginning.
3. Native adults have a *fondness* for children. Do you have a *fondness* for any particular kind of food?
4. *EXAMPLE:* He *relied on* his friend when he needed to borrow money.

   Who is the one person you can *rely on* when you need help?
5. *Matching:*

_____	1. *cosy*	**a.**	for always
_____	2. *rampant*	**b**	revival
_____	3. *clash*	**c.**	Aboriginal, belonging to First Nations
_____	4. *buy into*	**d.**	warm and comfortable
_____	5. *menial*	**e.**	disagreement or conflict
_____	6. *forever*	**f.**	without any checks or restraints
_____	7. *renaissance*	**g.**	low-skilled
_____	8. *indigenous*	**h.**	believe

REVIEW

Now that you have studied the vocabulary, reread or reskim the passage.

READING SEVEN

Look at the following title. Given what you have already learned about their traditional ways of life and about the history of Native–white relations, how do you think that Native North Americans probably live today? Write three questions that you hope will be answered in the following reading passage.

Reading process: For this reading you'll use skimming to build up your speed as well as your comprehension. Your teacher will give you exactly three minutes to skim the passage very quickly. Be sure to go all the way to the end in this period of time. Your purpose is just to catch some of the vocabulary and phrasing as a way of establishing the topic in your mind. Then you'll be given five minutes to skim again. Remember, it's skimming; don't try to read every word or sentence. Finally, you'll read the passage carefully.

NATIVE AMERICANS TODAY

1 In the 450 years between Columbus's arrival and the mid-twentieth century, the Native population of what is now the United States sank from one or two million to less than 250,000. There were people who believed that the Indian nations were going to "go the way of the buffalo." But in recent years the Indian population has risen greatly, to almost two million inhabitants again. The same trend of lessening and then growing populations has taken place in Canada, where the current Native population is estimated at somewhere between 700,000 and one million, depending on how it is figured. One reason for this increase is that the Indian birth rate is higher than the average: between 1980 and 1990 the total U.S. population grew at a rate of 10 percent, the white population at 6 percent, but the Native American population at a rate of 38 percent. Half of the Native population in the United States today lives in five states: California, Oklahoma, Arizona, New Mexico, and North Carolina. Just under half live on reservations, with the rest in cities, small towns, and the countryside.

2 The Indians who remain on the reserves often do so because they want to live in a community of others like themselves, where they can follow tribal customs. But some of the drawbacks[1] of reservation life are that unemployment is high, incomes[2] are low, health is poor, and social problems such as alcoholism are fairly common. Other Indians have moved to the cities or towns, hoping for better employment and perhaps looking for a different kind of life. And today a growing number are entering professions such as education, law, medicine, and engineering. Some of these professionals return to the reservations to provide advice and leadership to their tribes and to make their expertise[3] available[4] to the whole community.

3 Although living conditions on most of the reservations are difficult, a number of success stories can be told. On some reservations business corporations have been set up that employ local tribespeople in manufacturing jewellery or clothing, electronics parts, car parts, and cement. Other businesses include agriculture, hydroelectric generators, services, fish-packing, construction, airlines, forestry, mining, and four-star tourist resorts. Some Plains tribes are raising buffalo herds. Although these success stories are not frequent, they serve as encouragement[5] to other bands that Indians can establish[6] and operate their own businesses, providing employment and income for individual tribespeople and benefits[7] for the entire reserve community.

4 Interestingly enough, many Indians are very proud to consider themselves citizens[8] of the United States or Canada. During World War II, for example, more than 25,000 Indians served in the United States armed forces, and 30,000 more worked in war-related industries. The "Navajo Code Talkers" became famous: radio communications in the Pacific depended on using codes that could not be translated by outsiders. Navajo servicemen broadcast messages in their native language which were translated back into English by other Navajos

on the receiving end. Thus their native language was valuable to the country's war effort.[9]

5 Remember that it was the white settlers who grouped all Native populations under the single name "Indians"? The "Indians" thought of themselves only as members of their own band, and not as a part of the overall Native population. But in recent years they have found it useful to have not only individual identities as Crow, Blackfeet, Mohawk, but also a larger identity that joins them to all other Native American groups. By cooperating with other tribes, they gain power through numbers, power that can lead to improvements[10] in their lives. In the 1960s certain Native Americans joined forces to form a movement[11] which they called *Indian Power.* They forced the public to pay attention to the way they were treated by the government and by white society. Members of the American Indian Movement joined forces with certain members of the Oglala Sioux tribe, and armed with rifles, they took over the village of Wounded Knee, South Dakota, where U.S. soldiers had killed a large number of Sioux in 1890. Some Indians were for this movement and others were against it, but everyone had to agree that it focused the public's attention on some changes that needed to be made. And since the 1970s in both Canada and the United States, Indians have been given more and more control over their lands and their own future. Today the reserves are managed largely by the bands, not by white government agents. The local reservation communities have a greater voice in policy making.[12] And certain bands have talked the government into returning some lands to tribal control, particularly in Canada. The most notable example of this is the Canadian government's agreement to turn over a huge segment of the Northwest Territories to the Inuit peoples, who have renamed the area "Nunavut" ("Our Land"). This is by far the largest land settlement to date by either government.

6 In the 500 years between the coming of the Europeans and the end of the twentieth century, Native cultures were very badly treated. Their way of life was not valued: it was attacked, its economic base was destroyed, its traditions were belittled. But although some tribes completely disappeared, many have responded by becoming very adaptive in order to survive: that is, they have borrowed new ways and used them in their traditional lives without giving up some of the features that make them Indians. Their dress, their languages, their economic activities, their forms of housing, even their religions have changed in some cases, but they remain clearly and recognizably Indian. Many of them continue in some of their traditional beliefs and customs, and even those who live off the reservation may return to it periodically to attend ceremonies and to renew ties with their people.

7 One example of this cultural survival is a renewed interest in Native languages. Originally about 300 different Indian languages were spoken in what are now the United States and Canada. Sadly, almost half of these have completely disappeared. On many reservations in the past, children were taken away from their families to boarding schools where they were punished if they spoke their native tongues; so, many children grew up never knowing their tribal languages. But today on many reservations they are being instructed in these languages from a very young age, and it is hoped that soon some of the less common ones will be spoken in the home and will become children's first languages again. On other reservations the Native languages are widely spoken, as on the Navajo reservation in New Mexico and Arizona. Locals can tune in to a Navajo radio station, and bookstores sell *The Oxford Picture Dictionary* in Navajo/English.

8 Other areas in which traditions remain strong include keeping family and kinship ties and patterns, following the old ceremonies, joining tribal societies, eating Native foods, and bringing up children in traditional ways. Tribal ceremonies, songs, dances, arts, and crafts are valued and are taught, not only within the tribe, but from one tribe to another. There is a Native American Church which has about 140,000 members from many tribes. Some of its teachings are similar to Christian ones, but its ceremonies and rituals are distinctly Indian, including the importance attached to dreams and visions.

9 And what is the status[13] of American Indians in the larger society today? It must be said that stereotyping and discrimination[14] still exist, but there is also a more open and interested attitude toward Indians and their culture on the parts of many whites and in the media.[15]

After You Read

Identify the circled reference words.

IN WHICH PARAGRAPH CAN YOU FIND ...

1. The land of Nunavut ______
2. Renewed interest in Native North American languages ______
3. The Navajo Code Talkers ______
4. The return of buffalo herds ______
5. The Native American Church ______

IDENTIFYING TOPICS AND MAIN IDEAS

Reading Seven can be divided into the following sections. Each of these sections discusses a particular *topic,* or subject. Identify the topics.

Each section also has a *main idea,* which is what it says about the topic. The main idea can best be expressed in a complete sentence. Identify the main ideas.

Vocabulary

KEYWORDS

1. drawback ¶2
2. income ¶2
3. expertise ¶2
4. available ¶2
5. encouragement ¶3
6. establish ¶3

	TOPIC	MAIN IDEA
¶1	Population	After decreasing for many years, the Native North American population is now growing again.
¶s 2–3	________________	____________________________ ____________________________
¶ 4	________________	____________________________ ____________________________
¶ 5	________________	____________________________ ____________________________
¶s 6–8	________________	____________________________ ____________________________
¶ 9	________________	____________________________ ____________________________

7. benefit* ¶3
8. citizen ¶4
9. effort* ¶4
10. improvement ¶5
11. movement ¶5
12. policy ¶5
13. status ¶9
14. discrimination ¶9
15. media ¶9

KEYWORD EXERCISE

1. Almost every decision has advantages (results that you like) and *drawbacks.* Think about your decision to come to North America to study. What were some advantages, and what were some *drawbacks?*
2. Divide the word *income* into its two parts, and then explain the connection between the parts and the meaning of the whole.

   EXAMPLE: Most people who live on the reservations have low *incomes.*
3. Name three different kinds of *expertise* that a medical doctor needs.
4. If you were trying very hard to learn something for a class but you were having a hard time, what's something that your teacher might say to you that would give you *encouragement?*
5. Which of the following are elements of the verb *establish?*

   discover create locate begin business

   EXAMPLE: Many Indians *establish* and operate their own businesses.

6. Which invention of the twentieth century has *benefited* human life the most?
7. Name two things that only *citizens* of a country are allowed to do.

   EXAMPLE: Many Indians are proud to be *citizens* of the United States or Canada.
8. *Meanings:*
   - *Movement* is the act of moving.

     EXAMPLE: The cat saw a sudden *movement* in the grass and jumped on it.
   - A *movement* is a group of people who share the same beliefs and who work together to get what they want.

     EXAMPLE: The Indian Power *movement* succeeded in improving the treatment of Native Americans.
   - Explain the similarities between the two meanings.
9. Choose a world leader, and briefly explain his or her *policy* about something.

   EXAMPLE: Today local reservation communities have a greater voice in *policy* making.
10. Which of the following are examples of the *media?*

    cinema   books   television   radio   newspapers
11. *Matching:*

_____	**1.** *available*	**a.** position or level in society
_____	**2.** *effort*	**b.** better conditions
_____	**3.** *improvements*	**c.** unfair treatment
_____	**4.** *status*	**d.** possible to get or use
_____	**5.** *discrimination*	**e.** attempt

REVIEW

Now that you have studied the vocabulary, reread or reskim the passage.

Reading a Table of Information

Look carefully at the following table. Then answer the questions that follow.

LIFE EXPECTANCY AT BIRTH, BY SEX, AMERICAN INDIANS AND ALASKA NATIVES AND U.S. WHITE POPULATION, 1940–1980

	American Indians and Alaska Natives			U.S. White Population		
Year	**Both Sexes**	**Male**	**Female**	**Both Sexes**	**Male**	**Female**
1980	71.1	67.1	75.1	74.4	70.7	78.1
1970	65.1	60.7	71.2	71.6	67.9	75.5
1960	61.7	60.0	65.7	70.7	67.6	74.2
1950	60.0	58.1	62.2	69.0	66.3	72.0
1940	51.0	(51.3)	51.9	64.9	62.8	67.3

1. Does this table give information about Indians throughout North America?

____

2. Who lives longer: Native Americans or white Americans? ______________

____

3. Compare the difference in life expectancy between the two groups from 1940 to 1980. Then write a sentence about how the difference has changed over this period of time.

____

4. Look at the circled figure. Write a sentence expressing this information.

____

5. The table does not explain the reasons for the differences in life expectancy. Can you think of three factors that might shorten the life expectancy of Native peoples?

____

____

____

FREEWRITING: WHAT HAVE YOU LEARNED ABOUT NATIVE AMERICANS?

What are the most interesting or important things you've learned about Native Americans in this chapter? Identify information that you hadn't known before, or that you hadn't known much about.

Writing an Essay: The Best of Both Worlds

Look at your chart of cultural values again. Which ones from both sides do you most admire? How might a Native American or a non-Native American today combine some values from both sides in their life?

Evaluating Learning Strategies

Look back over the chapter at the learning strategies that were presented. Were there any that weren't especially helpful for you? What wasn't helpful about them? Which ones did you find especially helpful? Think about times and ways that you can keep using them in your future reading. If you know of other good strategies that were not suggested in this chapter, tell your classmates about them.

Evaluating Your Learning

	Very little	*Quite a bit*	*A lot*
You know more vocabulary.	________	________	________
Your comprehension is stronger.	________	________	________
You can read unsimplified passages.	________	________	________
You can guess vocabulary from context.	________	________	________
You can take notes from your reading.	________	________	________
You learned about Native Americans.	________	________	________

KEYWORDS FOR CHAPTER 3: NATIVE VOICES

Verbs
attack
attempt
attract
buy into
cooperate
destroy
establish
generalize
get ahead of
give up
heal
recognize
rely on
resist
retreat
shield

Nouns
attitude
benefit
ceremony
citizen
clash
climate
complexity
conflict
contradiction
depression
destruction
discrimination
diversity
drawback
effort
emptiness
encouragement
expertise
feature
fondness
game
generalization
herd
improvement
income
media
movement
nomad
policy
poverty
pride
relations
renaissance
ritual
spirit
status
survival
unemployment
variation
vision

Adjectives
adrift
ancestral
ashamed
available
clever
cosy
diverse
indigenous
menial
rampant

Adverbs
forever
instead of

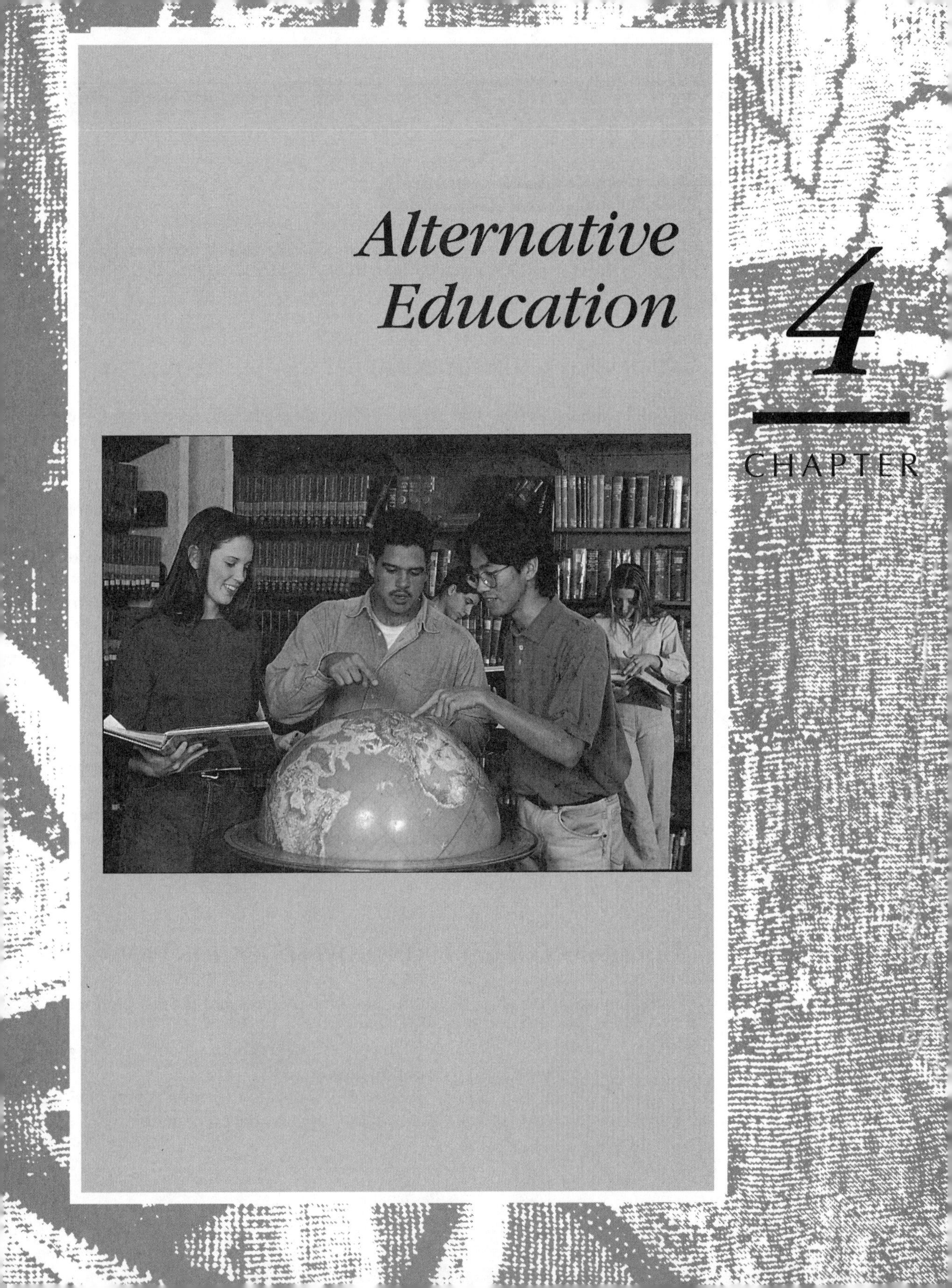

Alternative Education

4

CHAPTER

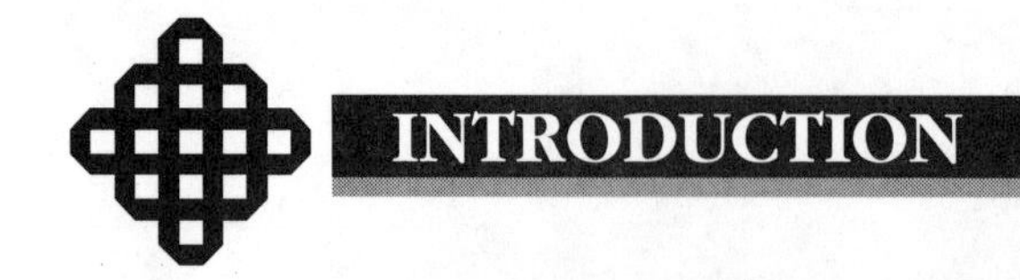

INTRODUCTION

LEARNING STRATEGY

Managing Your Learning: Using a checklist helps you see how well you are meeting your long-term and short-term goals.

PLANNING YOUR LEARNING

Review your overall goal statement. How much progress did you make toward it in the last chapter? Do you want to change it? Think about how you can work to meet your goal as you study this new chapter.

- How many words do you want to learn? (minimum 54, the number of keywords in the chapter)
- What grade would you like to make on the vocabulary section of the exam at the end of the chapter?
- What grade would you like to make on the reading comprehension section of the exam?
- What are you going to read outside of class?

PREVIEWING THE CHAPTER

- Think about the title of this chapter. What do you think "alternative education" is?
- Look in the Table of Contents at the titles of the five readings in this chapter. Look through the chapter at the pictures. What are some things that you expect to learn about?
- Which reading looks the most interesting?

DISCUSSION OF CARTOON: HOW EDUCATION WORKS

- What's the connection between the first nine pictures and the last picture? In other words, what's this cartoon about?
- What does each of the first nine pictures have to say about school? Does any one of these pictures describe your own feelings?
- What did (or do) you like about school? What didn't (or don't) you like? Either draw a picture of your own, or freewrite for about ten minutes.

Calvin and Hobbes
by Watterson © 1993
MOOOOO MOOO
MOOO
WHOOSH
KACHUNK
CHUG CHUG
SQUEAK
SQUEAK SQUEAK
CLANG
CLANG
WIZZ WIRP BOINGG
WIZZ WIRP BOINGG
AWKK!
HELLO!
HELLO!
RIP
GAAAA
GGHHH
BONK
BONK
GASP
GASP
BOY, AM I GLAD TO SEE YOU, HOBBES!
ANOTHER TYPICAL SCHOOL DAY?

FREEWRITING AND/OR DISCUSSION: THE PURPOSE OF EDUCATION

1. In your opinion, what is the most important purpose of education? (√)

	Most Important	*Important*	*Not So Important*
To train students for future careers	______	______	______
To prepare them to be good citizens	______	______	______
To make them better persons	______	______	______
To teach them information about things	______	______	______
To teach them how to do things	______	______	______
To teach them how to think for themselves	______	______	______
To teach them how to learn	______	______	______
To encourage and develop their creativity	______	______	______
To develop an understanding of their own cultures	______	______	______
To teach them how to get along together	______	______	______
Other: ______________	______	______	______

2. Think about your own experience in education. Did/does it serve the purposes that you believe are "most important," or did/does it serve other ones?

3. Did you study anything in school that you don't think was useful for you?
   - If so, what was it?
   - Do you think you should have had to learn it?
   - If so, why?

First Alternative for a Longer Project: Observing a Traditional Class

In this chapter, your teacher may assign you to choose a longer project that you could spend two or three weeks working on. Three of these projects will be described, but if you think of something else that you would rather work on, discuss it with your teacher. Here is the first alternative:

1. You will visit a traditional class at a level of your choice: kindergarten, elementary, secondary, or college/university. As you observe, answer the following questions:
   - **a.** What method is the teacher using? (lecture, discussion, individual reading/writing/problem solving, group or paired work, lab experiments, etc.)
   - **b.** Does the teacher expect the students to have completed homework or readings before the class?
   - **c.** Does the teacher conduct the class formally, or casually? Do the students behave formally, or casually? Give examples.
   - **d.** Do the students ask questions and give opinions during the class? If so, how does the professor react? (Is she or he pleased, or annoyed?)
   - **e.** What else do you notice that is interesting to you?
   - **f.** Which of the items on the "purposes of education" list do you think that this class fulfils?
   - **g.** In what ways does this class differ from a traditional class in your country?
2. If you wish, interview some students from the class that you visited. Beforehand, make a list of two or three questions that you wish to ask them. Write your questions here:

   ____

   ____

   ____
3. Write up a report of your observation. Include an introductory paragraph telling what you did and what your purpose was. In the next paragraph, tell what you observed. If you interviewed students, in the third paragraph summarize what you learned from them. Then in the last paragraph, give your conclusions about the whole experience, your reactions and opinions, and any comments that you wish to make.

PREPARING TO READ: VOCABULARY

The following questions provide practice in the basic vocabulary used to discuss education. Work with a partner. If you don't know an answer, use your dictionary or skip that question, but fill it in later when you compare your work with the rest of your classmates'.

1. What is the name for the school that children attend at:
   - around the age of 5? ______________________________
   - around the ages of 6 to 12? ______________________________
   - 13 to 18? ______________________________
2. What's the way of teaching in which the teacher does all the talking, giving information to the students?

   ____

3. What's another word for *way* of teaching?

____

4. What's the name for the list of all the courses that are taught at a particular school?

____

5. What do you call schools that are operated by the province?

____

What about the schools that are operated by another group, for instance, religious schools?

____

6. At the end of the course each student receives a ________________, e.g., A/B/C/D/F. A good one means the student ________________; a poor one means the student ________________ the course.

7. The person in charge of an elementary or secondary school is called the ____.

8. *Academic* subjects are (for example) ________________, ________________, ________________. ________________ is a *non-academic* subject.

9. ________________ tests are tests that all students in the city, province, or country take at a certain point in their education.

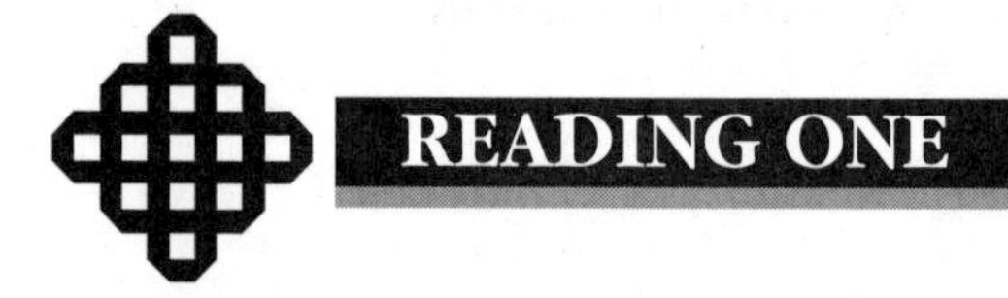

READING ONE

Sometimes people have an experience that suddenly teaches them something very important, something they'll remember all their lives. Usually these experiences take place outside the classroom. The following reading describes such a "learning moment" for one of the little boys in the story. Thirty years later he still remembered it so clearly that he told the story to Joseph Bruchac, an Abenaki Indian educator, who thought it was a perfect example of how the Native North American approach to education differs from the Euro-American one.

THANKING THE BIRDS

1 One day thirty years ago, Swift Eagle, an Apache man, visited some friends on the Onondaga Indian Reservation in central New York. While he was out walking, he heard sounds of boys playing in the bushes.

2 "There's another one. Shoot it!" said one of the boys.

3 When he pushed through the brush to see what was happening, he found that they had been shooting small birds with a BB gun. They had already killed a chickadee, a robin, and several blackbirds. The boys looked up at him, uncertain[1] what he was going to do or say.

4 There are several things that a non-Indian bird lover might have done: given a stern lecture[2] on the evil[3] of killing birds; threatened to tell the boys' parents on them for doing something they had been told not to do; or even spanked them. Swift Eagle, however, did something else.

5 "Ah," he said, "I see you have been hunting. Pick up your game and come with me."

6 He led the boys to a place where they could make a fire and cook the birds. He made sure they said a thank-you to the spirits of the birds before eating them, and as they ate he told stories. It was important, he said, to be thankful to the birds for the gifts of their songs, their feathers, and their bodies as food. The last thing he said to them they never forgot—for it was one of those boys who told me this story many years later: "You know, our Creator gave the gift of life to everything that is alive. Life is a very sacred thing. But our Creator knows that we have to eat to stay alive. That is why it is permitted to hunt to feed ourselves and our people. So I understand that you boys must have been very, very hungry to kill those little birds ..."

7 As the anecdote about Swift Eagle shows, children were taught the values of their culture through example and stories. Instead of scolding or lecturing them, Swift Eagle showed the boys how to build a fire and cook the game they had shot, giving the songbirds the same respect he would have given a rabbit or deer. He told stories that pointed out the value of those birds as living beings. The ritual activity of making the fire, thanking the spirits of the birds, hearing the stories, and then eating the game they had killed taught the boys more than a hundred stern lectures would have done, and the lesson stayed with them all their lives. Western education today tends[4] to be didactic. Children are told—in books, lectures, film scripts, and movies—*about* things, but rarely do they experience them. Adults then test the children by having them answer questions about what they have "learned." There is good reason for this method, of course. The world our children must know about is too broad[5] to allow them to learn everything through a hands-on approach. However, as many educators have observed, the result of such a method is too often learning that is more a conditioned reflex than a true understanding. Furthermore, the artificial[6] divisions between fields of study—with natural science alone being divided into botany, zoology, geology, astronomy, and hundreds of other areas—can lead to knowledge that is fragmented.[7] It is like what you learn by dissecting a frog: you know the parts, but you cannot put them together to understand the animal. And, in cutting the frog apart, you have killed it.

8 Native American education, in contrast, has always been experiential[8] and holistic.[9] If you wish to know how to make baskets, you go to a basket maker and watch that person at work. If you are patient and watch long enough, eventually the basket maker may ask you to do something—to hold onto this coil of sweetgrass here, to help shave down that strip of ash. If you return the next day, and the next, and the next, then one day you discover that you, too, know how to make a basket.

Threads

What is the task of all higher education? To make man into a machine. What are the means employed? He is taught how to suffer being bored.

F.W. Nietzsche

After You Read

Identify the circled reference words.

COMPREHENSION QUESTIONS

1. Why did Swift Eagle force the boys to cook and eat the songbirds?

____

____

2. What did he want the boys to learn from the experience?

____

____

LEARNING STRATEGY

Forming Concepts: Summarizing a reading in your own words requires you to think actively about the main ideas and helps you to remember them.

SUMMARIZING

1. Using your own words, summarize the first six paragraphs (the anecdote about Swift Eagle) into three sentences with a total of not more than 40 words.

____

____

____

____

____

____

2. If you were going to summarize ¶7, highlight not more than four sentences that contain the main points.
3. If you were going to summarize ¶8, which sentence contains the main idea?

____

What is the purpose of the other sentences? ______________________________

DISCUSSION AND FREEWRITING: "LEARNING MOMENTS"

1. Discuss with a partner: Have you learned more inside the classroom, or outside of it? Give examples of some of the most important things you've learned. Where did you learn them? Who did you learn them from?
2. Freewrite: Write about a "learning moment" of your own. What happened, and what did you learn?

DISCUSSION: HOW PEOPLE LEARN BEST

How do you learn best? How do you think most people learn best? (Through lectures, discussion, lab or field work, trial and error, observation, working with a partner, independent reading, etc.) Which of these methods are used in the style of education described in ¶7? In ¶8?

Vocabulary

VOCABULARY IN CONTEXT

Look at the following sentences from ¶7:

"It is like what you learn by dissecting a frog: you know the parts, but you cannot put them together to understand the animal. And, in cutting the frog apart, you have killed it."

Given the context, what do you think *dissecting* means?

LEARNING STRATEGY

Remembering New Material: Recording new words in a vocabulary notebook reserved for that purpose helps you remember them.

KEYWORDS

1. uncertain* ¶3
2. lecture ¶4
3. evil ¶4
4. tend ¶7
5. broad ¶7
6. artificial ¶7
7. fragmented ¶7
8. experiential ¶8
9. holistic ¶8

KEYWORD EXERCISE

1. Choose the synonym for *uncertain* from the following:
   sure   confident   doubtful   definite   positive

   EXAMPLE: The boys looked up at him, *uncertain* what he was going to do or say.

2. *Meanings:*
   - A *lecture* is a speech that someone gives in order to teach something.

     EXAMPLE: Our professor gave a *lecture* on the causes of the conflict in Northern Ireland.

   - If someone *lectures* you about something, they point out a bad thing you did and tell you how you should behave.

     EXAMPLE: Swift Eagle didn't *lecture* the boys.

   - Explain the similarities between the two meanings.

3. The following adjectives are all related to "bad," but some are worse than others. Rank them from the least bad (1) to the worst (6).

evil	wrong	unpleasant	poor	naughty	harmful
(1)	(2)	(3)	(4)	(5)	(6)

   EXAMPLE: Many religions teach about the difference between good and *evil* behaviour.

4. ***EXAMPLE:*** Today North Americans *tend* to pay with cheques or credit cards instead of carrying cash.

   Finish the sentences:
   - On rainy weekends I tend to ______________________________.
   - One stereotype of politicians is that they tend ____________________.
   - Cats ____.

5. If you define the word "family" in a *broad* way, whom does it include?
   If you define it in a narrow way, whom does it include?

   EXAMPLE: An educated person has a *broad* knowledge of the world.

6. Which of the following materials are not *artificial?*
   cotton   wool   nylon   wood   plastic   gold   stone   vinyl

   EXAMPLE: Computers make use of *artificial* intelligence.

   What word is a good antonym for artificial?

7. *Meanings:*
   - Something that is *fragmented* is made of a lot of different parts that seem unconnected with each other.

     EXAMPLE: My family moved around so often that my childhood is made up of *fragmented* memories of different cities, schools, and friends.

   - A *fragment* is a small broken-off piece of something.

EXAMPLE: When he dropped the cup, he had to sweep up all the *fragments* so no one would step on them and be cut.

- Explain the similarities between the two meanings.

8. The word *experiential* may not be in your dictionary. It's the adjective form of the noun *experience.* In ¶8, Bruchac says that Native North American education has always been *experiential* and holistic. Swift Eagle educated the boys through an experiential method. In what ways was his method related to the word *experience?*

9. *Holistic* is a word that may not be in your dictionary either. If you look at something *holistically,* you look at all of it in a connected way instead of just looking at separate parts of it. For instance, a holistic approach to medical practice considers not just the patient's temperature and pains, but also his or her eating habits, emotional condition, amount of regular exercise, etc.

   Look at Bruchac's example of basketmaking in ¶8. In what ways is it *experiential?* In what ways is it *holistic?*

REVIEW

Now that you have studied the vocabulary, reread or reskim the passage.

READING TWO

Reading process: As you read the following passage, look for the answers to the following questions (often called "journalists' questions"):

Who?	Why?	Where?
What?	How?	When?

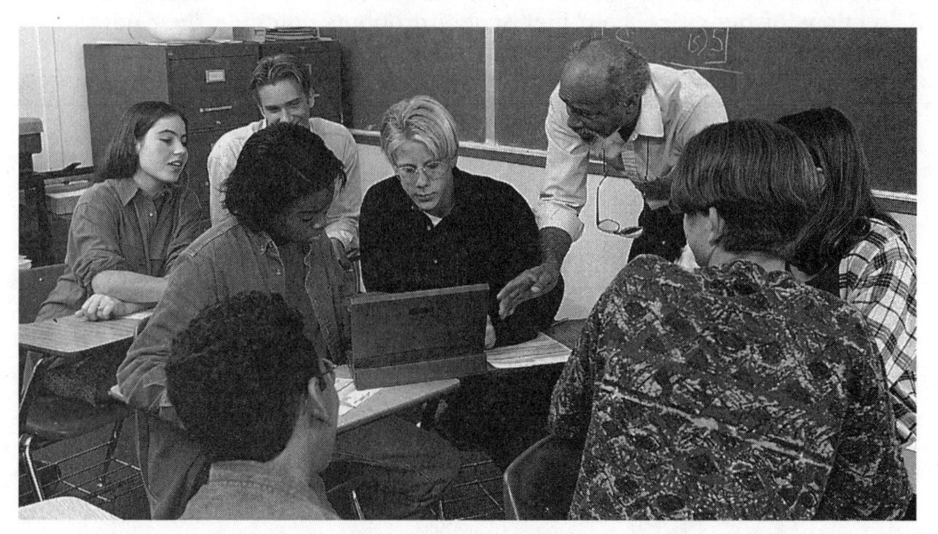

ALTERNATIVE SCHOOLS IN THE UNITED STATES

1 [An] alternative school is any public or private school that differs from traditional schools in curriculum, purpose, or teaching methods. Most alternative schools attempt to establish a less formal relationship between pupils and teachers. They also try to make greater use of community facilities outside the school and to involve[1] parents in the educational process. Alternative schools developed because of dissatisfaction[2] with the quality[3] and aims of traditional schools.

2 Alternative schools have voluntary enrollments. A typical alternative school has from 30 to 40 students. A school of this size can easily adjust[4] its program to fit individual needs and desires. Some alternative schools work only with children of elementary-school age, and others accept only teenagers. Many alternative schools put students of several ages into classes based on[5] subject interest.

3 Many alternative schools in the United States operate independently of the public school system. These schools, which are privately run, are usually called free schools. The word free refers to the independence of such schools. It also describes the emphasis[6] of these schools in allowing students to make their own decisions in various matters. Other alternative schools operate as part of the public school system. Such schools may be located in one area of a public school building or in a separate building provided by the school system. The separate buildings are often called *magnet schools* or *specialty schools.* They attempt to attract students from throughout[7] the school system.

4 The basic[8] principle[9] followed by alternative schools is that not all children have the same goals and the same ways of learning. Many of the people involved in operating these schools do not want to convert[10] the whole school system to their methods. They want to provide the opportunity for a different kind of education for children who would benefit from it.

5 The major feature of many alternative schools is the *open classroom.* The teacher of an open classroom, instead of lecturing most of the time, helps students find interesting ways to learn on their own.[11] Many kinds of educational materials are kept in the classroom. The students work with these materials alone or in groups. The teacher gives the students individual help ...

6 Many forms of alternative schools have developed in response to various needs. *Street academies* and *dropout centers,* which function in the poor sections of big cities, help high-school dropouts continue their education. *Storefront schools* have developed from child-care and kindergarten facilities. *Work schools* hold classes part of the day, and the students work at regular jobs the rest of the day.

7 The *school without walls* plan, used in some large cities, takes advantage of the educational opportunities[12] provided by businesses and institutions of the community. Students may spend part of the day at an artist's studio, a factory, a museum, a newspaper office, a repair shop, a theater, or a government or private agency. The purpose of this method is to make learning more realistic and enjoyable, and to broaden the experiences offered high-school students.

8 Some alternative schools emphasize[6] the study of the culture and history of a certain minority group.[13] Some accept only students from one such group. Others seek students from several cultures and races.

9 A number of alternative schools have been designed[14] for children from middle- or upper-class families. Usually such schools are in suburban or rural areas. Most of them stress[15] the independence of each student and have no required subjects.

Threads

In a natural learning environment a child is permitted to pursue whatever direction his curiosity takes.

Jane Williams, alternative educator

10 A trend[16] in the development of alternative schools has been the establishment of such schools within the public school system. One plan offers a variety of learning environments from which students, parents, and teachers may choose. At the elementary school level, parents can choose to place their children in a traditional classroom or in one of several kinds of open classrooms. High-school students decide whether to enter a free school with few course requirements, or one of several programs in the regular high-school program.

After You Read

Identify the circled reference words.

> What makes all this "alternative" is that the American public school system is not oriented to the fullest human development of students, but to preparing them to be loyal, obedient citizens, employees, and consumers. The social history of American education makes it clear that mass schooling, in the form we know it, was created to meet the needs of industrial capitalism. While many individual teachers are devoted to the needs and interests of their students, the system is mainly interested in sorting and controlling them.
>
> —*Ron Miller, alternative educator*
>
> Do you agree with this view of traditional schooling?

COMPREHENSION QUESTIONS

1. In ¶1 the authors tell why some people wanted to develop alternative schools. What might have dissatisfied them in traditional schools?

____

____

____

2. Based on the information in the reading, would it be accurate to say that alternative schools have a lot in common with each other?

____

3. According to the article, alternative schools can operate either within or outside of ____.

4. Reread the first sentence of ¶4. Who are the children who would want to attend alternative schools?

____

- In your experience, what goals and ways of learning would traditional schools serve?

____

5. Can you find anything in the article that suggests that the author believes that alternative schools are better—or are worse—than traditional schools?

____

____

____

____

TRUE–FALSE QUESTIONS

			¶ *number*
1. Most alternative schools are very small.	T	F	________
2. *Free schools* cost the students nothing.	T	F	________
3. *Magnet schools* are public schools.	T	F	________
4. In an *open classroom,* students study independently instead of all together.	T	F	________
5. In the *school without walls* plan, classes are held out-of-doors.	T	F	________

Second Alternative for a Longer Project: Observing an Alternative Class

Your teacher will take you to visit an alternative school in your community, and/or will invite an alternative educator to your class to be interviewed. If you visit a class, fill out the answers to these questions:

1. What method is the teacher using? (lecture, discussion, individual reading/writing/problem solving, group or paired work, lab experiments, etc.)
2. Does the teacher expect the students to have completed homework or readings before the class?
3. Does the teacher conduct the class formally, or casually? Do the students behave formally, or casually? Give examples.
4. Do the students ask questions and give opinions during the class? If so, how does the teacher react? (Is she or he pleased or annoyed?)
5. What else do you notice that is interesting to you?
6. Which of the "purposes of education" list items do you think that this class fulfils?
7. In what ways does this class differ from a traditional class in your country?

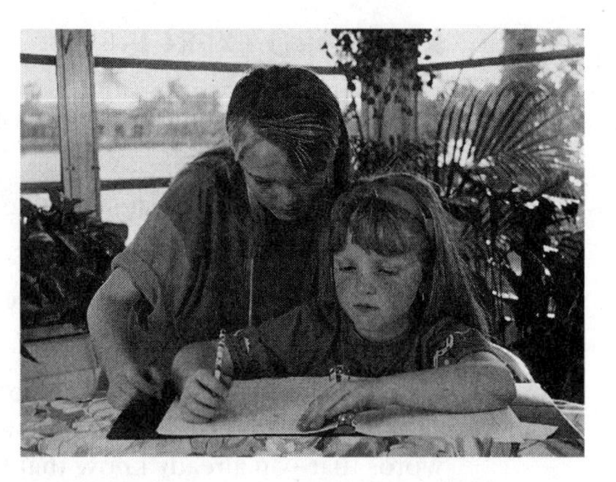

If an alternative educator comes to your class to be interviewed, work with your classmates to prepare a list of questions in advance. Each student should be responsible for asking one question. Advance preparation will help you to plan good questions and to make sure that questions aren't repeated.

Write a report on what you have learned. In the first paragraph, summarize what you did and tell your purpose. In the second, tell what you observed or summarize what the educator said. (If you both observed a class and interviewed an educator, devote a separate paragraph to each.) In your last paragraph, give your conclusions about the whole experience, your reactions and opinions, and any comments that you wish to make.

Vocabulary

VOCABULARY IN CONTEXT

1. Find the word *dropout* in ¶6. (It's used twice.) You can figure out its meaning in two ways: (1) by looking at the context, and (2) by dividing the word into its two parts and thinking about them. What do you think it means?

2. Find the phrase *learning environments* in ¶10. The context gives you several examples of learning environments. Name two.

   a. ______________________________

   b. ______________________________

KEYWORDS

1. involve ¶1
2. dissatisfaction ¶1
3. quality ¶1
4. adjust* ¶2
5. based on* ¶2
6. emphasis, emphasize* ¶s 3, 8
7. throughout* ¶3
8. basic ¶4
9. principle ¶4
10. convert ¶4
11. on their own* ¶5
12. opportunity ¶7
13. minority group ¶8
14. design ¶9
15. stress ¶9
16. trend ¶10

KEYWORD EXERCISE

1. ***EXAMPLES:*** Most alternative schools try to *involve* parents in their children's schooling.

   My roommate wants to *involve* me in all of his personal problems.

   Finish the sentences:
   Should religious leaders be involved ______________________________.
   A good teacher will become ______________________________.

2. The prefix *dis-* is often used to form the antonym of a word, as with *satisfaction/dissatisfaction.* Look in your dictionary and find three other words that you already know that form antonyms by adding *dis-*.

   a. ______________________________

   b. ______________________________

   c. ______________________________

   EXAMPLE: Alternative schools developed because of *dissatisfaction* with the quality and aims of traditional schools.

3. List four features that a high-*quality* school would have.

   a. ______________________________

   b. ______________________________

   c. ______________________________

   d. ______________________________

4. When you travel, list four things that you might need to *adjust* to.

   a. ______________________________

   b. ______________________________

   c. ______________________________

   d. ______________________________

   EXAMPLE: A small school can easily *adjust* its program to fit individual needs and desires.

5. When a scientist makes a discovery, what might it be *based on?*

   EXAMPLE: Many alternative schools put students of several ages into classes *based on* subject interest.

6. Which of the following words are elements of *emphasis* or *emphasize?*

   appear   barely   generalize   strong   important   true

   EXAMPLES: Native North American education *emphasizes* teaching through stories.

   My high school put a lot of *emphasis* on examination scores.

7. ***EXAMPLES:*** It rained *throughout* the night.
Spanish is spoken *throughout* Latin America.

Finish the sentences:
The soldiers kept watch throughout ______________________________.
Around this time of year, students ______________________________.

8. Which of the following are elements of the word *basic?*

the most important   the simplest   the most available
the most diverse

EXAMPLE: The *basic* elements of good art are imagination and technique.

9. *Meanings:*

- A *principle* is a general belief that you have about the way you should behave. This principle governs your behaviour. An example: "Friends should always have time for each other."
- A *principle* is also a general rule about how something should be done, or a general scientific law that explains how something happens or works.
- Which meaning is used in this sentence from ¶4?

"The basic *principl*e followed by alternative schools is that not all children have the same goals and the same ways of learning."

10. ***EXAMPLE:*** She won't marry him if he doesn't *convert* to her religion.

Finish the sentences:
After I left home, my parents converted my bedroom to ______________.
The children converted the large cardboard box ______________________.

11. Which of the following is an antonym for *on their own?*

independently   alone   without help   cooperatively

EXAMPLE: The teacher helps students find interesting ways to learn *on their own.*

12. Which of the following is the best representation of an *opportunity?*

money   a good friend   a prison   an open door   a key

EXAMPLE: Businesses and institutions in the community also provide educational *opportunities.*

13. Name some *minority groups* that live in North America.
Name some *minority groups* that live in your country.

EXAMPLE: Some alternative schools emphasize the study of the culture and history of a certain *minority group.*

14. Which of the following is not an element of the word *design?*

accidental   plan   prepare   decide   details

EXAMPLE: A number of alternative schools have been *designed* for children from middle- or upper-class families.

15. In ¶8, find a synonym for the verb *stress.*

EXAMPLE: Some alternative schools *stress* the independence of each student and have no required subjects.

16. One synonym for *trend* is *fashion,* a popular style that people are doing (or wearing) these days. We can speak of *trends* in clothing, in cars, in eating or exercise habits, in television and films, and also in education, government, and medical practice. Choose one of these areas and describe some recent trends. Remember, if it's a trend, it must be something that wasn't happening several years ago.

REVIEW

Now that you have studied the vocabulary, reread or reskim the passage.

LEARNING STRATEGY

Managing Your Learning: Every evening, organize your handouts and pages of notes from that day. These papers can't help you if you can never find them. Review them every week or two.

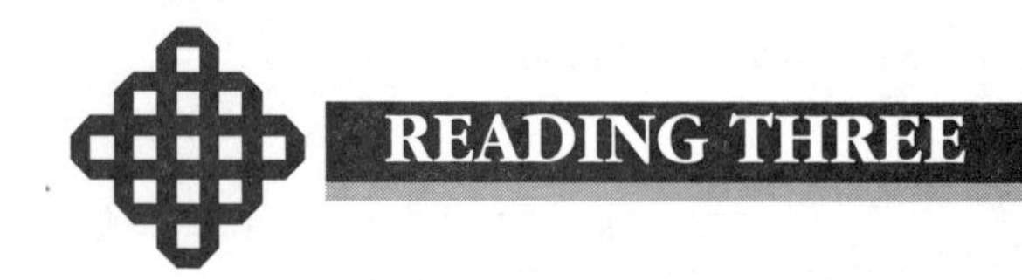

READING THREE

Reading process for Readings Three and Four: Your teacher will ask half of the class to read Reading Three, and the other half to read Reading Four. If you read Reading Three, you will answer questions that a partner who hasn't read it will ask you. Then you will ask your partner questions about Reading Four, which she or he will have read. The questions follow the readings.

When each of you has finished, read the other passage.

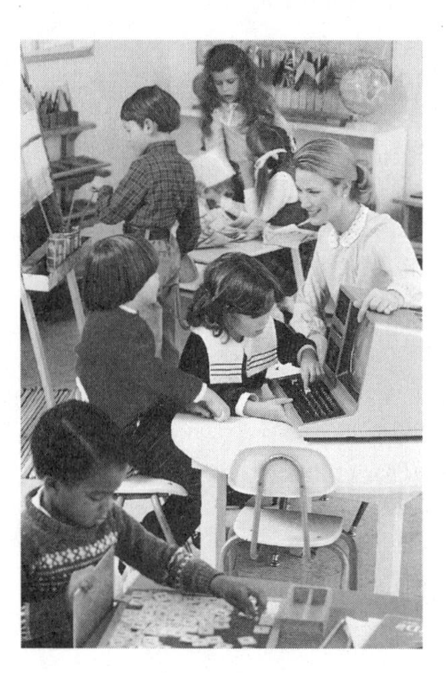

THE MONTESSORI METHOD

1 The Montessori method of education, used worldwide today, was developed by Dr. Maria Montessori (1870–1952). She was the first woman in Italy to receive a medical degree, but found it difficult to practise medicine because Italians at that time were not ready to accept female doctors. So she turned to education, working with children who had been locked away in mental institutions because they were considered[1] unable to learn. Through her thoughtful observations[2] and through her experience with these children, she developed a method of educating them that was so successful that they were able to pass reading and writing examinations designed for normal children. She wrote several

books about her methods, the best-known of (which) is entitled *The Absorbent Mind.* These books form the basis for[3] "the Montessori method" which is still in use today in Montessori schools.

2 Montessori schools do not group children as traditional schools do. Instead of all the six-year-olds studying together in the first grade, taking examinations, receiving grade reports, and then either passing to the next grade or repeating the first grade, Montessori children are grouped in larger age groups—say, three- to five-year-olds together, or six- through nine-year-olds together in one classroom. The teachers keep careful records of each child's development[4] and activities, but they do not grade the children. If a child is having difficulty with an activity, the teacher will spend extra time with her until she succeeds[5] in learning it. Parents are welcome to observe classes at any time, and parents and teachers meet to discuss the child's development at regular intervals throughout the year.

3 Children are carefully taught how to do things, beginning at the earliest ages. For example, in kindergarten, each day a different child may be in charge of preparing a snack for all the children. The child would be taught how to cut up apples safely and how to pour and serve glasses of milk without spilling them. If a Montessori school has any space around it, the children will usually be taught how to plant and care for a garden. There are often small animals in the classroom: maybe fish, birds, white mice, guinea pigs, kittens. Even the smallest children are taught how to respect and care for these pets. But children are also taught traditional academic subjects. Part of their course of study is independent research into topics of their choice, which they write papers and give oral reports on.

4 Dr. Montessori based her method on observing each child to see when he was ready to learn a new concept[6] or process[7] instead of making the whole class do the same thing at the same time. She believed that children begin to learn best when they can see and touch something, can experience it through their senses. Concepts are always taught by exposing the children to a real-life, concrete[8] experience first, before the abstract[9] idea is introduced. For instance, when learning about mathematics, the children begin by counting and arranging coloured beads or other small objects, then later move on to working with abstract numbers on paper. Everything they learn should be made real.

Threads

Maria Montessori believed that education begins at birth, and that the first few years of life are especially important.

Mark and Helen Hegener, alternative educators

Threads

In a classic Montessori school four areas of development are addressed: care of self and the environment, sensory and motor education, reading and writing skills, and premath teaching.

Mark and Helen Hegener, alternative educators

After You Read

Identify the circled reference word.

> One of the objectives of Montessori is to assure that the child does not fail when attempting new tasks. Montessori believes that failure can have negative effects on the child, so Montessori instructors do everything they can to assure that this doesn't happen.
>
> —*Jane Williams, alternative educator*

COMPREHENSION QUESTIONS

1. Who was Maria Montessori?

___

___

2. Why didn't she practise medicine, as she was trained to do?

___

___

3. Identify two features of the Montessori method.

___

___

4. Would you have enjoyed learning this way? Would you have liked it better than the way that you learned in school?

___

___

IN WHICH PARAGRAPH CAN YOU FIND ...

1. A description of the principles that the Montessori method is based on ___
2. A description of what children learn in a Montessori school ___
3. A history of how the Montessori method developed ___
4. A description of the organization and policies of a Montessori school ___

TAKING NOTES AS YOU READ

In the last chapter (on pages 65 to 69) you made notes of the important points in the reading passage. Now practise this again, in a slightly different way.

1. Look at ¶1. Pick out the three most important pieces of information in this paragraph, and highlight or underline them.
   - How is ¶1 organized: chronology, examples, cause and effect, comparison/contrast, or problem/solution? (See the Appendix on page 250, for a list of markers that will help you answer this question.)
   - Circle the markers that tell you the organization.
2. Pick out the three most important pieces of information in ¶2.
   - How is it organized?
   - Circle the markers.

3. What are the two most important pieces of information in ¶3?
   - What's the organization?
   - The markers?

4. What are the three most important parts of ¶4?
   - The organization?
   - The markers?

5. Now make notes on a piece of paper. Use abbreviations and symbols instead of writing complete sentences. For instance:

   Maria Montessori: MM
   children: chdrn
   learn: lrn
   school: schl
   students: sts

6. Choose one of these graphic formats for each paragraph:

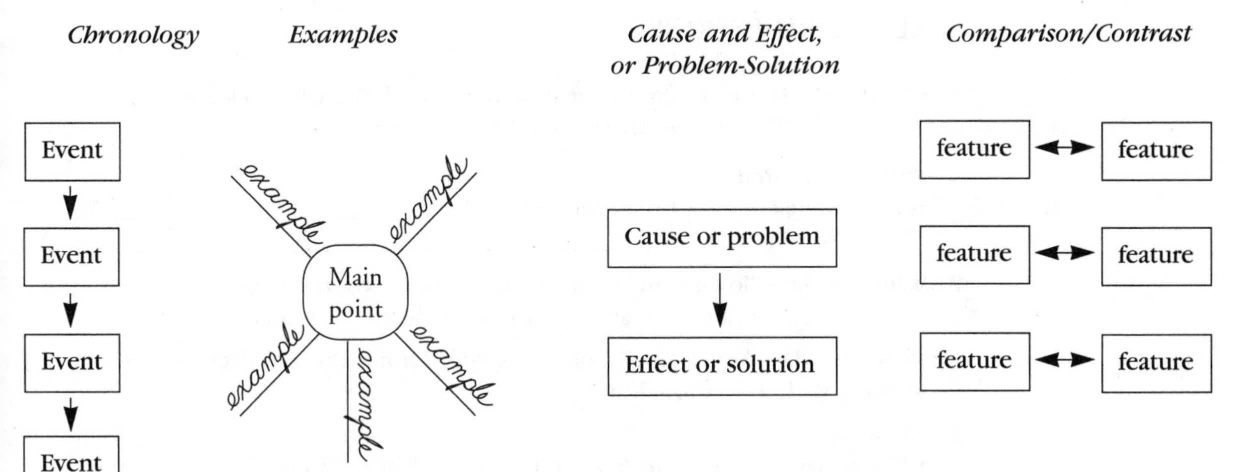

Use the appropriate format to make notes of the most important points and details on a separate piece of paper. When you finish, compare your work with a classmate's and then show it to your teacher.

Vocabulary

VOCABULARY IN CONTEXT

1. ¶2 says, "Parents and teachers meet to discuss the child's development at *regular intervals* throughout the year." What do you think *intervals* are? If you can't think of a definition, give an example.

2. ¶3 says that children are taught how to pour and serve glasses of milk without *spilling* them. Using your arms and hands, show what happens when you *spill* milk.

3. ¶4 says that Dr. Montessori "believed that children begin to learn best when they can see and touch something, can experience it through their *senses*." What can you understand about the word *senses?*

KEYWORDS

1. consider ¶1
2. observation ¶1
3. form the basis for ¶1
4. development ¶2
5. succeed* ¶2
6. concept ¶4
7. process ¶4
8. concrete ¶4
9. abstract ¶4

KEYWORD EXERCISE

1. *EXAMPLES:* Those children were *considered* (to be) unable to learn.
We *consider* these figures to be accurate.

Finish the sentences:
Some people consider Columbus to have been ______________________.
This tourist resort is ______________________________________.

2. Which of the following are elements of the word *observation?*
offer   watch   think   learn   notice

EXAMPLE: Dr. Montessori's *observations* about the children she was working with were thoughtful.

3. *Meanings:*
   - If something *forms the basis for* a method or decision, it provides the reasons for doing it.

     EXAMPLE: Maria Montessori's books *formed the basis* for her educational methods.
   - We say that the most important and simplest parts of something are its *basics.*

     EXAMPLE: Children are not ready to learn algebra until they have mastered the *basics* of arithmetic.
   - Explain the similarities between the two words.

4. Which of the following are elements of the word *development?*
slow   sudden   step by step   growth   change

EXAMPLE: The teachers keep careful records of each child's *development.*

5. *EXAMPLE:* The teacher worked patiently with the little boy until he *succeeded* in learning to tie his shoes.

Finish the sentences:
After many attempts, the athlete finally succeeded in ____________________.
I hope to ____.

6. Remember when you were a child, how it took you a long time to understand the idea, the *concept,* of time? At an early age you had no clear idea of how long a year would be, nor a week, nor even the hour that your parents asked you to be quiet so they could take an afternoon nap. An understanding of those *concept*s came with experience.

   What are some other *concepts* that children have difficulty understanding? Can you remember any from your own experience?

   EXAMPLE: Dr. Montessori introduced children to new *concepts* and processes as they became ready to learn them.

7. What are the steps in the *process* of winning an Olympic gold medal in your favourite event?

   a. ____

   b. ____

   c. ____

   (etc.)

8. Divide the following words into *concrete* and *abstract* nouns.

   diary ambition knowledge belief hero controversy
   inhabitants report value loads encouragement nomads

Concrete	*Abstract*
____________________	____________________
____________________	____________________
____________________	____________________
____________________	____________________
____________________	____________________
____________________	____________________

REVIEW

Now that you have studied the vocabulary, reread or reskim the passage.

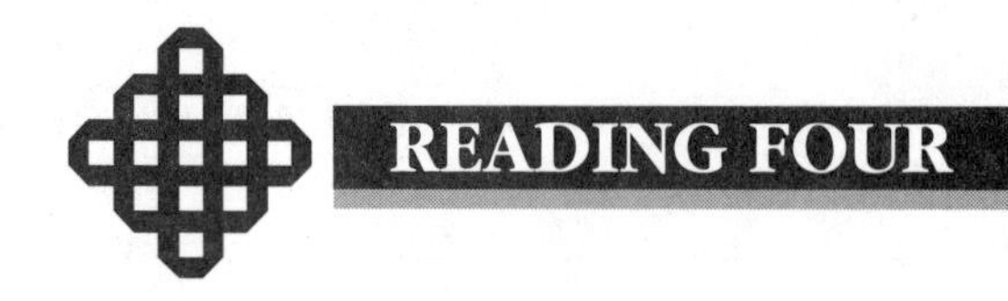

READING FOUR

STRESSING TEAMWORK IN SCHOOLS: QUÉBEC TRIES CO-OPERATIVE EDUCATION

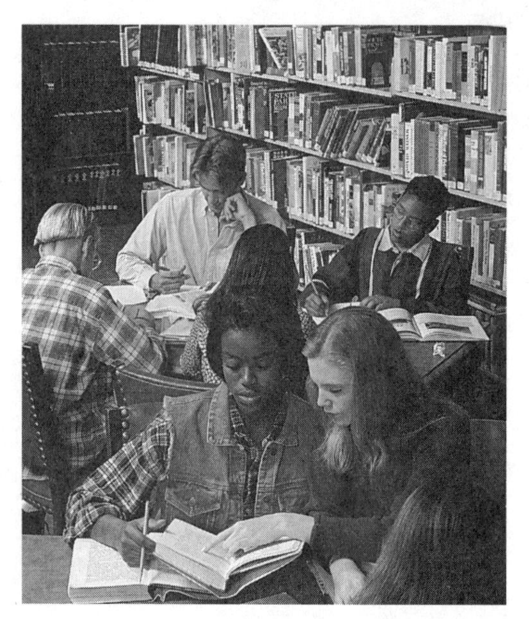

1 At Meadowbrook School in Lachine, Lesley MacLeod's Grade Two students are busy exploring African literature. Some sit cross-legged in groups of two or three on cushions at the back of the class. Others are huddled together at their desks or sprawled out on the floor, perched on their elbows expressing the emotions the poignant folk story has evoked. Team members take turns[1] talking and writing. And when it's time for the designated speakers to read each of the essays aloud, there are encouraging pats on the back and a few high fives on the side. At the end of the class, the teams rate their own performances and discuss how to do better next time. And then the bell rings and it's time for lunch. It's called co-operative[2] learning ...

2 Across most of Canada and the United States, [co-operative learning] has been changing the face of the classroom and the very way children have been taught. It was pioneered[3] nearly 20 years ago by researchers at the University of Minnesota in response to mounting evidence that the traditional mode of teaching, with students competing against each other for grades and the teacher's approval, was proving inadequate ...

3 In the co-operative classroom, long tidy rows of desks with quiet, acquiescent students sitting and listening dutifully while the teacher lectures from the front are history. Instead, students are grouped in small teams of mixed gender, race and academic ability. Each team member is assigned a specific role and all are equally responsible[4] for completing the task. "Young children can be self-centred, egocentric little beings. Working together this way helps them see that their peers have interesting ideas that are worth sharing," said MacLeod ... "But we can't just throw them into groups together. They need to be taught social skills." So among the flags of the world and painted murals lining the walls of MacLeod's cheery classroom are posters outlining the how-to's of working together and listening to each other: "Make eye contact. Nod your head. Smile. Lean toward your partner. Say, 'That's great, I like that, good idea.'"

4 Down the hall, another Meadowbrook teacher, Maria Hruby, said the students in her multi-level class are more willing to take risks and are less terrified of giving the "wrong" answer since she began organizing them in teams three years ago. And they seem to be having more fun ... "They are willing to share and take risks. They have a confidence they didn't have before," said Hruby, who has been teaching for more than 30 years. "No matter what their level of academic skills or their language level, they all get a chance to participate."

5 ... Critics worry that co-operative learning allows weaker students to become too dependent on their stronger peers, and that stronger students are held back by being obliged to work with weaker ones. (Some) say teachers are too overloaded to handle the extra preparation and organization time it takes to keep co-operative learning sessions from turning into free-for-alls. But when implemented effectively, proponents say co-operative learning promotes higher self-esteem, higher achievement and greater collaborative[5] skills and more positive attitudes among students, while cutting down on disruptive classroom behaviour ...

6 Charley Levy, director of instructional services at the Protestant School Board of Greater Montréal (PSBGM), said nobody is looking to replace existing teaching methods altogether. But he says the values[6] promoted by co-operative learning are becoming increasingly important in the new global[7] economy. The Conference Board of Canada lists teamwork as one of the most important assets for students preparing to enter the work force. "The values that are promoted in a co-operative learning setting are what we want to see in students of the 21st century—awareness and respect for the opinions of others and the ability to work together," Levy said.

After You Read

Identify the circled reference words.

COMPREHENSION QUESTIONS

1. Identify two ways in which co-operative education differs from the traditional classroom.

___

___

2. Why was there a need to rethink the traditional way of teaching?

___

___

3. How similar to or different from Meadowbook School was your elementary or high school?

___

___

TAKING NOTES AS YOU READ

Each of the paragraphs in the above reading contains what's called a *topic sentence*; that is, a single sentence that identifies the main idea of the paragraph. Can you find them?

HINT: The most common place it might appear is at the beginning of the paragraph. The second most common place is the last sentence. The third would be somewhere in the middle. And finally, many paragraphs don't have an actual topic sentence, although they do have a main idea or purpose.

Everything else in the paragraph *supports* the topic sentence by giving details about it. As you did with the reading on the Montessori Method, look at each paragraph and identify the way this information is organized: chronology, examples or features, cause and effect, comparison/contrast, or problem/solution.

Paragraph 1: ____________________

Paragraph 2: ____________________

Paragraph 3: ____________________

Paragraph 4: ____________________

Paragraph 5: ____________________

Paragraph 6: ____________________

Make notes of the most important points and details in the margin, using one of the formats from page 107 for each paragraph. When you finish, compare your work with a classmate's and then show it to your teacher.

Vocabulary

1. In ¶1, Lesley MacLeod's students are described as being "*busy exploring* African literature." What does *exploring* mean in this context?
2. In ¶4, "In the co-operative classroom, long tidy rows of desks with quiet, acquiescent students sitting and listening dutifully while the teacher lectures from the front *are history*."

   What does the expression *to be history* mean?

VOCABULARY STUDY: A CONFUSING PAIR

Here's a sentence from the article "Alternative Schools in the United States," on page 98:

> "The basic *principle* followed by alternative schools is that not all children have the same goals and the same ways of learning."

Now look at this sentence:

> *Principal* Howard Jones believes in giving students the opportunity to express their ideas and opinions freely and without fear of censure.

You looked up the word *principle* earlier, so you know what it means. From the context, what can you tell about the word *principal*? What part of speech is it? What does your dictionary say about the word *principal*? Is there any difference in pronunciation? Look them up and pronounce both.

KEYWORDS

1. take turns ¶1
2. co-operative ¶1
3. pioneered ¶3
4. responsible ¶4
5. collaborative ¶8
6. values* ¶9
7. global ¶9

KEYWORD EXERCISE

1. Students at Meadowbrook School *take turns* talking and writing in class. Complete the following sentence:

   My sisters and I used to *take turns* ______________________________

   ____.

2. Have you ever participated in *co-operative* activities either at school or in your community? If you have, list two of them.

   ____

   ____

   EXAMPLE: The Smiths are generous and *co-operative* members of the community.

3. *Pioneer* is the noun form of the verb *pioneered*. Below are the names of some well-known *pioneers*. Look them up in a reference book, such as an encyclopedia, to see what they are noted for.

   Alexander Graham Bell
   Wilbur and Orville Wright
   James Naismith
   Marie Curie
   Frederick Banting
   Paul de Chomedey sieur de Maisonneuve
   Samuel de Champlain
   Roberta Bondar
   Henry Ford

4. What are some things that you are *responsible* for doing at home? Write them here.

   ____

   ____

   EXAMPLE: Johnny does his homework diligently and very seldom misses classes. He is a very *responsible* student.

5. Give an example of a school project that you and a partner or partners *collaborated* on in the past, or any project that persons would need to *collaborate* on.

EXAMPLE: The teacher is the *collaborator*, team leader, and guide, rather than the boss.

6. Look up the word *values* in the dictionary. How is it defined?

   ____

   What are some *values* that you consider important to have?

   ____

7. Some people call the earth today a "*global* village." What do you think they mean?

   ____

   ____

   EXAMPLE: *Global* weather patterns are driven mainly by the oceans.

Third Alternative for a Longer Project: Doing an Oral History

Find an older person in your community, and do an oral history of something interesting that that person can tell you. Here are some ideas:

- How ______________ was different when she or he was a child (education, childhood, daily life, etc.)
- Something she or her parents learned how to do that isn't often done today
- Personal or family values when he was young
- Hard times in her life
- Celebrations when he was young

Once you and the person have decided on a topic, make a tape recording of the person talking. Feel free to record your own questions and comments as you go along.

Later, listen to the recording and write down anything that you want to include, *but you must write it down exactly as the person said it.* If you want to leave anything out, write three periods, with spaces before and after: ... (this is called an *ellipsis*) to indicate that something was omitted. When you finish, listen to the recording as you read along, and make corrections as needed. This word-for-word written copy is called the *transcript* of the recording.

For your final report, write an introduction telling what you did, what your purpose was, and who the person was. Then give the transcript. Finally, write a concluding paragraph telling what you learned, your opinions, and/or your comments.

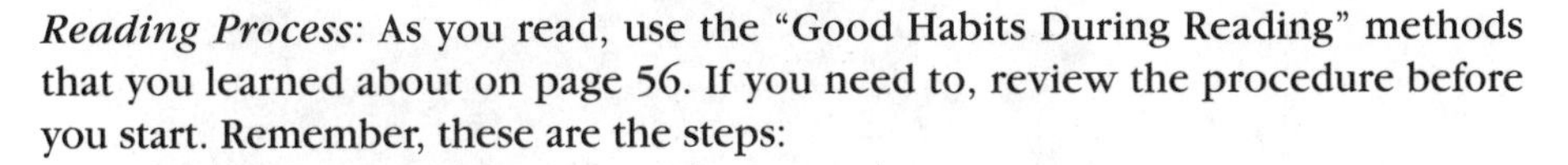

READING FIVE

Reading Process: As you read, use the "Good Habits During Reading" methods that you learned about on page 56. If you need to, review the procedure before you start. Remember, these are the steps:

- Make predictions
- Form mental pictures
- Make connections with your own experience, or with something you already know
- Recognize your reading problems
- Solve these problems

NOTE: This reading is also on the tape.

SPECIAL EDUCATION PROGRAM MAKES THE GRADE

1 Well, I've finally done it. After six years of high school, I've finally completed my secondary school requirements and graduated. Six years? Yes, it has taken me a little longer than most to graduate, and I probably wouldn't have graduated at all had it not been for the Carleton Board's Alternative Education Program.

2 I began my secondary education at Sir Wilfrid Laurier Secondary School on Carson Road in September 1988. My Grade 9 education went well despite[1] my failure to attend classes. Grade 10 started out OK, then spring hit. I just couldn't seem to stay in school. In Grade 11, I ran into some heavy trouble. I was suspended three times for skipping,[2] and failed most of my classes. The classes I didn't fail reflected my absences, with mid-50s averages. Then the school moved to Orleans and so close to my home, I assumed I could sleep in every day and still make it to school on time. Of course, it was so easy to go home for lunch that I was either late or absent nearly every afternoon. When nobody noticed I was absent, I decided that I might as well spend the nicer days of the school week at the beach. Needless to say, I failed miserably.

3 So in '92 I returned to school to graduate. I was certain that this was the year. I would finish for sure and that would be the end of it, on to bigger and better things. I'm sure you all remember how unusually warm and sunny it was that year I was expelled for my absences, a whopping[3] 50-some days. I thought I should get a job and skip my Grade 12. That decision lasted all of about three months. Nobody would hire me because I was a dropout.[4] I decided to go back to school, this time at the Norman Johnston Alternative Education Site on Cyrvill Road.

4 I arrived at the school in September, and had a lengthy[5] interview with the school's principal, Bob Mercer. During the interview, he informed me that I was welcome to learn at the school, but if I pulled my old tricks I would be removed from the program. I believed him and made a mental note to stay in school.

5 Every student who comes to the Alternative Program is enrolled in a personal life management course, commonly known as "life skills." This isn't so

bad, I thought. It was even kind of enjoyable. All the students would sit around in a large room and discuss current issues and events. This way, if you had an opinion on something, or you were displeased with the way you were treated, or you were just plain having a bad day, you could share your experiences and feelings with your peers[6] and usually leave feeling much better. Since the course was so enjoyable, I kept a near perfect attendance record. The days I was absent were legitimate as proven with medical certificates; without them it would have been skipping, period. I earned[7] one credit for that course, with a final mark of 84 percent, probably the highest mark I had ever achieved.[8]

6 Then I proceeded to a co-operative education placement[9] at Uplands Air Force Base. I was required to attend my placement for seven days a week, eight hours a day. Through frequent meetings with the school's co-op supervisor, as well as a series of reports and assignments, I was judged on my performance in the workplace[10] and given a grade of 76. I was awarded two credits for my co-op education.

7 At this point, I required only one more credit to qualify for my Ontario secondary school diploma. I was enrolled in a computer literacy course, and earned my last credit in six weeks. I was graded and given a high-90s mark, a fine ending to my long years as a high school student.

8 I once thought that I was beyond hope. I believed that I would never amount to anything simply because I could not learn in a normal classroom environment. The program at Norman Johnston provided me with a comfortable and effective learning environment, and allowed me to achieve personal levels of development I had not thought possible. Because of the firm, yet relaxed environment, I was able to explore[11] levels of education I thought previously unattainable.[12] I firmly believe that there should be more educational programs like the one at the Norman Johnston site. If this form of education was used in more schools, there would be far fewer dropouts and far more graduates. It is simply a more effective way to learn. And it helped me change my life.

After You Read

Identify the circled reference words.

PARAPHRASING AND SUMMARIZING THE MAIN IDEAS

First, identify the most important information in each paragraph. It may be one topic sentence, or it may be just parts of two sentences. Compare your choices with those of a partner.

Now summarize the article by writing a sentence that contains the main idea of each paragraph. Don't just copy the author's sentences; paraphrase them in your own words. When you finish, compare your work with your partner's and make whatever changes you think would improve both. Your teacher can help you too.

Paragraph 8 has been done for you as an example.

¶1 ______________________________

____

____

¶2 ______________________________

____

____

¶3 ______________________________

____

____

¶4 ______________________________

____

____

¶5 ______________________________

____

____

¶6 ______________________________

____

____

¶7 ____

____

____

¶8 For many students, an alternative education program is more effective than the traditional high-school program.

A DIFFICULT IDIOMATIC EXPRESSION

From ¶2:

"In Grade 11, I *ran into* some heavy trouble."

What do you think the author means?

____

How different from the above are the following expressions in meaning? Try to use them correctly in a sentence.

1. *run into* a telephone pole

   ____

2. *ran into* a long-lost friend

   ____

3. the colours *ran into* one another

   ____

FREEWRITING: EXPRESSING YOUR OPINION

What do you think of Robert Alex Moerman's experience at the Norman Johnston Alternative Education Site? Could you see yourself in a similar situation? Would you take it as seriously as you would a traditional high-school program? Do you know anyone who might do better in such a program? Why do you think so? What are the advantages of such a program? What are its disadvantages? Do you agree with Moerman's view that having more alternative education programs would result in fewer dropouts and more graduates?

Vocabulary

KEYWORDS

1. despite* ¶2
2. skipping ¶2
3. whopping ¶3
4. dropout ¶3
5. lengthy ¶4
6. peers ¶5
7. earned ¶5
8. achieved ¶5
9. placement ¶6
10. workplace ¶6
11. explore ¶8
12. unattainable ¶8

KEYWORD EXERCISES

1. ***EXAMPLE:*** My Grade 9 education went well *despite* my failure to attend classes.

   What other expression can you use for *despite?*

   ____

2. ***EXAMPLE:*** I was suspended three times for *skipping.*

   Rewrite this sentence in your own words to show what the author did.

   ____

   ____

3. *Whopping* is an informal word that means much larger than usual.

   EXAMPLE: I was expelled for my absences, a *whopping* 50-some days.

   In ¶3, *whopping* is used to refer to the number of absences. Rephrase the sentence in the example using a synonym for *whopping.*

   ____

4. Is there a high *dropout* rate in your school? If so, what, in your opinion, are some of the reasons for this problem?

   ____

   ____

5. ***EXAMPLE:*** Moerman had a *lengthy* interview with the principal.

   Finish the sentences:

   His talk was so *lengthy* ______________________________.

   ______________________________ such a *lengthy* explanation.

6. List four groups of people you consider your *peers.*

   ____________ ____________ ____________ ____________

7. To *achieve* means to successfully accomplish something.

   What do you hope to *achieve* in the next five years?

8. ***EXAMPLE:*** He *earned* a living selling magazine subscriptions.

   Finish the sentences:

   ________________________ his place in history.

   ______________________________ to earn a living.

9. From the text you just read, what do you think a co-operative education *placement* can give students like Robert Moerman?

   ____

   HINT: Look up the meaning of *placement*.

10. Identify the *workplace* of these professionals:

    teacher ________________________

    chef ________________________

    teller ________________________

    doctor ________________________

    scientist ________________________

    pilot ________________________

    pharmacist ________________________

11. Divide the word *unattainable* into three parts:

    __________ + __________ + __________

    What's the connection between the meaning of the three parts and the meaning of the whole word?

    Meaning of the three parts: ________________________________

    ____

    Meaning of the whole word: ________________________________

    ____

12. ***EXAMPLE:*** Nicolas wants to *explore* the world before he settles down.

    Here are the names of three well-known *explorers*. What are they most noted for?

    - Christopher Columbus
    - Ferdinand Magellan
    - Samuel de Champlain
    - Sir Edmund Hillary

REVIEW

Now that you have studied the vocabulary, reread or reskim the passage.

WRITING AN ESSAY: HOW WOULD YOU HAVE LEARNED BEST?

Write an essay on the following topic: Compare the way that you were educated with one of the three ways described in this chapter.

1. The Montessori method
2. The co-operative education method
3. The alternative education method

Do you think that you would have gotten a better education if you had gone to one of these three schools? Or, on the other hand, do you think that the education you received was better? Explain your opinion, giving specific examples.

LEARNING STRATEGY

Managing Your Learning: Reading on your own outside of class improves your reading skills.

Evaluating Learning Strategies

Look back over the chapter at the learning strategies that were presented. Were there any that weren't especially helpful for you? What wasn't helpful about them? Which ones did you find especially helpful? Think about times and ways that you can keep using them in your future reading.

Evaluating Your Learning

	Very little	*Quite a bit*	*A lot*
You've increased your vocabulary.	________	________	________
Your comprehension is stronger.	________	________	________
You can identify the topic sentences of paragraphs.	________	________	________
You can take good notes from your reading.	________	________	________
You've learned something about alternative education.	________	________	________

KEYWORDS FOR CHAPTER 4: ALTERNATIVE EDUCATION

Verbs
achieve
adjust
consider
convert
design
earn
emphasize
explore
involve
pioneer
skip
stress
succeed
take turns
tend

Prepositions
on one's own
throughout

Nouns
basis
concept
development
dissatisfaction
dropout
emphasis
evil
lecture
minority group
observation
opportunity
peers
placement
principle
process
quality
trend
value
workplace

Adjectives
abstract
artificial
based on
basic
broad
co-operative
collaborative
concrete
global
experiential
fragmented
holistic
lengthy
responsible
unattainable
uncertain
whopping

Adverb
despite

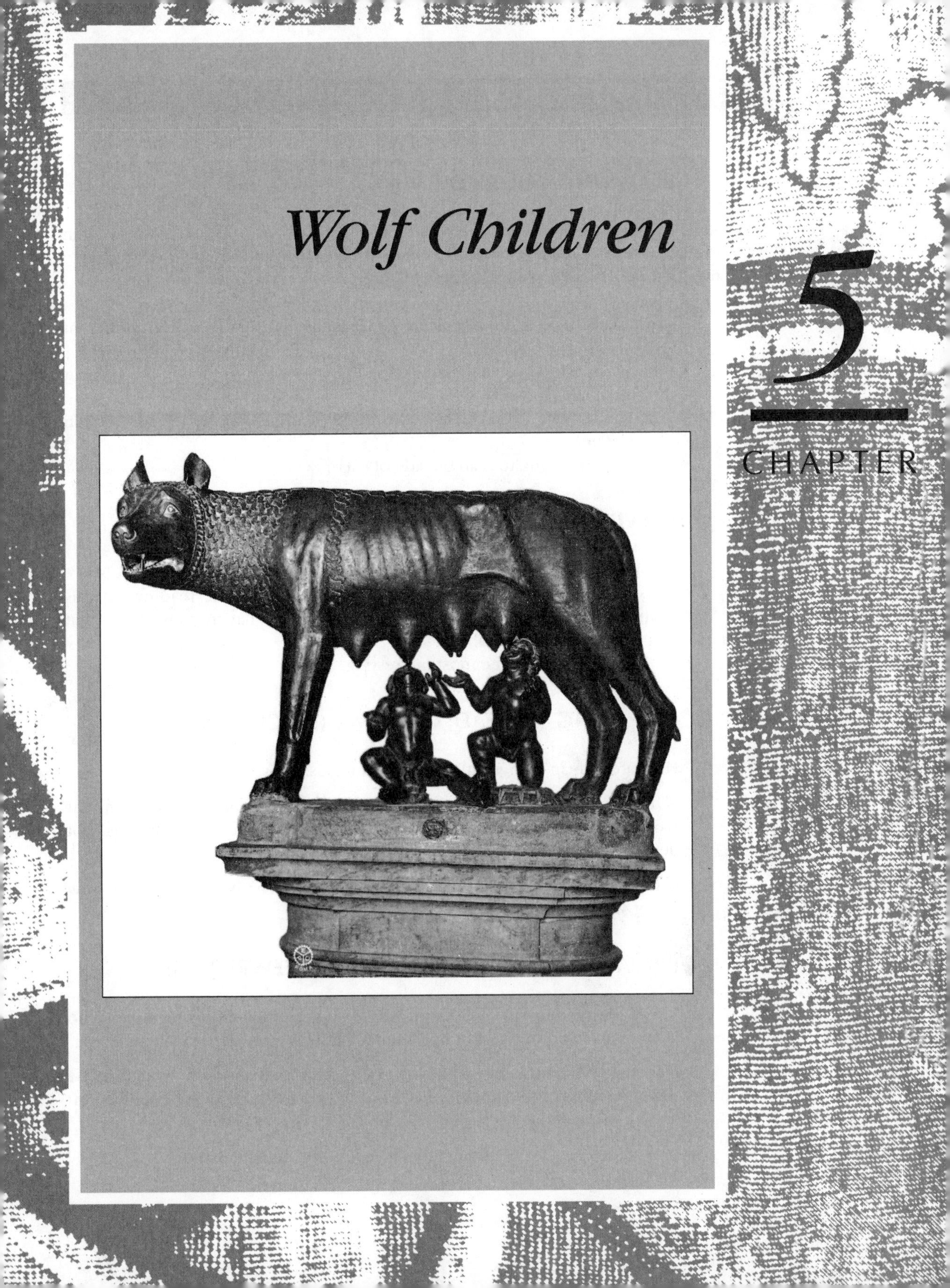

Wolf Children

5

CHAPTER

INTRODUCTION

PLANNING YOUR LEARNING

Review your overall goal statement. How much progress did you make toward it in the last chapter? Do you want to change it? Think about how you can work to meet your goal as you study this new chapter.

- How many words do you want to learn? (minimum 37, the number of keywords in the chapter)
- What grade would you like to make on the vocabulary section of the exam at the end of the chapter?
- What grade would you like to make on the reading comprehension section of the exam?
- What are you going to read outside of class?

PREVIEWING THE CHAPTER

- Think about the title of this chapter. What do you think a "wolf child" is?
- Look in the Table of Contents at the titles of the three readings in this chapter. Look through the chapter at the pictures. What are some things that you would like to learn about?
- Which reading looks the most interesting?

PREPARING TO READ: CONTENT (DISCUSSION)

1. How are human beings different from animals?
2. Which of these human characteristics are "learned" (for example, from our parents), and which are truly "biological" (automatic to all humans, not dependent on being taught)?
3. If we wanted to find out which are learned and which are biological, how might we do this?

PREPARING TO READ: CONTENT (FREEWRITING)

1. Think about your own childhood before you read the following story. Who taught you to do the human behaviours that you listed above in Item 2?
2. If you had been brought up by wolves instead of humans, how would you be different? What could you do that you can't do now, and what couldn't you do that you can do now?
3. Do you believe stories about animals "adopting" human babies?

PREPARING TO READ: VOCABULARY

You will encounter these words in this chapter's readings. Work with a partner. If you don't know an answer, use your dictionary or skip that question.

1. Horses, cattle, sheep, and goats are called *tame* or *domestic* animals. What's the adjective used to describe animals that aren't tame? w _______________
2. If humans wanted to bring a wolf child back into human society, they would probably have to catch it and force it to come. What's another verb for this action? c _______________
3. A wolf child would b _______________ more like a wolf than like a human. What's the noun form of this verb? _______________
4. A wolf child would have to l _______________ to do all the things that normal humans are taught by their parents when they are very young.
5. Learning to walk, to talk, to laugh, etc., is part of the process of human d _______________.
6. Parents teach their children to live comfortably in human society. This process is called s _______________. (It's the verb form of the noun *society*.)

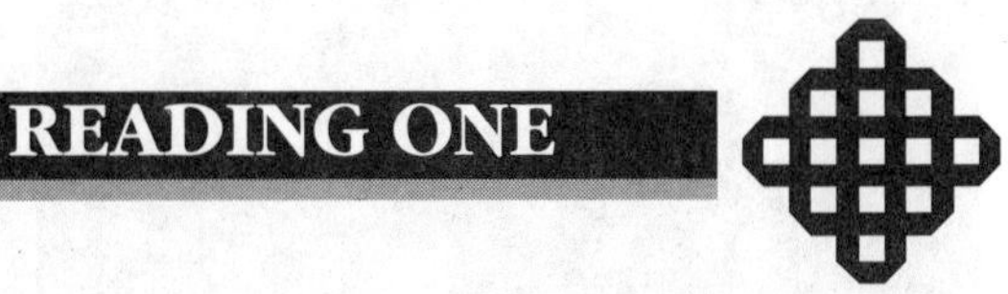

READING ONE

Reading process: This reading has been divided into four parts. Everyone will read the first part, but then your teacher will assign each of you to read Part Two, Three, or Four in a limited time. When you finish, you will meet with two students who read the other parts, and you'll tell each other what you learned.

NOTE: Parts of Mr. Singh's journal are on the tape.

KAMALA, A WOLF-GIRL OF INDIA

Part One

1 In the year 1920, in an isolated part of India, a missionary named J.A.L. Singh was visiting some isolated villages. One of the inhabitants complained to him of an evil spirit, a "man-ghost" that was living nearby with a family of wolves. The villagers were very frightened of this creature. Singh asked to see it, so

Amala and Kamala asleep overlapping

they took him to the place late one afternoon. In the half-light of evening he saw a group of wolves emerging one by one from their "home," a hole in a mound of earth. Singh counted three adult wolves and two young cubs. Then he saw the "man-ghost," which did indeed have the body of a small human, but whose head "was a big ball of something covering the shoulders," as he later wrote in his journal. Immediately after it came another, smaller version of the same kind of creature. Singh immediately realized that these two beings were human children, even though they acted exactly like the wolves, looking around to the right and left before coming out of the hole and walking on all fours. The villagers wanted to shoot them, but Singh stopped them from doing this. Instead, he suggested that they frighten the wolves away and capture the man-ghosts. This they did, but not easily; the human children were wilder than the wolves, and tried to attack the people.

Part Two

2 The two "man-ghosts" turned out to be two little girls, one around one and a half and the other about eight years of age. Mr. Singh took the children home with him to the city of Midnapore, where he directed an orphanage. He and his wife named the younger "Amala" and the older "Kamala." They were a terrible sight, covered with dirt and sores. After the Singhs bathed them and cut off their filthy matted hair, the children looked more human, although they certainly did not behave[1] in any human way. They could not stand up at all. They moved around mostly on their elbows and knees; when they "ran" on their hands and feet, it was almost impossible to catch them. The only food they would eat was raw meat and raw milk; they chased chickens and tried to eat the bodies of any dead animals that they found on the grounds of the orphanage. Their tongues hung out through their thick red lips, and they growled and showed their teeth when anyone came near them. During the day they stayed in the darkest corners of the room with their backs to the other children, showing not the least interest in anything that was going on. It was obvious[2] that they wanted nothing to do with human company. They repeatedly tried to escape, and they bit any of the other children who tried to stop them. Clearly they missed the company of wolves and wanted nothing more than to rejoin their "family." At night they livened up, howling and barking noisily like wolves, but they were unable[3] to speak or to understand human speech.

Kamala receiving biscuits from Mrs. Singh's hand

> They had a powerful instinct and could smell meat or anything from a great distance like animals. On the fifteenth of September, 1922, Kamala smelled meat from a distance of seventy yards and ran quickly to the kitchen veranda, where meat was being dressed. With a ferocious look, she tried to grab it, her eyes rolling, jaws moving from side to side, and teeth chattering while she made a fearful growling sound, neither human or animal.
>
> —From the journal of J.A.L. Singh

3 Amala and Kamala had very sharpened senses[4], as wolves and some other animals do. They could see perfectly well on the darkest night when humans could see nothing. Their sense of smell was very sensitive, especially for raw meat, which they could detect from a long distance away. Like wolves, they always used to smell their food carefully before they would eat it. They also had very sharp hearing. When they were fed, they would not sit at the table; they ate from dishes set on the ground or the floor. When they were thirsty, they would crouch in front of their bowls on the floor and lap up the milk or water with their tongues, like dogs. They seemed insensitive to heat or cold. Singh wrote in his diary, "In cold in winter we used to make them wear clothing, but they resented it very much and used to tear it to pieces as soon as they were left alone. We tried to cover them up with blankets at night, but they threw them away, and if repeated, they used to tear them off. They did not feel cold at all, and used to love to be without any covering or clothing on their body, even in the coldest weather. They were never seen shivering in the most chilly season, nor perspiring in the hottest day or night." Like animals, they feared fire. They hated being given baths.

Threads

Experience is the mother of all things.

John Florio

Kamala standing up for the first time

Part Three

4 Coming to the orphanage was a traumatic[5] experience for the little girls, but a worse one followed about a year later. They both became very ill, and Amala died. At first Kamala did not appear[6] to understand what had happened, but eventually[7] she seemed to comprehend that her "sister" was gone, and a single drop of water fell from each eye. They were the only tears she ever shed. Afterwards she seemed to be very lonely, and she began to keep company with the animals of the orphanage. She first developed[8] an affection for the kid goats, then for the cat and for the dogs, with whom she ate from the same plate at feeding time. The Singhs then removed the animals to a farm, leaving Kamala with no other choice but human company. At this point she seemed in danger of going crazy from loneliness, but still she wanted nothing to do with humans.

5 The Singhs thought hard about how to win Kamala over. Mr. Singh believed that her human nature[9] had been replaced by wolf nature so early in her life that she really thought of herself as a wolf. In order to become human, she would have to unlearn that whole first nature and replace it with something very foreign to her. This could only happen if she came to want to do it. It seemed to the Singhs that the person with the best chance of getting through to her was Mrs. Singh, a loving and motherly woman. She worked with incredible patience to build a feeling of trust in Kamala. This unbelievably slow process involved eliminating[10] some of her wolf habits and replacing them with human ones, but she fought so bitterly against the change that it took years to happen. When she came to the orphanage, Reverend Singh noted, it was as though "she had to begin life from her very infancy over again."

Threads

Every man has a wild animal within him.

Frederick the Great

6 One of the ways which Mrs. Singh used to try to awaken a sense of trust and affection in Kamala was by massaging her, a common practice by Indian mothers with their children. She also talked with her tenderly and patiently. The first time that Kamala indicated[11] an understanding of what she said was about three months after Amala's death. Kamala approached[12] Mrs. Singh, who asked her if

she was hungry, and she nodded yes and stayed by her side instead of trying to move away. At this point Kamala must have been around nine years old, but in terms of human development she behaved like a child of one and a half.

Part Four

7 As the years passed, Kamala very gradually[13] began to behave in a more human way, taking food with her hand instead of with her teeth, drinking from a glass, bathing herself. She seemed to be intelligent, and the adults who observed her concluded that her odd behaviour was the result not of stupidity, but of growing up with the wolves instead of with human models of behaviour. As Reverend Singh wrote in his journal,

> First of all, her dislike to all that was human presented itself in a very strong form, as we have seen before, and then gradually and very very slowly, it changed into a liking, and then the pleasure in that liking attracted her to new things and actions so that she acquired new knowledge and new practice to the making up of a different life altogether. All this came to pass during her stay with us during those years from 1920 to 1929.

Within three years she no longer wanted to go outside at night; indeed, she came to fear the night and preferred to be inside. At around the same time she first stood up on her two legs, but it took about three more years for her to learn to walk, and she never was able to run upright[14] like a human child. By 1925 she had developed a taste for salt with her food. A year later the Singhs noticed that she seemed to be enjoying her baths. She developed a strong preference for the colour red, both of toys and of clothing. She would pick red toys out of all the rest and would run away with them in her mouth.

8 Over the years she began to understand language more and more. By 1923 she could nod and shake her head to indicate "yes" or "no," though she could not speak yet. Within another year she had learned to say a number of words which meant *yes, no, rice, all right, red, I,* and some of the children's names. Reverend Singh kept a list of the words and the simple sentences as Kamala spoke them (such as—in Bengali—"Mama come" when Mrs. Singh approached). By 1926 she could carry on a very limited conversation with a vocabulary of about three dozen words. However, her understanding was better than her speaking, and she had no trouble following instructions. By 1929, at the end of her short life, she had a speaking vocabulary of about fifty words and she was able to talk easily with the others who lived at the orphanage and to call them by their names. Her pronunciation was never clear, however.

9 As she took on more human habits, it was observed that her ability to see in the dark, her keen hearing and sense of smell, and her insensitivity to heat and cold left her. She began to like her blanket at night, and insisted on wearing clothes, especially red ones. She would eat and drink only from *her* plate and glass. By 1926 she began to feel affection towards the younger children in the orphanage and would do her best to take care of them, though in very limited ways. By 1927 her relationship with the dogs had changed: they barked at her as though they recognized her as a human, not one of themselves; and she responded[15] with fear and avoided[16] them.

10 Unfortunately, Kamala's health began to fail almost exactly nine years from the date of her capture. On November 14, 1929, she passed away. By this time she must have been around seventeen years old, though in terms of human development she behaved more like a child of about two and a half.

After You Read

COMPREHENSION QUESTIONS

Questions for Part Two:

1. What were the names and ages of the two children?

   ____

2. Tell four ways in which they behaved like animals.

   a. ______________________________

   b. ______________________________

   c. ______________________________

   d. ______________________________

3. What was their attitude toward human beings?

   ____

Questions for Part Three:

1. What happened to Amala?

   ____

2. How did Kamala react to this event?

   ____

3. Which human being did Kamala feel closest to?

   ____

4. How did this human being win Kamala's trust?

   ____

   ____

Questions for Part Four:

1. Give four examples of human behaviour that Kamala learned.

   a. ______________________________

   b. ______________________________

   c. ______________________________

   d. ______________________________

2. Give two examples of animal behaviour that Kamala unlearned.

   a. ______________________________

   b. ______________________________

3. What happened to Kamala at the end of the story? How old was she when this event happened?

___

REVIEW: COMPLETING THE READING

Now read the whole passage.
Identify the circled reference words.

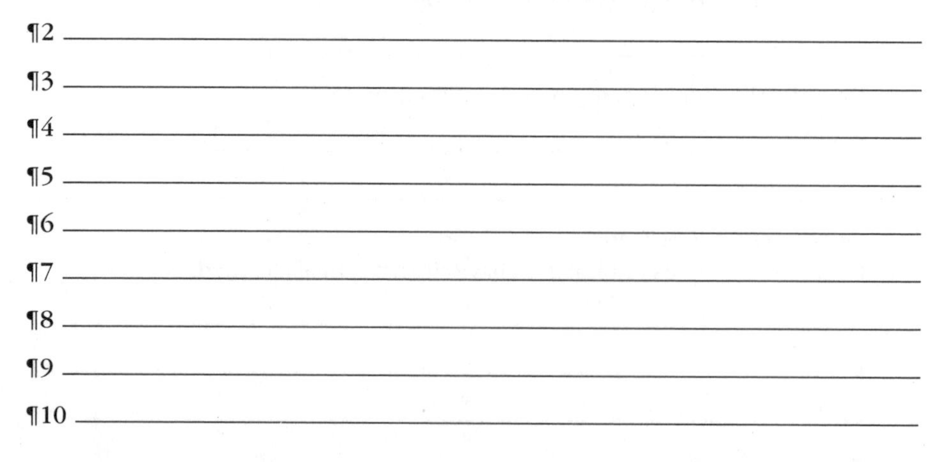

LEARNING STRATEGY

Forming Concepts: Outlining helps you comprehend information in a simple way.

OUTLINING THE READING PASSAGE

There are ten paragraphs in the story, and each one has one main idea or purpose (as in all good English writing). See if you can identify them. The first has been done for you.

¶1 The children were discovered and were removed from the wolves.

¶2 ___

¶3 ___

¶4 ___

¶5 ___

¶6 ___

¶7 ___

¶8 ___

¶9 ___

¶10 ___

Now read your list from start to finish. It will provide you with a quick summary of the story. Compare it with a partner's list and discuss any differences. Revise your list if you need to.

Vocabulary

KEYWORDS

1. behave ¶2
2. obvious ¶2
3. be unable to* ¶2
4. senses ¶3
5. traumatic ¶4
6. appear ¶4
7. eventually ¶4
8. develop ¶4
9. human nature ¶5
10. eliminate* ¶5
11. indicate* ¶6
12. approach* ¶6
13. gradually ¶7
14. upright ¶7
15. respond ¶9
16. avoid* ¶9

KEYWORD EXERCISE

1. Name some things that (1) you, (2) infants, or (3) wolves are *unable* to do.

EXAMPLE: Kamala was *unable* to walk upright at first.

2. Name the five *senses*. In your own culture do you have five, or do you have more or fewer? Do you know what a *sixth sense* is?

EXAMPLE: Kamala's wolflike *senses* enabled her to see in the dark.

3. *Meanings:*

- To *approach* someone means to come near them.

  EXAMPLE: Kamala *approached* Mrs. Singh when she felt hungry.

- An *approach* to a problem is one way of thinking about it or trying to solve it.

  EXAMPLE: One *approach* to learning vocabulary is to write the words on little cards and then study them.

- Explain the similarities between the two meanings.

4. Which of the following objects are *upright?*

a wall   a road   a rug   a tree   a door

5. Which of the following would you most like to *avoid?*

a bad meal   a war   an examination   a job   an argument

EXAMPLE: Kamala *avoided* human company as much as possible.

6. Which of the following words does not mean the same thing as the others?

obvious   balanced   clear   plain

EXAMPLE: It was *obvious* that Kamala wanted to rejoin her wolf family.

7. Which of the following experiences would be most *traumatic* for a small child? For an adult?

getting lost in a shopping centre   being in an earthquake
moving to another country

EXAMPLE: Amala's death was a *traumatic* experience for Kamala.

8. *Meanings:*
   - *Nature* is all the living beings, things, and processes in the world that were not made or caused by people.

     QUESTION: Name your favourite event or process in nature.
   - *Human nature* is the basic qualities and behaviour that most people have.

     QUESTION: Name two characteristics of *human nature.*
   - Explain the similarities between the two meanings.
9. Which of the following words are connected with the idea of *eliminate?*

   realize misuse remove delete subtract

   EXAMPLE: As the years passed, Kamala *eliminated* her wolf nature and took on a human nature.
10. Which of the following words does not mean the same as the others?

    point out show require *indicate*

    EXAMPLE: Kamala's responses to Mrs. Singh *indicated* that her attitude had begun to change.

REVIEW

Now that you have studied the vocabulary, reread or reskim the passage.

LEARNING STRATEGY

Personalizing: Identifying yourself with a person in a story helps you to understand the material better because it becomes more real to you.

Writing: Kamala's Memoirs

Kamala never learned to write, but if she had, she might have written her own story before she died. Imagine that you are Kamala, and write your story. Consider the following questions, but feel free to write this any way that you wish to.

1. What happened to your human parents? How did you come to live with the wolves?
2. Describe what happened when you first came to the orphanage. What did you think of the people? What did they want you to do? How did you feel about this?

3. As the years passed, how did your feelings about your new life change? Why did you decide to learn to walk and talk? Did you like it?

4. Which do you like better, life among humans or life among wolves? Do you miss your wolf family? Do you think you'll ever return to live with them or perhaps to visit them?

READING TWO

As you will see in the following passage, the term "wolf children" is used not just for children brought up by wolves or other animals. In a more general way, it applies to any children who grow up isolated from human society and human models. How was the next child's background different from Kamala's? How were their behaviour and development similar?

Reading process: This reading has been divided into six parts. Your teacher will assign you a part in addition to the first part.

THE MYSTERY OF KASPAR HAUSER

Part One

1 One pleasant May evening in 1828, a very strange-looking young man appeared up on the streets of the German city of Nuremberg. At first it looked as though he were drunk: he was unable to stand upright or to walk well. In his hands he held a letter addressed to a military captain in the city, and he kept repeating a sentence that sounded like, "I want to be a soldier like my father," though the words seemed to mean nothing to him, as though he had merely memorized the sounds. He was given some meat and beer, but he reacted violently to the taste, as though they were poison. Bread and water were all he could take. He was unable to comprehend questions about what his name was and where he came from.

2 He was taken to the captain, who opened the envelope which the young man carried. Inside were two letters. One of them was written by an unnamed person who said that when the young man was an infant, he had been left with him by the mother, who asked him to bring the boy up with his own children. This he had done, but he had been told to bring the boy to Nuremberg when he was seventeen years old so that he could serve in the military. The letter-writer did not identify himself and said that the place where he lived must also be kept secret. In the same envelope was a shorter, much older piece of paper on which someone had written, "You must educate the child. ... When he is seventeen years old send him to Nuremberg

Kaspar Hauser,
as he appears in Feuerbach's 1832 book

to the sixth [military] regiment, for there his father also was ... He was born the 30th April, 1812. I am a poor girl and cannot support him. His father is dead."

3 The young man did indeed appear to be about seventeen years of age, in spite of the fact that he behaved more like a child of two. To everyone's surprise when someone offered him a pen and paper, he took them and wrote in clear letters the name "Kaspar Hauser," though he could not say it.

Part Two

4 No one knew what to do with him, so they took him to a local prison, where the kind prison-keeper took him into his family. The man's children began to teach Kaspar how to speak and to sit with them at the dinner table. He could eat only bread and water at first, and only gradually[1] was he able to take other foods. If anyone put even a tiny amount of beer, wine, or coffee in his water, he became sick. He seemed to have had no experience at all with social customs or human ways of thinking. His face at first looked stupid and animal-like, though as the months passed it took on an expression of interest and intelligence and became completely human. When the sun went down he went to bed, but all day long he simply sat on the floor with his legs stretched out straight in front of him. He hardly knew how to use his hands and fingers at all. He was good-natured and sweet-tempered, however, and those who spent time with him became very fond[2] of him.

5 Kaspar's senses seemed much sharper than ordinary people's. He could see so well in the dark that he could even read (later, after he learned to read); in fact, his eyes were oversensitive and sunlight hurt them. His sense of hearing was also as sharp as an animal's. But his sense of smell was so sensitive that it caused him discomfort: some smells that most people consider pleasant, such as the fragrance of flowers, were terrible to him, and the smell of fresh meat made him sick. Years later, after he had learned to eat normal food, he commented that since he had begun to eat meat, his sense of sight had grown much weaker and he was no longer able to see in the dark.

Threads

The smell of fresh meat was, to him, the most horrible of smells.

Anselm von Feuerbach

6 He showed great interest in horses, and in particular[3] in toy horses. Noticing this, someone brought him some little wooden horses, and he was overcome with happiness. He would pet them, would decorate them with everything shiny and beautiful that he could find, and always put his bread to their mouths before eating and their mouths in his water cup before he took a drink. But as he began to learn more about people and the world around him, he lost interest in these toys.

Part Three

7 Kaspar was an intelligent, reflective person. When faced with a new object, idea, or behaviour, he would withdraw into some inner place in his mind, standing very still and completely lost in thought until he could make sense of it by connecting it to something that he already understood. If the new thing were very hard for him to comprehend, his face would begin to twitch and he would become upset. Not surprisingly, after a few weeks of adjusting to so much newness, he actually fell ill. At this point a secondary-school teacher named Daumer offered to give him a home so that he could have a professional tutor and could live a quieter and calmer life. The household consisted of Daumer, his sister, and their mother, and they welcomed the young man into their little family.

8 As Kaspar began his education, one of the most interesting features was his inability to distinguish[4] reality from unreality, living beings from inanimate

objects,[5] animal behaviour from human behaviour. He began to dream at night for the first time in his life, but he was not aware[6] that what he dreamed had not really happened: to him the memory of a dream was like the memory of real events. Someone brought him a mirror, and when he saw his reflection, he looked behind it to see who was hiding there. He treated toy animals as though they were alive, and once he became angry because a dirty statue in a garden did not wash itself. If a sheet of paper was blown away by the wind, he thought that it had run away from the table. He became angry at a cat for not sitting up straight and taking its food with its "hands"; he spoke to it as he would have to a human, and believed that it was simply unwilling to learn. He felt that animals ought to have to learn the same behaviours as he. At the beginning he used only two words for living creatures: all humans were "bua," and all animals were "ross" (a German dialect word for *horse*). Only their clothing enabled[7] him to distinguish men from women, and he refused to believe that children would one day become adults, or that this had happened to him.

9 He had strong feelings about particular colours: he feared anything that was black, disliked green and yellow, cared nothing about white, liked gold very much, and loved anything that was red. The sight of natural beauty did not move him at all; he greatly preferred a view of beautifully painted red houses through his bedroom window to another window's view of a green garden, which appeared to him like so much confusion.

> I directed [K]aspar to look out of the window, pointing to the wide and extensive prospect of a beautiful landscape that presented itself to us in all the glory of summer; and I asked him whether what he saw was not very beautiful. He obeyed; but he instantly drew back, with visible horror, exclaiming, "Ugly! ugly!" and then pointing to the white wall of his chamber, he said, "There are not ugly." To my question, Why was it ugly? no other reply was made, but "Ugly! ugly!"
>
> —*Anselm von Feuerbach*

10 Eventually Kaspar Hauser learned to speak very well, but his process of learning language was similar to the process that little children go through with their native language. The first words that he learned were nouns and verbs, then adjectives and adverbs. Words such as prepositions, articles, and conjunctions came much later. He used verbs in the infinitive rather than in tenses. It was a long time before he could understand or use the pronouns "I" or "you"; he would refer to himself as "Kaspar" and would speak to other people always using their names. He would apply a word to anything that it reminded him of, as when he spoke of a fat man as "the man with the great mountain."

Part Four

11 But what was the story of Kaspar's earlier life, that lost period when he could neither understand nor speak? How had he lived, and what accounted for his condition when he first appeared in Nuremberg? Once he had learned to speak, he was able to tell the story. His only memories were of living in a very small locked room which he sometimes called a "hole" and sometimes a "cage." The only other human whom he knew he called "the man with whom I had always been," whose face he never saw but who left bread and water beside him when he was sleeping. In his cage Kaspar sat all day on the floor, barefooted, wearing only a shirt and a pair of trousers. He heard no sounds, saw no one except "the man," and never saw the sunlight. Sometimes his water

tasted bitter, and then he fell into a deeper than normal sleep, and when he awoke, he would find himself wearing clean clothing and with freshly cut nails. The only objects in the hole with him were two wooden horses that he played with all day. He knew nothing, saw nothing, thought nothing. Because he had known nothing else, he was content.

Threads

Man really knows nothing save what he has learned from his own experience.

C.M. Wieland

> As long as he can recollect, he had always lived in a hole (a small low apartment which he sometimes calls a cage), where he had always sat upon the ground, with bare feet, and clothed only with a shirt and a pair of breeches. In his apartment he never heard a sound, whether produced by a man, by an animal, or by anything else. He never saw the heavens, nor did there ever appear a brightening (daylight) such as at Nuremberg. He never perceived any difference between day and night, and much less did he ever get sight of the beautiful lights in the heavens.
>
> *—Anselm von Feuerbach*

12 One day the man brought a small table into his room, stood behind him, and taught him to write his name with a pencil. Kaspar had no idea what this meant, what writing was, nor even that it was his name; but he enjoyed the activity and copied the letters over and over. Another time the man took hold of him around his waist from behind and tried to teach him to stand upright, but without much success, because Kaspar's legs and feet would not co-operate and it was very painful for him.

13 Then one day the man came and carried him out of his prison and took him on a journey. Even then he never showed his face. He put new clothes on Kaspar, including boots, which hurt his feet very much. He forced the boy to walk, but insisted that he look only at the ground and at his feet, so that he could see neither the man nor the countryside they were walking through. Eventually they stopped and the man put an envelope into his hand and left him. That was how he came to Nuremberg.

Part Five

14 Even so, Kaspar had no hard feelings for "the man with whom he had always been," and he was surprised when other people suggested that he should hate him. For a long time he defended the man. He said, "Man not bad, man me no bad done," and his only complaint was that the man had not returned to take him back "home," where his life had been simple and he had never had to adjust to so much that was unknown to him. He often commented that it seemed unfair that the people he had met since coming to Nuremberg knew so much, even the little children, while there were so very many things which he had yet to learn.

15 This attitude did not change until he had been in human society for about a year and a half. One clear August night, Professor Daumer took Kaspar outside to look at the stars. He had never seen or imagined anything so beautiful. For a long time he stood speechless as his tutor pointed out the different constellations and named the individual stars. Then he said, "That is, indeed, the most beautiful sight that I have ever yet seen in the world. But who has placed all these numerous beautiful candles there? Who lights them? Who puts them out?" When these questions had been answered, he fell silent again and began to cry. He asked bitterly why "the man with whom he had always been" had kept him locked up for so many years so that he could never see such wonderful sights. He said that the man ought to be locked up himself, so that

he could learn what it felt like. This was the first time that he ever said anything against the man.

16 Later he commented to a friend, who asked him why he looked sad,

> I was just thinking how many beautiful things there are in the world, and how hard it is for me to have lived so long and to have seen nothing of them; and how happy children are who have been able to see all these things from their earliest infancy, and can still look at them. I am already so old, and am still obliged to learn what children knew long ago. I wish I had never come out of my cage; (he) who put me (there) should have left me there. Then I should never have known and felt the want of any thing; and I should not have experienced the misery of never having been a child, and of having come so late into the world.

17 During his stay in Professor Daumer's household he became aware of the deeper meanings of family ties,[8] and asked what it meant to have or to be a father, a mother, a brother, or a sister. Upon thinking of the answers that were given to him, he again shed tears at the thought of how unfair it was that he had no family, and was completely alone as though he were a member of a separate species,[9] the only one of his kind in existence.

Part Six

18 In October of 1829, about a year and a half after he came to Nuremberg, the newspapers announced that the famous Kaspar Hauser was planning to write the story of his life. It was probably this news article that brought on a terrible event and that eventually brought his short life to its tragic end. One day Professor Daumer went out, leaving Kaspar at home. Around midday Daumer's sister noticed spots of blood and bloody footprints on the stairs. She and her mother went looking for Kaspar and found him lying downstairs in a corner of the cellar. He was very weak and was covered with blood, and he kept saying, "Man, man." They called a doctor and carried him to his bed, where he lay in a very bad condition for two days. His forehead had been cut open and he had lost a great deal of blood. But in time he recovered[10] and was able to tell what had happened: He was in the hall of the house when he discovered a stranger whose face was covered with a black handkerchief. The man struck him on the head and he fell to the floor unconscious. When he came to himself, he found that he was bleeding, and became frightened that the man would return to finish him off. He could hardly move, but somehow he managed to pull open the heavy cellar door and found a dark corner to hide in. There he lost consciousness again.

The gravestone of Kaspar Hauser in Ansbach

19 No one knew for sure who had tried to kill Kaspar, but people assumed that it was "the man with whom he had always been," and various people reported seeing a stranger come out of Daumer's house, wash his hands in a nearby watertrough, and (several days later) ask someone on the street whether Kaspar were dead or alive.

20 Kaspar recovered fully and continued to learn about the world, surrounded by friends, tutors, and others who wished him well. Everyone who knew him was impressed by his honesty, openness, and sweet nature. But this was

not the end of the story. In December of 1833, five years after he had discovered the outside world, a stranger approached him in a park and told him that he had news of Kaspar's mother. The man gave him a lady's handbag which had a note in it. When Kaspar opened the purse to look inside, the man stabbed him in the chest with a knife, then ran away. Kaspar, badly hurt, just managed to walk back to his home. He lived for three days, but then he died of his wound.

21 The note in the handbag was written backwards and said, translated into English,

> Hauser can tell you exactly
> How I look and who I am.
> If Hauser will not take this trouble
> Then I will myself say
>
> I come __ __ __ __ __ __
>
> I come from __ __ __ __
>
> Of the Bavarian border __ __ __
>
> At the river __ __ __ __
>
> And I will even tell you my name M. L. O.

22 Who was this man, and why did he want to kill Kaspar Hauser? Was he, as most people assume, "the man with whom he had always been"? It remains a mystery, but the most popular answer is that he was killed for political reasons. This theory is extremely complicated, but it concludes that he was killed by someone who did not want Kaspar's real identity to be guessed. It is not clear why the killer, if it was "the man," had not killed him when he was a child, nor why he had brought him to Nuremberg if he feared that Kaspar's identity would become known. Many questions remain unanswered, leaving us with only the puzzling but charming story of a kindhearted young man who came late into life and who left it tragically early.

After You Read

COMPREHENSION QUESTIONS

Questions for Part One:

1. Name two things that Kaspar Hauser couldn't do when he was discovered.

a. ____________________

b. ____________________

2. Who wrote the two letters?

a. The newer letter: ____________________

b. The older letter: ____________________

3. What surprising thing could Kaspar do?

____

Questions for Part Two:

1. Who were Kaspar's first teachers?

2. Compare Kaspar's senses with ordinary people's.

3. What was something that he liked very much at this point in his life, and what did he do with these objects?

Questions for Part Three:

1. Where was Kaspar's second home after he came to Nuremberg?

2. Give an example of how he confused living beings with nonliving objects.

3. Give an example of how he confused reality with unreality.

Questions for Part Four:

1. Where had Kaspar lived before he came to Nuremberg?

2. Who took care of him?

3. Describe Kaspar's life at that time.

4. What did his keeper teach him to do?

5. Describe his journey to Nuremberg.

Questions for Part Five:

1. At first, what was Kaspar's attitude toward his former keeper?

   How and why did this attitude change?

2. What were Kaspar's negative feelings about having come into human society?

____

Questions for Part Six:

1. Describe Kaspar's first attack.

____

____

2. Describe Kaspar's second attack, and tell the result of it.

____

____

3. Who was probably responsible for these events?

____

REVIEW: COMPLETING THE READING

Now read the whole passage.
Identify the circled reference words.

IN WHICH PARAGRAPH CAN YOU FIND ...

1. The point at which Kaspar turned against "the Man" _______________
2. A description of the final attack on Kaspar _______________
3. Mention of Kaspar's loneliness _______________
4. A description of Kaspar's trip to Nuremberg _______________
5. A paragraph in Kaspar's own words _______________

Distinguishing Between Topic and Main Idea

The *topic* is the general subject of a paragraph; the *main idea* is what the author says about that topic. The topic is usually expressed as a noun or a noun phrase, while the main idea should be expressed in a complete sentence.

Identify both the topic and the main idea of each of the following paragraphs:

Topic	Main Idea
¶5 Kaspar's senses	Kaspar's senses were much more sensitive than normal people's.
¶10 ________________	____
¶11 ________________	____

DEVELOPING GOOD HABITS DURING READING

Practise the "Good Habits During Reading" methods that you learned about on page 56. If you need to, review the procedure before you start. Remember the steps:

- Make predictions
- Form mental pictures
- Make connections with your own experience, or with something you already know
- Recognize your reading problems
- Solve these problems

When you finish, fill out the chart on the handout that your teacher gave you earlier.

UNDERSTANDING GRAMMAR

There is one grammar point that may give you a little trouble in this chapter. Here's an example of it:

> If the new thing were very hard for him to comprehend, *his face would begin* to twitch and *he would become* upset. Not surprisingly, after a few weeks of having to adjust to so much newness, *he actually fell ill.*

One of the ways that we use *would + verb* is to describe a past habit, an action repeated many times in the past. It is not used in this way to describe present habits. Thus it carries two meanings: one, that the action was habitual in the past; and two, that it is not being done now. Contrast the two examples of this with the final clause *he actually fell ill,* which uses the simple past because it describes one action, not a habit.

Now scan Kaspar's story and mark five examples of *would + verb.* Read them over and note that they inform you of Kaspar's habitual behaviour. If you'll take a look at Kamala's story, you'll find similar examples. (You'll notice that Kaspar himself sometimes says *should + verb,* which is an old form that means the same thing. *Should* isn't often used that way today.)

Vocabulary

KEYWORDS

1. gradually ¶4
2. fond ¶4
3. in particular* ¶6
4. distinguish* ¶8
5. object ¶8
6. aware* ¶8
7. enable* ¶8
8. tie ¶17
9. species ¶17
10. recover* ¶18

LEARNING STRATEGY

Forming Concepts: Forming a mental picture of new vocabulary items helps you remember them better.

KEYWORD EXERCISE

1. Which of the following sentences can be said to have happened *gradually?*
   - **a.** She learned Arabic.
   - **b.** The superpowers destroyed their nuclear weapons.
   - **c.** My grandfather grew old.
   - **d.** The boy broke his leg.
   - **e.** We went to Toronto on our vacation.

   EXAMPLE: Kaspar *gradually* learned to speak and even to write.
2. *EXAMPLE:* I like outdoor activities, *in particula*r hiking and camping.

   Finish the sentences:
   She's allergic to animals, in particular ________________________________.
   He enjoys movies, ____.
3. *EXAMPLE:* Colour-blind people cannot *distinguish* between red and green.

   Finish the sentences:
   When the twins were born, their parents dressed them in different colours until they could distinguish ____.
   Doctors may have trouble distinguishing ______________________________.
4. In ¶8, find and list three inanimate *objects.* ______________________________

   ____

   ____
5. Name some environmental problems that people have gradually become *aware* of over the past several years. ____

   ____

EXAMPLE: Kaspar was not *aware* of the larger world until he was about seventeen years old.

6. *EXAMPLE:* Their differences in clothing *enabled* Kaspar to distinguish men from women.

   Finish the sentences:
   Winning the lottery would enable me to ______________________________.
   Taking the summer off enabled ______________________________________.

7. A *species* is a group of living beings that share the same characteristics and are able to reproduce together. This is the biological classification of human beings:

   Kingdom: Animal
   Phylum: Chordates
   Class: Mammals
   Order: Primates
   Family: Hominids
   Genus: Homo
   Species: Sapiens

   Human beings are a *species.* National and ethnic categories such as *Japanese, Jews,* and *white people* describe groups within the human species, not separate species.

   EXAMPLE: Kaspar felt as though he were the only member of a *species* because there was no one else like him.

8. Which of the following conditions might a person *recover* from?
   malaria good news bad news culture shock a broken bone

   EXAMPLE: Kaspar eventually *recovered* from his first attack.

REVIEW

Now that you have studied the vocabulary, reread or reskim the passage.

LEARNING STRATEGY

Forming Concepts: Making a chart of related information from different sources helps you learn the material and forms a very helpful study guide.

A Chart Comparing the Wolf Children

The cases of Kamala and Kaspar provide us with interesting similarities and differences that help us to understand human development. A useful study habit is to *synthesize* and reorganize information from two readings in a way that makes it easy to compare them.

Take a piece of paper and turn it sideways (horizontally). You'll use it to make a chart. Down the left side put three categories:

Kamala
Kaspar
Victor ... and leave three or four blank lines under each.

Across the top, you're going to write categories of points on which you can compare and contrast the three children. Start with Kamala and Kaspar; later you'll add Victor. Try to come up with at least six categories (for example, "Age at Discovery"). You can work alone or with a partner, but after a time, your teacher will ask you to compare your work in a small group. Use your partners' lists to improve your own.

Writing a Summary of Kaspar's Life

Write a brief article that might have appeared in a newspaper the day after Kaspar's death. Write only three paragraphs: The first will announce his death, the second will describe his background before discovery, and the third will describe his development after discovery. Then count the words. Try to limit your article to 200 words: if it's longer than that, cut it down (without breaking grammar rules).

READING THREE

The third major type of "wolf child" is one who seems to bring himself up with the help of neither humans nor animals. How old do you think such a child would have to be in order to do this? What might cause such a situation to exist? The following story is a classic case of this kind of child. Notice the similarities between his behaviour and development and Kamala's, and then Kaspar's.

VICTOR, THE WILD CHILD

Part One

1 In the late 1790s several people in a region of south central France reported seeing a "wild boy" in the forest. This youngster wore only a torn shirt, avoided human contact, climbed trees like a monkey, and seemed to survive[1] on such foods as nuts, roots, and raw potatoes that he stole from farms. He appeared to be about twelve years old. Several times he was captured, and several times he escaped; eventually, however, he approached a house and acted as though he wanted to be taken in. The people in the house kept him for a few days and then sent him to a children's hospital in

Paris. There he was observed,[2] and the following behaviour was noted: He showed little interest in his surroundings; his eyes moved restlessly and did not follow anything; his hearing responded neither to loud noises nor to sweet music; he could not speak; he showed no reaction to either bad smells or fine perfume; and he could not use his hands as normal humans do. He was unable to open a door or to climb onto a chair in order to reach objects that he wanted; he seemed to have no memory; and he would not or could not imitate actions or sounds. The doctors at the hospital concluded[3] that he was an idiot, even less intelligent than an animal.

2 At this point the doctors wanted to send the wild boy to a special hospital for mentally retarded children, but a Doctor Jean-Marc-Gaspard Itard stepped forward and asked to take over his case. He removed the child to his own house, put him under the care of his housekeeper, Madame Guérin, and attempted to educate him. He gave the boy the name Victor.

The Wild-boy of Aveyron

Part Two

3 No one ever learned how Victor had come to live in the woods, nor at what age, nor how he had survived with no help from humans or from animals. He had been seen more than five years earlier, so he must have been at least five or six years old when he was abandoned[4] or lost. His body was covered with scars, some apparently the marks of animal bites; but there was one particularly large scar across his throat, and Dr. Itard thought that perhaps someone had tried to kill him and then had left him for dead in the forest. Somehow the boy had survived and had managed[5] to develop the skills for finding food and avoiding humans. Whether he was retarded or not was hard to tell, but he had clearly been isolated[6] from human society long enough that he could not speak or respond to situations in the usual human ways. His interests and thought processes were quite different from those of normal humans.

4 When found, Victor could walk and run easily, though he disliked wearing clothing, especially shoes, and he could run much faster in his bare feet. He seemed insensitive[7] to cold or heat: he would go outside barefooted in the snow, and he could pull burning wood from the fireplace with his bare hands. Although there was no evidence[8] that he had been assisted by animal foster-parents, he did share with animals the habit of smelling everything he came across. His only two emotions were happiness and anger: when happy, he would laugh; when angry, he threw around the room everything that he could lay his hands on. He would spend hours rocking backwards and forwards, his eyes fixed on the window, very much like a caged animal in a zoo. He loved nature and liked nothing more than to be out in the garden or taking walks, and he responded with great joy to thunderstorms and heavy snow. He frequently attempted to escape, but was always found and brought back. Itard remarked, "Indeed, when we consider the little time he has been in society, [Victor] is much less like a simple youth, than an infant of ten or twelve months old … "

5 Gradually he learned some clever ways to make people do what he wanted. For instance, if he tired of visitors, he would bring them their hats and coats and show them to the door. He loved being pushed around the garden in a wheelbarrow, and he would bring it out before guests and put their hands on the handles, then get in it himself. When he wanted to eat, he would put the tablecloth on the table and set out the plates and wait expectantly.

Part Three

6 As time passed, Victor became very fond of Madame Guérin, who was part caretaker, part teacher, and part mother to him. She was extremely patient and understanding. He disliked leaving her side, and rejoining her always filled him with happiness. In his interactions with her, Itard could see evidence of Victor's progress[9] in observing human behaviour and in becoming more socialized.[10] A very touching example of this took place when Madame Guérin's husband fell ill and died. That evening at dinnertime, Victor set the usual number of places at the table. When Madame Guérin came into the room and saw her husband's place set out, she burst into tears. Victor, realizing that his actions had upset her, quickly removed the plate and put it away. He never repeated the mistake.

7 He also developed an affection[11] for Itard, in spite of the fact that some of the doctor's methods[12] in educating him might seem cruel to people today. Many times Itard would try to force Victor to perform tasks which he either did not comprehend or simply did not want to do. From time to time Victor would explode in anger and would begin to throw objects around the room. But Itard's will was as strong as his, and the doctor was bigger and was on familiar ground. Once, knowing Victor's fear of heights, he held him upside down out of a fourth-storey window until the terrified boy did as he wished.

Part Four

8 Victor never did learn to speak, and Itard finally abandoned attempts to teach him to repeat sounds and even to understand language as others spoke it to him. He did not respond to spoken words in a way that showed that he attached any meaning to them; but he did respond to gesture, expression, tone, and volume of voice. Interestingly enough, Itard's only success with language was in teaching him to make the connection between certain objects and their *written* representation, which seems as though it would have been extremely difficult since Victor had no oral language, and since the very idea of language and of writing was unknown to him.

9 In attempting to teach Victor language, Itard tried to show him the connections between drawings of objects and the objects themselves. If he showed the boy a picture of a comb, for example, Victor was to go and get an actual comb and bring it back. Once Victor understood this, he showed enough intelligence to "overgeneralize": that is, when showed a book, he might bring a newspaper, a letter, or any other example of writing on paper. Itard progressed to showing Victor new ideas in sets of three: a book, a picture of a book, and the written word *book*. Making the connection between the object and the letters was a painfully slow and difficult process for Victor, who of course had no interest in learning to read and write, but eventually he did learn these skills at a very simple level. They did not enable him to tell any interesting details about his past history, but he was able to communicate some of his needs.

Part Five

10 Eventually Victor developed enough responses to heat and cold that he would feel his bath water to make sure it was warm enough; and he would dress himself warmly in cold weather. He learned to perform simple household tasks and to eat "normal" human food at the table with others. But he never really lost his "wild" side, as Itard explains in the following description:

> I would go so far as to say that he has always kept a distinct preference for water. The way he drinks it seems to suggest that it is one of his greatest pleasures ... Almost always at the end of dinner, even when he is no longer very thirsty, we see him like a gourmet before a glass of some exquisite liqueur—he fills his glass with pure water, takes a sip and swallows it drop by drop. What adds interest to this scene is its setting. He drinks his water standing at the window, eyes turned towards the countryside as if in this moment of sheer delight this child of nature seeks to unite the only two things which remain from his lost freedom, a drink of clear water and the sight of the sun on the countryside.

11 After several years of working with Victor, Itard moved on to other projects, leaving him in the care of Madame Guérin for the rest of his life. He lived to be about forty years of age.

Threads

Train up a child in the way he should go, and when he is old, he will not depart from it.

Proverbs 12:6, the Bible

After You Read

COMPREHENSION QUESTIONS

Questions for Part One:

1. How old was the "wild boy" when he was found?

____

2. Tell two observations that his doctors made.

   a. ______________________________

   b. ______________________________

3. What was the doctors' conclusion about him?

____

4. Where did the boy go after he left the hospital, and what name was given to him?

____

Questions for Part Two:

1. What might have happened to have caused Victor to live alone in the forest?

____

2. How might he have gotten his largest scar? Where was it?

____

3. Tell three ways in which Victor was different from a "normal" boy.

   a. ______________________________

   b. ______________________________

   c. ______________________________

4. Tell one way in which Victor showed his intelligence when he wanted something from people.

   ____

Questions for Part Three:

1. How did Victor feel about Madame Guérin?

   ____

   What functions did she fill in his life?

   ____

2. What did he do that upset her?

   ____

   What did he do as a result of having upset her?

   ____

3. How did Dr. Itard force Victor to perform tasks?

   ____

Questions for Part Four:

1. How much success did Victor have in learning to speak?

   ____

2. What did Victor respond to when people spoke to him?

   ____

3. Tell about Itard's experiments with drawings, objects, and printed words.

   ____

   ____

4. Eventually, what were people able to learn about Victor's history in the forest?

   ____

Questions for Part Five:

1. Name two ways in which Victor became more "normal."

   a. ______________________________

   b. ______________________________

2. In your opinion, did he become very socialized? Why do you think he did or didn't?

____

3. What happened to Itard and to Victor in the end?

____

REVIEW: COMPLETING THE READING

Now read the whole passage.

TRUE–FALSE QUESTIONS

			¶ *number*
1. Victor was an idiot, even less intelligent than an animal.	T	F	______
2. Someone may have tried to kill Victor when he was five or six years old.	T	F	______
3. When Victor became angry, he lost control of himself.	T	F	______
4. Victor's favourite person was Dr. Itard.	T	F	______
5. Victor never learned to speak, but he could understand what other people said to him.	T	F	______

LEARNING STRATEGY

Forming Concepts: Thinking about what information *isn't* included in a reading passage makes you a better reader.

CRITICAL THINKING: WHAT ISN'T THERE?

Working alone or with a partner, make a list of three questions about each child that the reading passages do not answer. Your questions should be about information that you would really like to know. Write them on the blackboard. Why do you suppose that information was not included in the passages?

EXAMPLE: Why couldn't Victor learn to talk?

Vocabulary

VOCABULARY IN CONTEXT

1. Look at ¶1 and find the word *idiot.* Read the sentence in which it appears. What do you think an idiot might be?
   What information in the sentence leads you to that guess?
2. Look at ¶3 and find the word *scars.* Read the sentence in which it appears (twice). What do you think a scar is?
   Which part of the sentence is most useful in helping you guess?
3. Look at ¶4 and find the word *bare.* Read both of the sentences in which it appears (three times). What does it probably mean?
   Which parts of the sentence are most useful in helping you guess?

KEYWORDS

1. survive* ¶1
2. observe ¶1
3. conclude* ¶1
4. abandon ¶3
5. manage ¶3
6. isolated ¶3
7. insensitive ¶4
8. evidence* ¶4
9. progress ¶6
10. socialize ¶6
11. affection ¶7
12. method ¶7

KEYWORD EXERCISE

1. *Meanings:*
   - If you *observe* someone or something, you carefully notice what they're doing or what's happening.

     QUESTION: In ¶1, what did the doctors *observe* about Victor?
   - If you *observe* a law or a custom, you obey it or follow it.

     QUESTION: Name a law or custom that is *observed* in your country but not in Canada.
   - Explain the similarities between the two meanings.
2. Which of the following are important elements of the word *conclude?*
   evidence   because   claim   deceive   decide

   EXAMPLE: The doctors *concluded* that Victor was an idiot.
3. Which of the following are important elements of the word *isolated?*
   accurate   separate   lonely   distant   useless

   EXAMPLE: Victor grew up *isolated* from human society.
4. Which of the following could be called *sensitive* or *insensitive?*
   a movie   a person   your skin   a camera   a drink

EXAMPLE: At first Victor was *insensitive* to extreme heat and cold.

5. Which of the three wolf children became the most *socialized?* Give evidence for your answer.

   EXAMPLE: Parents *socialize* their children through direct teaching and also through example.

6. If you were lost in the jungle, what would you need in order to *survive?*

   EXAMPLE: Victor *survived* by eating nuts, roots, and raw potatoes.

7. *Meanings:*
   - If you *manage* to do something, you succeed in doing it (even if it is difficult).

     QUESTION: What did Victor *manage* to do before he entered human society? After?
   - If you *manage* a business, you direct its operations.

     QUESTION: Who *manages* the school or institute where you are studying English?
   - Explain the similarities between the two meanings.

8. If a detective were investigating a murder, what *evidence* might she look for?

   EXAMPLE: The large scar across Victor's throat was *evidence* that someone may have tried to murder him.

9. What are some ways that you can measure your *progress* in English?

   EXAMPLE: Victor's *progress* in socialization was very limited.

10. Name two different *methods* of learning a language. Which do you prefer?

    EXAMPLE: Some of Itard's educational *methods* seem cruel to us today.

11. What happens if you *abandon* your exercise program?
    If you *abandon* your car on the freeway?
    If you *abandon* your attempts to keep in touch with your old friends back home?

REVIEW

Now that you've studied the vocabulary, go back and reread or reskim the story.

LEARNING STRATEGY

Overcoming Limitations: Trying to figure out the cause or the pattern of your errors helps you improve your language skills.

Discussion: An Interview with Victor

Victor was the wolf child we know the least about because he never learned to talk at all. But what if he had? Work with a partner and imagine that one of you is Victor, and the other is a reporter who will interview him. Before you begin the interview, together you should write out four or five questions that you want to use, and you should think about (and maybe make notes of) the answers that "Victor" will give. Then practise role playing the interview. The next time this class meets, your teacher will ask each pair of partners to take turns performing your interviews for the class.

Completing Your Chart

Add information about Victor to the categories on your chart. Then compare your entries with a partner, revising them if you wish to. You will use the information on this chart as the basis for a paper that you will write, so make it clear and easy to follow.

> We must not forget that the human child learns more during the first two years of his life under the influence of his living surroundings than in all the entire period afterwards.
>
> —*Robert M. Zingg, anthropologist*

Writing an Essay: Comparing the Wolf Children

FREEWRITING: THE MOST INTERESTING WOLF CHILD

Which wolf child was most interesting to you, and why?

COMPARING THE WOLF CHILDREN

Write a paper comparing and contrasting the three children. Mention all three, but provide the most detail about your favourite. Consult your chart, but use only the information that you find most interesting: don't use everything. You can organize your paper either this way …

I. Similarities
- **A.** Kamala
- **B.** Kaspar
- **C.** Victor

II. Differences
- **A.** Kamala
- **B.** Kaspar
- **C.** Victor

... or this way:

I. Category (for example, Age at Discovery)
- **A.** Kamala
- **B.** Kaspar
- **C.** Victor

II. Category
- **A.** Kamala
- **B.** Kaspar
- **C.** Victor
- (et cetera)

Don't forget to write an introduction and a conclusion.

LEARNING STRATEGY

Managing Your Learning: Finding out what resources can be useful to you enriches your language. Your teacher and your classmates can suggest some good ones, such as dictionaries, thesauruses, grammar books, encyclopedias, cultural guides, radio and TV programs, and videotapes.

Evaluating Learning Strategies

Look back over the chapter at the learning strategies that were presented. Were there any that weren't especially helpful for you? What wasn't helpful about them? Which ones did you find especially helpful? Think about times and ways that you can keep using them in your future reading.

Evaluating Your Learning

Look at the following list of items that you practised in this chapter. How did you do on each one? Check your answers (√).

	Very little	*Quite a bit*	*A lot*
You built up your vocabulary.	______	______	______
You can read and understand long passages.	______	______	______
You can explain what you read about.	______	______	______
You can distinguish between topic and main idea.	______	______	______
You can write an essay based on your notes.	______	______	______
You learned about wolf children.	______	______	______

KEYWORDS FOR CHAPTER 5: WOLF CHILDREN

Verbs
abandon
appear (seem)
approach
avoid
behave
conclude
develop
distinguish
eliminate
enable
indicate
manage
observe
recover
respond
socialize
survive

Nouns
affection
evidence
human nature
method
object
progress
senses
species
tie

Adjectives
aware
fond
insensitive
isolated
obvious
traumatic
unable

Adverbs
eventually
gradually
in particular
upright

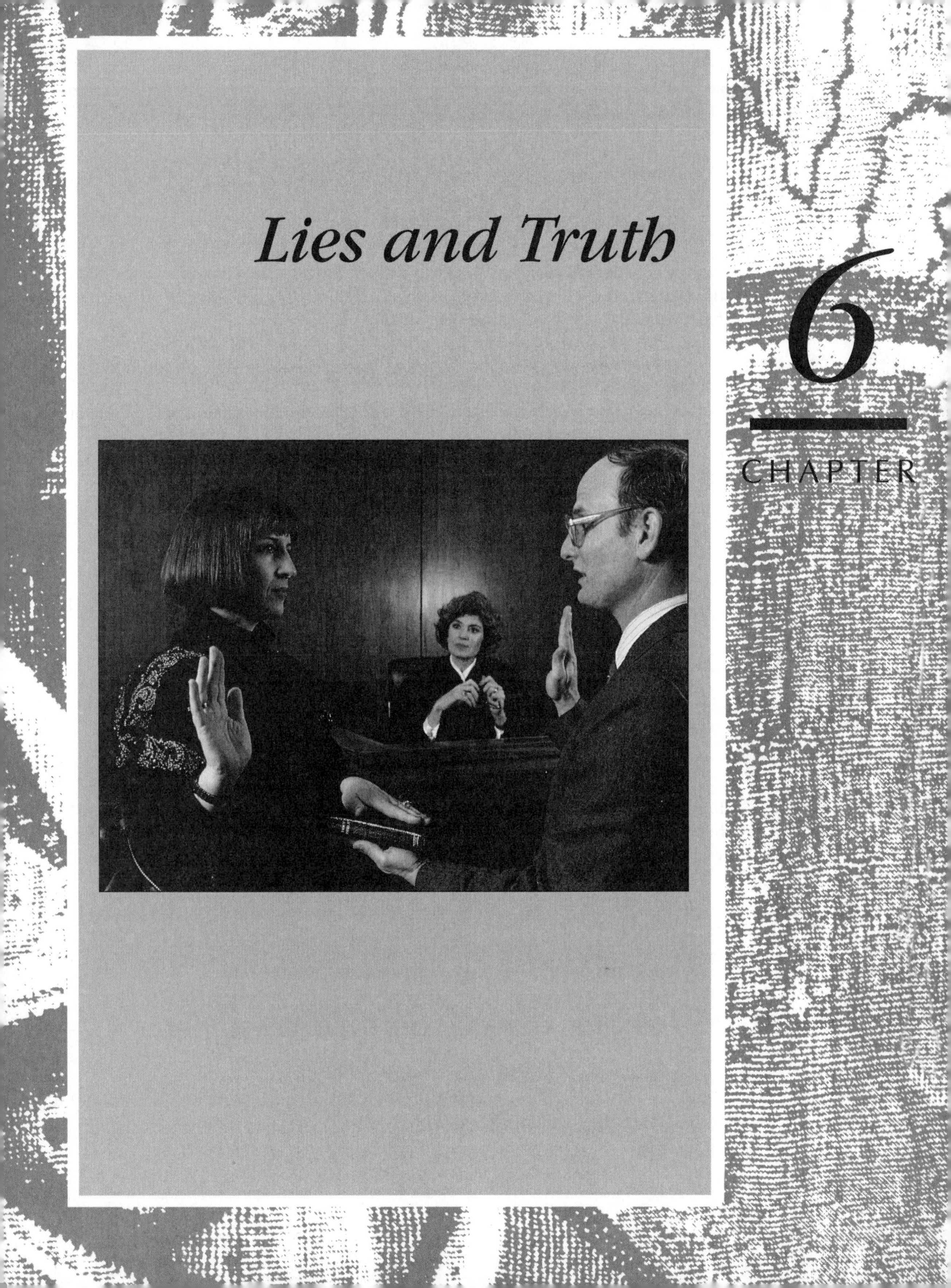

Lies and Truth

6

CHAPTER

PLANNING YOUR LEARNING

Review your overall goal statement. How much progress did you make toward it in the last chapter? Do you want to change it? Think about how you can work to meet your goal as you study this new chapter.

- How many words do you want to learn? (minimum 57, the number of keywords in the chapter)
- What grade would you like to make on the vocabulary section of the exam at the end of the chapter?
- What grade would you like to make on the reading comprehension section of the exam?
- What are you going to read outside of class?

PREVIEWING THE CHAPTER

- Think about the title of this chapter. Look in the Table of Contents at the titles of the four readings in it. Look through the chapter at the pictures. What are some things you expect to find out?
- Which reading do you think you'll be most interested in?

PREPARING TO READ: CONTENT (DISCUSSION)

Is hiding the truth from your parents wrong?
Imagine yourself in this situation: You are a high-school student, and you have just been caught cheating on an examination at school. You return home looking worried. Your parents want to know what happened.

- Will you tell them the truth?
- Would most friends from your culture?
- If you were your mother or father, would you want to know the truth?
- Would you prefer to tell only one parent and not the other?

PREPARING TO READ: CONTENT (FREEWRITING)

A World Where No One Lies
Imagine a world in which everyone always told the truth. What would it be like? Would it be better than this world?

PREPARING TO READ: VOCABULARY

Look at the following vocabulary items. Fill in the blanks with the opposite meaning of the word in the other column. The first one has been done for you.

lie (verb)	tell the truth
dishonest	honest
false	true
lie (noun)	the truth.
a liar	truth-teller
distrust	trust
fact	fantasy?

LEARNING STRATEGY

Testing Hypotheses: Asking yourself what you expect to find in new material helps to activate your mind and prepare it for the new content.

READING ONE

The following is a general article on lies and lying. Before you look at it, work with a partner and make a list of questions that you might expect such an article to discuss.

Reading process: Now scan the passage for about three minutes, checking off any of your questions that it answers. Then go back and read it carefully.

LIES AND TRUTH

1 What is truth?—and the opposite question that goes with it, What makes a lie? Philosophers, teachers, and religious leaders from all cultures and all periods of history have offered many answers to these questions. Among Euro-North-American writers, there is general agreement on two points. The first is that what we call "a lie" must have been told intentionally[1]—that is, if someone tells an untruth but they believe it to be true, we don't consider them a liar. The second point is that practically everyone lies, and lies frequently. But there the agreement ends.

Threads

No man is really honest.

Aristophanes

2 One rather extreme point of view is that lying is always bad and that we should try to find ways to avoid doing it. The reason is that lying hurts not only the listener, but also the liar. Each lie makes the next one easier to tell, and the liar comes not only to disrespect herself, but to mistrust others, whom she believes will lie as easily as she. In a society where lying is common, trust[2] becomes impossible, and without trust, cooperation cannot exist. Furthermore, by lying to people, we remove their power to make important choices about (for example) how to spend money, what future career to take, what medical treatment to choose.

3 Toward the opposite extreme is the position that although some lies are evil, many others are not—in fact, they are necessary to hold our society together. We lie in harmless ways to protect each other's feelings and to better our relationships. These are not lies that try to hurt others. We laugh at the boss's joke which we have heard before and which she doesn't tell very well; we pretend interest in a friend's story of something uninteresting that happened to him. If someone asks us a question that is very personal and is none of their business, we may lie in response. Sometimes we lie to protect the reputation or even the life of another person. On a larger scale, government may protect national security by lying.

4 Many people's positions are somewhere between these two extremes. It's common for North American parents to tell their children that lying is bad, that they shouldn't do it and should feel guilty if they do. In Euro-American cultures, a traditional punishment for a child who lies is to wash the child's mouth out with soap. Yet through their actions, parents also teach their children that there are circumstances[3] under which most people do lie. Consequently the children grow up following both teachings—they occasionally lie, but they feel guilty[4] and don't want people to know they've done it.

5 Each person seems to have some point at which they draw the line between an acceptable lie and a bad lie. Obviously, this point varies from individual to individual and from culture to culture. A sometimes painful part of growing up is realizing that not everyone shares your own individual definition of honesty. Your parents and your culture may teach you that liars will suffer,[5] but as you go through life, you find that often they don't: in fact, dishonest people often seem to prosper[6] more than honest ones. What are you to do with this realization? It may make your moral beliefs look weak and silly in comparison, and you may begin to question them. It takes a great deal of strength and courage to continue living an honest life in the face of such a reality.

6 There are many ways to categorize lies, but here is a fairly simple one:

7 *Little white lies:* This is our name for lies that we consider harmless and socially acceptable. They are usually told to protect the liar or the feelings of the listener. Most of them would be considered social lies, and they include apologies and excuses: "I tried to call you, but your line was busy." "You're kidding! You don't look like you've gained[7] a pound." Some people, however, would consider it acceptable to lie to save themselves from responsibility in a business transaction: "After I got it home, I noticed that it was broken, so I'm returning it and would like my money back."

8 Occasionally a "little white lie" may have a very profound[8] effect on the lives of the listeners, and may even backfire.[9] Author Stephanie Ericsson tells of the well-meaning U.S. Army sergeant who told a lie about one of his men who had been killed in action. The sergeant reported the man as "missing in action," not killed, so that the military would continue sending money to the dead man's family every month. What he didn't consider was that because of his lie, the

Threads

In time and place a harmless lie is a great deal better than a hurtful truth.

Roger Ascham

family continued to live in that narrow space between hope and loss, always watching for the mail or jumping when the telephone or the doorbell rang. They never were able to go through the normal process of sorrowing for, and then accepting, the death of their father and husband. The wife never remarried. Which was worse, the lie or the truth? Did the sergeant have the right to do what he did to them?

9 What we really mean when we call an untruth a "little white lie" is that we think it was justifiable.[10] Into this category fall many of the lies told within the walls of government. A person may lie to government, or a government official may lie to the public, and believe that by doing so, he becomes a hero. Clearly, however, one person's "little white lie" is another person's "dirty lie." Which brings us to the second category:

10 *Dirty lies:* These are lies told with intent to harm[11] the listener or a third party and to benefit the liar. Into this category fall the lies of some dishonest salespersons, mechanics, repairmen; husbands or wives who are having an affair with someone else; teenagers who lie to get out of the house in order to do things that their parents would die if they knew about; drug addicts who beg family members for money to support their habit. Dirty lies may be told to improve one person's reputation by destroying another's, to hurt a colleague's chances of promotion so that the liar will be advanced.

Threads

The cruelest lies are often told in silence.

Robert Louis Stevenson

11 *Lies of omission:* Some people believe that lying covers not only what you say, but also what you choose not to say. If you're trying to sell a car that burns a lot of oil, but the buyers don't ask about that particular feature, is it a lie not to tell them? In the United States a favourite place to withhold the truth is on people's income tax returns. The government considers this an unquestionable lie, and if caught, these people are severely punished. If omission can be lying, history books are great liars. Until recently, most U.S. history textbooks painted Christopher Columbus purely as a hero, the man who "discovered America," and had nothing to say about his darker side. Moreover, most Native American and African-American contributors to science, technology, invention, literature, art, discovery, and other areas of civilization used to be omitted from children's schoolbooks. Many people considered this a lie, and today's history books usually mention at least some of it, though not as much as some people might like.

12 *False promises:* This category is made up of promises that the promiser knows are false, that he has no intention of keeping even as the words leave his lips. While some are fairly harmless and social, others are taken more seriously and can hurt the listener: "I'll never do it again, I promise." Advertisers and politicians suffer from terrible stereotypes because of the false promises of some of their number: "Lose 50 pounds in two weeks." "Read my lips: No new

taxes." Probably everyone would agree that if we make a promise but have no intention of keeping it, we lie. But what if we really do plan to keep it, and then something happens to prevent[12] it? Consider the journalist who promises not to identify his sources, but then is pressured by his newspaper or by the law. How far should he go to keep his word? If he breaks his promise, is he dishonest?

13 *Pathological lies:* Pathological liars are persons who lie constantly and for no apparent reason. They will lie about anything. They seem to be unable to control the impulse to lie. Studies of such people find that many of them were badly treated as children, many come from families in which one member was an alcoholic or was mentally ill, many grew up in families in which the truth was simply never valued or practised. They seem to have an unusually strong need to be liked and admired by others. But not everyone of whom this is true becomes an uncontrollable liar, and no one knows why some do and some don't. Pathological liars tend to have few if any close or long-lasting personal relationships, because people catch on to them and drop them; they are very careful not to introduce their acquaintances to each other for fear that they might begin to compare stories.

Threads

The most common sort of lie is that by which a man deceives himself.

F.W. Nietzsche

14 *Lies to oneself:* This is perhaps the saddest and most pathetic kind of lying. These are the lies that prevent us from making needed changes in ourselves: "I know I drank/spent/ate too much yesterday, but I can control it any time I really want to." But there is a fine line between normal dreams and ambitions on the one hand, and deceiving ourselves on the other, and we have to be careful where we draw it. It's common for young people to dream of rising to the top of their company, of winning a Nobel Prize, of becoming famous or rich; but is that self-deception,[13] or simply human nature? The term "mid-life crisis" is used to describe the point when some people realize that their life is half over and they are never going to achieve some of those dreams. But were they lying to themselves? More likely, they really believed that such a future was open to them, because they had seen it happen to others. We shouldn't be too hard on ourselves, but if we have turned a blind eye to our faults, we should take an honest look in the mirror.

15 There is no question[14] that the terms "lying" and "honesty" have definitions that vary across cultural boundaries.[15] Members of one culture may stereotype members of another as "great liars," "untrustworthy," or "afraid to face the truth." But what may lie behind these differences is that one culture values factual information even if it hurts, while another places more value on sensitivity to other people's feelings. While the members of each culture believe that of course their values are the right ones, they are unlikely to convince members of other cultures to change over. And that's "the truth."

After You Read

Identify the circled reference words.

DEVELOPING GOOD HABITS DURING READING

Practise the "Good Habits During Reading" methods that you learned about on page 56. If you need to, review the procedure before you start. Remember the steps:

- Make predictions
- Form mental pictures
- Make connections with your own experience, or with something you already know
- Recognize your reading problems
- Solve these problems

When you finish, fill out the chart on the handout that your teacher gave you earlier.

DISCUSSION: COMPREHENSION QUESTIONS

From your own imagination, give an example of each of the categories of lies from the reading.

1. What's a *lie of omission* that a mother might not tell her daughter? Why might she do this?
2. What's a *little white lie* that a daughter might tell her mother? Why?
3. What's a *lie* that you remember having told *yourself?* Why did you do it?
4. What's a *false promise* that a child might tell a parent? Why?
5. Imagine that you're a *pathological liar,* and tell about something incredible that happened to you the other day.
6. What's the *dirtiest, most hurtful lie* that you can think of?

Now let's review: Try to answer these questions from memory, without looking back at the reading. The answers are the six categories that you just talked about.

1. This kind of lie is like a psychological illness.
2. Some people think that if everything they say is true, they're not lying. But according to the reading, they could still be guilty of what kind of lie?
3. These lies are told by people who don't want to face reality.
4. People tell this kind of lie when they want other people to quit bothering them.
5. Which kind of lie is considered the least serious?
6. Which kind of lie is considered the ugliest and meanest?

Explain this sentence from ¶4: Yet through their actions, parents also teach their children that there are circumstances under which most people do lie.

Paraphrasing and Summarizing

If you really understand something, you ought to be able to explain it to someone else. That's why much academic work in North American universities and colleges requires you to express information from your reading in words of your own. This skill is called *paraphrasing,* and you'll use it every time you write a report, a research paper, a thesis, a dissertation, or any paper that uses other people's writings.

Your ability to paraphrase well depends strongly on your ability (1) to summarize (see pages 94 and 117) and (2) to express the same information in different ways. Let's practise with something fairly simple from the reading above:

> There is no question that the terms "lying" and "honesty" have definitions that vary across cultural boundaries.

A bad method: Here's what you *don't* want to do: Don't keep the same grammar and just substitute synonyms or similar words. That makes for very bad paraphrasing.

Here are two good methods.

Good method one: Read the original sentence several times to make sure you understand it. (Do this now.) Then cover it up with a piece of paper and try to write down the general idea. (Do this now.) When you finish, compare your sentence with the original. Is the meaning the same? If not, revise it. Are the grammar and vocabulary too similar to the original? If they are, try to change them around without changing the meaning of the sentence.

Now try something else.

Good method two: Highlight the words in the original sentence that can be changed. In this case you can change ...

There is no question that: ____________________

terms: ____________________

definitions: ____________________

vary: ____________________

boundaries: ____________________

Write synonyms or equivalents for these words and phrases. Feel free to use your dictionary or a thesaurus.

There's no reason you can't change these words and phrases. But you shouldn't change the words *lying, honesty,* and *cultural,* because there aren't any good equivalents. You must change everything you can, but sometimes you're allowed to keep some words.

Now paraphrase the sentence in your own words, changing the grammar around. When you finish, compare your work with that of a couple of your classmates. Working together, revise your sentences any way you want to. Then your teacher will ask you to write some of your sentences on the blackboard.

Now practise something on your own. Look at the second and third paragraphs; highlight the topic sentence of each. Then paraphrase each one.

Paragraph two
Topic sentence, paraphrased:

___

___

Type of support (reasons? examples? definitions? facts? statistics? comparisons?):

___

How many supporting details?

___

Paragraph three
Topic sentence, paraphrased:

___

___

Type of support:

___

How many supporting details?

___

Identifying Issues

An *issue* is a moral question that different people have very different answers to. There are many issues suggested by the reading above; for instance:

Is lying always wrong?
Where does truth end and a lie begin?
Are some lies worse than others?

Issues are questions of morality, not questions of fact. This is *not* an issue:

What do most Euro-North-American writers agree on?

And finally, issues are questions that apply to everyone, not just to the people in one case. So this also is *not* an issue:

Should the sergeant have lied about his man who was killed in action?

But you could convert this question to an issue by making it apply more generally to everyone:

Is it justifiable to tell a lie in order to benefit people, even though that lie itself might cause them problems?

Look back at Reading One and write another issue-question that it suggests:

___

FREEWRITING: YOUR OPINIONS ON LYING

Which category of lie is worst? What would you teach your children about lying? What did your parents teach you?

Vocabulary

VOCABULARY IN CONTEXT

1. Find the word *acceptable* in ¶5. Read the sentence it's in. What do you think it means?
2. Find the word *omission* in ¶11. What do you think it means?
   Which sentence explains the meaning?
   Can you find a synonym for *omit* in the third sentence?

KEYWORDS

1. intentionally, intention ¶1
2. trust ¶2
3. circumstances ¶4
4. guilty ¶4
5. suffer ¶5
6. prosper ¶5
7. gain ¶7
8. profound ¶8
9. backfire ¶8
10. justifiable ¶9
11. harm* ¶10
12. prevent* ¶12
13. deception ¶14
14. there is no question that ... * ¶15
15. boundary ¶15

KEYWORD EXERCISE

1. Which of the following are elements of *intention?*
   accident planning affection function decision

   EXAMPLE: He has no *intention* of keeping that promise.
2. Find the antonym for *trust* in ¶2.

   ____

   EXAMPLE: In a society where lying is common, *trust* becomes impossible.
3. Look at ¶10. What part of speech is *harm* as used in the first sentence?

   ____

   Find the adjective form of *harm* in ¶12.

   ____

What does this adjective mean?

HINT: the suffix will tell you.

It's not given here, but do you know an adjective that is the antonym of this one, formed of *harm* + a different suffix?

EXAMPLE: Dirty lies are told with intent to *harm* the listener.

4. Do you think that animals are capable of feeling *guilty?* If so, what makes you think so?

EXAMPLE: Most of us feel *guilty* when we lie.

5. Describe the ideal *circumstances* for learning how to dance.

EXAMPLE: There are *circumstances* under which most people lie.

6. Give an example of how a liar might *suffer.*

EXAMPLE: Our parents and our culture may teach us that liars will *suffer.*

7. Give an example of how liars might *prosper.*

EXAMPLE: Dishonest people don't always suffer for it; sometimes they *prosper.*

8. The word *gain* has several meanings. Which one applies to this sentence?

EXAMPLE: You don't look like you've *gained* a pound.

9. We can use the word *profound* to describe many things: profound ideas, profound hatred, a profound thinker, a profound book, profound silence. The word came into English from Latin, where it originally meant *deep,* as in a deep hole. What's the connection between the idea of depth and the English meaning of *profound?*

EXAMPLE: Sometimes a little white lie may have a *profound* effect on the listener.

10. *EXAMPLE:* Occasionally a "little white lie" may *backfire*, as in the case of the sergeant who lied.

The word *backfire* was originally used in which of the following activities?
fire control automobile repair unemployment shooting a gun

11. If someone lies and says, "You don't look like you've gained an ounce," how would they *justify* this lie?

Do you think it's justifiable? ______________________________

Have you ever said anything like this? ______________________________

12. Note that *prevention* is used before something might happen, not after it has happened. The whole idea is that you don't want it to happen.
What might you do at your house to *prevent* burglars from breaking in?

____

What do travellers do to *prevent* seasickness or airsickness?

____

What can people from different cultures do to *prevent* misunderstanding?

____

13. The oppossum is a very common but peculiar North American animal. Opossums cannot defend themselves very well with teeth or claws, nor can they run very fast. They protect themselves with an unusual kind of *deception* that we call "playing possum." If you don't know what this phrase means, ask a North American. Then write the answer here:

____

____

EXAMPLE: Lying to oneself is a form of self-*deception.*

14. *EXAMPLE:* *There is no question that* these words have different meanings in different cultures.

Did you find this phrase in your dictionary? It means that something is so obvious that no one could doubt it. Note that it comes at the beginning of a sentence.

From the following list, choose one statement that you *would* begin with this phrase, and one that you *wouldn't.*
... overpopulation is a serious global problem.
... everyone learns languages the same way.
... a cure for AIDS will eventually be found.

15. What states or provinces share *boundaries* with the one you are now in?

EXAMPLE: These beliefs vary across cultural *boundaries.*

REVIEW

Now that you have studied the vocabulary, reread or reskim the passage.

Optional Longer Project: Interviewing Businesspeople in Your Community

Choose a partner. Together, you will survey two businesspeople in the community where you live. You want to find out how important honesty is in their line of work, and whether they trust the people they do business with. Make up a list of three or four questions that you want to ask them.

Now get together as a class and discuss

1. how to select a businessperson to interview.
2. what kinds of things you could say to introduce yourself and your interview to the businessperson.
3. what each partner will do during the interview.

After the interviews, each partner will write up a report. Your teacher will tell you when it is due. You may be asked to summarize your findings orally to the class as well as writing a report.

LEARNING STRATEGY

Managing Your Learning: Review old vocabulary regularly, doing so more frequently at first, then gradually less frequently.

READING TWO

PARENTING TROUBLE LIES IN CHILDHOOD DECEPTION

1 Parents will overlook a lot of misbehaviour[1] of their children, but one thing most cannot abide is when their children lie to them. Parents want a special relationship with their children. They want their home to be a place where children can feel safe, tell the truth, get help, where love is unconditional. Parents also want to know what's going on in their heads and in their lives, in case a little help or guidance is needed.

2 Children aren't born with morals,[2] however. They have to learn them. So, all children lie. It's simply a part of normal child development, something all parents will face. When my daughter was six years old, she told me she didn't break the glass that was in pieces at her feet on the kitchen floor. Her mother had seen it slip out of her hand. When I asked her why she told me she didn't

do it, her answer was as innocent as could be: "Because I thought I would get in trouble." It took a long time to teach her how lying can jeopardize[3] relationships, why it's important to tell the truth even when you've done something wrong, how apologizing[4] (and meaning it) can do more to undo misbehaviour than trying to cover it up[5] with lies and then wondering what other people are thinking.

3 The research literature is quite clear on how to stop lying and how to increase truth-telling, by using praise, explanations and consistent consequences, beginning at a very young age. Unfortunately,[6] however, the literature never defines lying. It deals only with the most obvious cases—when a child says he didn't have homework when he did, the child who took something or did something wrong and refused[7] to admit it, the child who says someone else started the fight when he did. Yet, lying is much more than that. It is deception in all its forms. As a psychologist and a parent, I am much more concerned with the notion of deception. If a child has learned only that he should not say it is white when it is black, he has learned nothing about lying.

4 Children can be deceptive by exaggerating or embellishing[8] the truth, by not telling us parts of the story they know we need to get an accurate picture. Children can attribute[9] positive motives to their behaviour when there were none, distract us from the issue by bringing up lesser problems, blame others, or pretend to feel they are never believed even when they are telling the truth. Lying is deception in its broadest sense, and it is important that parents teach children that deception is wrong.

5 I see many children from good, caring families who rarely[10] get in trouble at school. Yet, when something does go wrong, they turn out to be masters of deceit[11] and what started out as a minor problem turns into a major trial for the parents, the school and the child. The child starts concocting tales to cover his tracks, putting the best spin on it so his motives were pure, blaming others for starting it, dealing with everything except his own wrongdoing. New deceptions are then needed when parts of the story are forgotten and the child has to explain why he changed his story. Other children and their parents are interviewed and feel accused.[12] Everyone starts to feel like a detective instead of a parent or a teacher. Often, the whole thing gets dropped because no one can prove it.

6 It is important, when we teach our children about lying, that we teach them the morals behind it. The key issue is deception, in any of its myriad faces. If parents teach children how to tell the truth when they've done something wrong, to apologize and try not to do it again, then perhaps the need for lying will be reduced.

After You Read

Identify the circled reference words.

TAKING NOTES FROM YOUR READING

In very brief form, write the main idea of each paragraph. Then show how the supporting details are related to it. Try to use your own words. Abbreviations can be used. The first one has been done for you.

¶1: *Pts can never accept lying from their children—need to know what chn are thinking to give help (pts=parents; chn=children)*

¶2: ______________________________

____

____

¶3: ______________________________

____

____

¶4: ______________________________

____

____

¶5: ______________________________

____

____

¶6: ______________________________

____

____

TRUE–FALSE QUESTIONS

			¶ number
1. Most parents can put up with lying from their children from time to time.	T	F	______
2. Lying is more than not telling the truth.	T	F	______
3. Children often lie because they don't want to get into trouble.	T	F	______
4. Children from good homes may lie, but they don't often get away with it.	T	F	______
5. One form of deception is hiding parts of a story.	T	F	______

ANTICIPATING TEST QUESTIONS: MULTIPLE-CHOICE, TRUE–FALSE, FILL-IN-THE-BLANK

One of the best methods of studying for a test is to write your own practice questions. By imagining yourself in your teacher's place, you're better able to anticipate what questions she or he might ask on the actual test. Practice: You write the comprehension questions for this reading. Try three different approaches, each of which is a very common kind of test question in North American education:

1. Write a multiple-choice question.

EXAMPLE: It is important to teach children that lying in all its forms is bad because …

a. they tell many lies.
b. it can hurt people.
c. they don't know the difference between right and wrong.

Your question: ____

____

____

____

2. Write a true–false question.

EXAMPLE: The author believes it is important to teach children the principles underlying good conduct. T F

Your question: ____

____ T F

3. Write a fill-in-the-blank question.

EXAMPLE: One way of encouraging children to tell the _______ is by praising them.

Your question: ____

____

When you finish, find a couple of partners and "test" each other.

TAKING POSITIONS ON ISSUES

This reading discussed a number of issues about raising children. How do you feel about children lying to their parents? Your answer is known as your *position* on the issue. You will give and explain your position in the Discussion/Writing activity that follows.

DISCUSSION/WRITING

How should parents deal with children who lie? What's the custom in your culture, and what values does it represent? In answering these questions, use some of the concepts and vocabulary from Reading Two.

Vocabulary

VOCABULARY IN CONTEXT

1. Find the expression *slip out of* in the second paragraph. What do you think it means? What in the context makes you think so?
2. Find the word *minor* in the fifth paragraph. Find an antonym that is nearby.
3. Find the word *tale* in the fifth paragraph. Then find a synonym in a nearby sentence.
4. *To put a spin on* something, which is used in the fifth paragraph, is a relatively recent expression that comes from political jargon. What do you think it means? What in the context makes you think so?

KEYWORDS

1. misbehaviour ¶1
2. morals ¶2
3. jeopardize ¶2
4. apologize ¶2
5. cover up ¶2
6. unfortunately ¶3
7. refuse ¶3
8. embellish ¶4
9. attribute ¶4
10. rarely ¶5
11. deceit ¶5
12. accused ¶5

KEYWORD EXERCISE

1. What is one form of *misbehaviour* that is not tolerated in school?

   ____

   EXAMPLE: Have you ever been guilty of this *misbehaviour?*

2. ***EXAMPLE:*** *Morals* refer to principles of conduct and right living in our society.

   Do you think you have good *morals*?

   ____

3. ***EXAMPLE:*** In some large cities, you *jeopardize* your life every time you cross the street.

   Can you name some things that can *jeopardize* your health?

   ____________ ____________ ____________

4. If you bumped into someone as you were walking to class, how would you *apologize* for your awkwardness?

EXAMPLE: He *apologized* for having forgotten to call his friend on the weekend.

5. Which of the following are synonyms for *cover up*? Underline them.

   travel over protect hide conceal accept include

   EXAMPLE: She tried to *cover up* the fact that she didn't do her homework.

6. *Unfortunately* has a prefix *un-* and a suffix *-ly*. What do these tell you about the word?

   ___

   EXAMPLE: Unfortunately, there is not a great deal of literature on what exactly lying means.

7. What are some things you would *refuse* to do even for a friend?

   ___

   EXAMPLE: He *refused* to admit his guilt during the trial.

8. Look up the words *embellish* and *exaggerate* in the dictionary. How do they differ in meaning? Think of an incident or event that happened to you while you were on vacation. How would you *embellish* the incident to make it more exciting?

9. Success in school can be *attributed* to many qualities. What are some of these qualities?

   ___ ___ ___

   EXAMPLE: She *attributed* his bad temper to his upset stomach.

10. What are some things that you *rarely* do on weekends?

    ___

    EXAMPLE: He is *rarely* late for appointments.

11. *EXAMPLE:* Many people consider politicians to be masters of *deceit*.

    Deception appeared in the first reading, in ¶14. What do you think *deceit* means?

    ___

12. Have you ever been unjustly *accused* of some wrongdoing?

    EXAMPLE: He was *accused* of having given false information.

REVIEW

Now that you have studied the vocabulary, reread or reskim the passage.

Freewriting: A Personal Experience

Write about a time when someone lied to you. Did you believe the liar? What happened?

LEARNING STRATEGY

Managing Your Learning: Reading aloud for five minutes each day helps you make connections between the printed language and the spoken language.

READING THREE

Reading process: Scanning for information

In which paragraph can you find the following information?

1. The name of the person whose research this essay is based on ____________
2. A list of the four kinds of behaviour that can give a lie away ____________
3. Examples of body behaviours that can't be controlled ____________
4. A discussion of different kinds of smiles ____________
5. A list of precautions ____________

HOW CAN YOU TELL[1] WHEN SOMEONE IS LYING?

1 In the children's story, the wooden puppet Pinocchio could never hide a lie because when he told one, his nose grew longer. Wouldn't it be convenient if that happened every time anyone told a lie?—or at least everyone except ourselves? But since it doesn't, how can we decide whether someone is lying to us or telling the truth?

2 Psychologist Paul Ekman has made a lifetime study of how people act when they lie. Usually they not only want the hearer to believe the words they are saying; they also want to cover up some strong emotion that they are feeling such as guilt, shame, fear, anger, pain, or even pleasure. In addition to telling the lie, they want to conceal that emotion, and the easiest way to do this is by trying to substitute the signs of a different emotion. By noticing the

contradictions between their words and their behaviour, Ekman found that he could often catch them in the act of lying.

3 Ekman concludes that there are four kinds of behaviour that can give a lie away[2]: the liar's words, voice, body, and face. He says that liars try hardest to control their words and face, since they assume that that's what the listener will be paying attention to. Consequently "lie catchers" should also pay close attention to the speaker's voice and body signals, which she may forget to control. He then points out what the lie catcher should look for in deciding whether he is being deceived.

4 Obviously most lies are untruthful words, and it's these words that we focus on. A common problem for liars is keeping their story straight. As we all know, one lie leads to another, and before the liar knows it, someone will comment, "But that's not what you said a few minutes ago." A less common but more fatal giveaway is what's called a "slip of the tongue," in which the liar accidentally tells the truth instead of the lie she intended to tell. Additionally, frequent pauses may indicate that she is making up the story as she goes along.

Threads

A liar must have a good memory.

Quintilian

5 The liar's voice can also give her away, and the voice is much harder to control than the words. When telling a lie, she may speak unusually loudly or softly, may speed up or slow down her speech for no apparent reason. This can be because of the emotion she's hiding or because she feels self-conscious[3] telling a lie. The voice clue that seems to be the most reliable[4] is that when people are upset, their voices tend to become higher. But Ekman points out that vocal changes such as these are not always signs of lying; they simply indicate strong emotion that the person may be trying to conceal.

6 Some body behaviours can be controlled, but others can't. When telling a lie, a person may swallow frequently, sweat, or breathe faster. Gestures can give her away: nervous gestures, such as swinging the foot, scratching or rubbing parts of the body, or twisting the hair often increase when a person is self-conscious or under stress.[5] The normal gestures that usually accompany speech are often used less when someone is lying. Or the liar may accidentally use a gesture that contradicts her words, such as nodding "yes" while saying "no."

7 The final thing that can give a lie away is the liar's face. Some facial behaviour is impossible to control and can indicate that a person is emotional or self-conscious. Such signs include changes in facial colour (reddening or paling), increased blinking, and enlargement of the pupils of the eyes. Some people find it impossible to hold back tears, and almost everyone finds it hard to produce tears in the absence of genuine[6] emotion. But facial expressions fall into both categories: some of them are hard to control, while others can easily be falsified.[7]

8 Since the liar often wants to mask her true emotion, she is likely to try to substitute a false one through her facial expression. The most common and successful mask is a smile. Ekman's research has identified more than fifty different kinds of smiles, to which he has given names like the "felt smile" (this is a genuine smile), the "fear smile," the "miserable smile," the "embarrassed smile." What distinguishes these smiles from each other is the tension and shape of the lips and also the behaviour of the muscles around the eyes and in

the eyebrows, forehead, and chin. A false smile tends to be a "mouth only" smile, rather than a "full-face" smile that includes the eyes. In addition, the false smile may linger on the person's face longer than a felt smile would. (Think of how uncomfortable you feel holding a smile for the camera, and how unnatural such smiles usually look in pictures.)

9 In addition to smiles, the "lie catcher" should notice the forehead, eyebrows, and eyes. Facial muscles showing anger and surprise are easy to control and are commonly falsified, something we often do during a polite conversation. But forehead muscles that show real sadness and fear are almost impossible to hide, and are equally difficult to falsify.

10 How reliable are these "giveaways"? Taken alone, not very. Ekman provides a list of precautions[8] that can keep the lie catcher from jumping to the wrong conclusion. Here are some of them:

1. Try to identify exactly what the person is doing that makes you suspicious. Doing this will help you to recognize your own mistakes.
2. Keep in mind that you are risking two mistakes: one, that you might believe a lie; the other, that you might disbelieve the truth. Think carefully about both possibilities.
3. Some liars don't give off the signs described above, and some truthful people give them off regularly. In other words, everyone has an individual style of communicating. Looking for changes in a person's usual behaviour is more useful than comparing her behaviour to other people's.
4. Don't let your own emotions influence your judgment. Are you looking for a lie because you are jealous or angry? If so, you may "see" a lie that isn't there.
5. Bear in mind that a truthful person may "act guilty" if he feels that you believe he is lying.
6. Does the speaker know that you suspect[9] her? If so, what would she gain[10] if you caught her, and what would she lose?
7. Do you know something that only the liar would know? If so, you might catch her with a question about it.
8. Never decide that a person is lying purely on the basis of the behavioural clues described above. Use them as the reason for further investigation.

11 A further precaution concerns cultural differences. Interestingly enough, Ekman's research has convinced[11] him that most facial expressions (of fear, anger, happiness, etc.) are culturally universal, though their frequency and the company in which they are shown may vary from culture to culture. For example, Ekman observed Japanese subjects watching emotional films and found that when alone, their facial expressions were identical to North Americans'; but when a person of authority was in the room with them, they masked any expression of negative emotions with a polite smile, as one should in Japanese culture. Euro Americans are taught to make eye contact when they speak as a sign that they are being truthful; such eye contact may be a sign of disrespect in some other cultures. If you observe a Korean in a conversation with a Brazilian, you'll see great differences in body movements and gestures. As Ekman points out, "When liar and target[12] come from different cultures and do not share a language, detecting deceit is, for a number of reasons, much more difficult." A lie catcher who is not aware of these differences is likely to

misinterpret some signals and to miss others completely, leading to serious errors[13] in judgment.[14]

12 As we all know from experience, there are "good" liars and "bad" ones. Some people can "get away with murder," while others somehow fail to make us believe in them no matter how honest they are. But the one group of liars who always succeeds is liars who deceive themselves, who believe their own lies. Ekman says that these people are "undetectable."[15]

After You Read

Identify the circled reference words.

TRUE–FALSE QUESTIONS

			¶number
1. At the same time as they are lying, most liars are trying to keep you from seeing their true emotions.	T	F	________
2. A liar tries hardest to control her voice and body signals, often forgetting to control her face and words.	T	F	________
3. It's easier to control your words than it is your voice.	T	F	________
4. People can't control how often they swallow.	T	F	________
5. There are many different kinds of smiles.	T	F	________
6. You can always catch a liar by watching for these "giveaways."	T	F	________
7. Ekman believes that the facial expressions for particular emotions vary from culture to culture.	T	F	________

ANTICIPATING TEST QUESTIONS: IDENTIFICATION AND DEFINITION

Two other common kinds of test questions are *identification* and *definition.* Each one generally requires a response of a few sentences, maybe a brief paragraph. For instance, these questions might be asked on a test over Reading One:

QUESTION: Define a *pathological liar.*

Example of a good answer:

A pathological liar is a person who lies about everything, and to everyone. He can't control his lying. He generally doesn't introduce his friends to each other because they might compare stories and realize that he's lied to them all. It's unclear what causes this condition, but it's often related to a bad family background or to a great need to be liked.

QUESTION: Identify the two extreme moral positions on lying.

Example of a good answer:

The two extreme moral positions on lying are (1) that people should never lie, because lying hurts both the listener and the liar; and (2) that some kinds of lies are justifiable and even helpful to society.

You want your answer to be long enough to convince your teacher that you have a clear understanding of the topic.

Write one definition or identification question about Reading Three. Then get together with a couple of classmates and "test" each other orally.

RECOGNIZING THE STRUCTURE OF THE READING PASSAGE

Reading Three can be divided into four main parts: The introduction, two parts of the body, and the conclusion. Where do these parts begin and end, and what information is contained in the body?

Introduction: ¶s ______________________________

Part I of the body: ¶s ______________________________

Topic of Part I: ______________________________

How many main points are there in Part I? ______________________________

Part II of the body: ¶s ______________________________

Topic of Part II: ______________________________

How many main points are there in Part II? ______________________________

Conclusion: ¶s ______________________________

DISCUSSION: "BODY LANGUAGE" FOR LYING

In Euro-North-American culture, crossing the first two fingers of one hand is a gesture whose meaning is related to lying (especially if you hold that hand behind your back, where the listener can't see it). Do you know what it means? If not, ask a native. Winking (closing one eye) as one speaks is also related to lying. Find out what it means, too. Are there gestures that carry similar meanings in your culture?

In your culture, what's a traditional punishment for children who lie?

Vocabulary

VOCABULARY IN CONTEXT

1. In ¶4, find the phrase *keeping their story straight.* Read that sentence and the next one.
What do you think it means?
What makes you think that this is the meaning?

2. Here's a challenge: Find the phrase *culturally universal* in ¶11. Read the sentence carefully. What do you think it means?
What makes you think so?

KEYWORDS

1. tell* (distinguish) (title)
2. give something away ¶3
3. self-conscious ¶5
4. reliable ¶5
5. stress ¶6
6. genuine ¶7
7. falsify ¶7
8. precaution ¶10
9. suspect* ¶10 #6
10. gain ¶10 #6
11. convince* ¶11
12. target ¶11
13. error ¶11
14. judgment ¶11
15. undetectable ¶12

KEYWORD EXERCISE

1. ***EXAMPLE:*** How can you *tell* if someone is lying?

   Did you find this meaning of *tell* in your dictionary? Which of the following sentences uses it?
   - He told everyone my secret.
   - His face told me that he was lying.
   - I can't tell the twins apart.

   This meaning of *tell* is a synonym for a keyword introduced in the story of Kaspar Hauser in the last chapter. Can you find it?

2. *Meanings:*
   - If something *gives something away,* it shows everyone something that someone is trying to hide.

     EXAMPLE: The liar's voice can *give his lie away.*

   - If someone has something but they don't want it, they may *give it away.*

     EXAMPLE: After the children grew up and left home, their mother *gave away* some of their old toys.

   - Explain the similarities between the two meanings.

3. Which of the following are elements of the adjective *self-conscious?*

    uncomfortable   relaxed   natural   nervous   embarrassed

    EXAMPLE: Some people feel very *self-conscious* when telling a lie.

4. Compare the noun *stress,* which means the worry that a person feels when they're under pressure, with the verb *stress* (a keyword from Chapter 4), which means to emphasize something.

    Example of verb: Most parents *stress* the importance of honesty to their children.
    Example of noun: Nervous gestures may increase when a person is under *stress.*

    In this reading we consider the noun. Which of the following situations (or another one that you might name) causes you the most *stress?*
    • taking an examination
    • moving to a new place
    • making a major decision

5. The verb *falsify* is related to the adjective *false.* Note the suffix *-ify,* which makes it a verb. Name three things that a person can *falsify* (you can use examples from this reading if you like).

    EXAMPLE: Some facial expressions can be easily *falsified.*

6. ***EXAMPLE:*** Ekman provides a list of *precautions* to keep the lie catcher from jumping to conclusions.

    A *precaution* is something you do if you want to *prevent* (Reading One, ¶12) something unpleasant or dangerous from happening. The expression is to *take a precaution.* As you can see from the sentence above, a *precaution* is also a *warning.*
    What's the connection between the two meanings (preventing and warning)?

7. ***EXAMPLE:*** What would the liar *gain* if you caught him, and what would he lose?

    What did Columbus hope to *gain* when he was planning his first voyage?

8. Note the differences in the grammar that follows *convince:*

    EXAMPLES: His face *convinced* me that he was telling the truth.
    The salesclerk *convinced* me to buy the more expensive item.

    Finish the sentences:
    The weather report ______________________________________.
    My teacher ______________________________________.

9. *Meanings:*
    • A *target* is a mark that you try to hit when you are practising shooting a gun or throwing darts.

    EXAMPLE: A good dart thrower can hit the centre of the *target* nine times out of ten.

- A *target* can also be a person whom someone is trying to deceive, usually for the deceiver's gain.

  EXAMPLE: When liar and *target* come from different cultures, detecting deceit is much more difficult.

- Explain the similarities between the two meanings.

10. Note that *judgment* can also be spelled *judgement.* Both are acceptable. In Chapter 1, what was the king's *judgment?*

11. *Matching:*

_____	**1.** *reliable*	**a.**	not noticeable
_____	**2.** *genuine*	**b.**	real
_____	**3.** *suspect*	**c.**	dependable
_____	**4.** *error*	**d.**	a person whom you believe has done something wrong
_____	**5.** *undetectable*	**e.**	mistake

REVIEW

Now that you have studied the vocabulary, reread or reskim the passage.

LEARNING STRATEGY

Managing Your Learning: Work a little bit each day on what's hardest for you.

READING FOUR

NOTE: This reading is also on the tape.

Reading process: Scanning for information

In which paragraph would you expect to find the following information?

HINT: Use the *headings* to help you locate these items.

1. A computer company lied to an advertising agency ____________________
2. You just have to take chances sometimes ____________________

3. Honest businesspeople are proud of their clean names ______________
4. Most victims don't do anything about it ______________
5. Most businesspeople trust each other ______________

HONESTY[1] AND DISHONESTY IN THE BUSINESS WORLD

1 *Are most business people honest?* When they were children, the businesspeople of today were taught by their parents that honesty pays[2] and that the dishonest will suffer. Their parents and teachers told them moral[3] stories about honest people who were rewarded and dishonest people who were punished. Then they grew up and went out into the cold hard world of business. Faced with a choice between honesty and dishonest profit,[4] which road do these people take? According to a study conducted by *Harvard Business Review,* most U.S. businesspeople do conduct their affairs honestly. They also are willing to trust other businesspeople, because their experience has taught them that most of them are honest too.

2 *Who is dishonest?* But the Harvard team found numerous examples with a different outcome: sometimes dishonesty was greatly profitable. A computer company deceived an advertising agency in order to get good terms, and that single ad helped them sell $150,000 worth of software. Expensive department stores in New York City have a reputation[5] for breaking their promises to suppliers and costing the suppliers a great deal. Some investment brokers deceive their clients[6] and lose all their money. Yet more clients come along, the suppliers keep working with the department stores, and ad agencies take new chances with unknown firms.

3 *Why does anyone believe them?* Given examples like these, it may seem strange to you that businesses would be so trusting. It's partly due to an assumption[7] in the business world that some dishonest people are going to come your way, and you just have to take it in stride.[8] In other cases the reason is greed[9]: the investor convinces the client that he will make such incredible profits that the client can't resist. The smooth talk of the sales rep may win over[10] the customer. Clients have their lawyer go over the contract with a fine-toothed comb, hoping that they can outfox the deceiver. And another reason that dishonesty pays is because most businesspeople believe that most others are as honest as they themselves are.

4 *How do they get away with it?* You might think that dishonest companies and businesspeople would be sued,[11] but they seldom are. The victim[12] may be afraid of the person's power, they may just not want to spend the time and money and effort, or they might not want to endanger their own reputation.

5 *So why be honest?* It sounds bad, doesn't it? Crime pays, honest people suffer. Yet these stories do seem to be in the minority. It's true that you can always find ways to lose your money if you want to take foolish risks with people who have bad track records,[13] but the truth is, most businesspeople told *HBR* that they generally trusted people and that they were very rarely burned. Most of them also said that they themselves were honest in their own business dealings.[14] Why? Not because they believed that it would bring them higher profits, but because of their own self-respect and moral principles. They "took pride in their good names." Said one: "We keep promises because we believe it is right to do so, not because it is good business."

Threads

Honesty is the best policy.

English proverb

After You Read

Identify the circled reference words.

DISCUSSION: COMPREHENSION QUESTIONS

Work with a partner and take turns answering these questions. Try to do it without looking back at the reading.

1. Are most businesspeople honest?
2. Give three examples of dishonest businesses.
3. How are dishonest businesspeople able to find anyone to trust them?
4. How do dishonest businesspeople get away with their deceptions?
5. Why are honest businesspeople honest?

A CULTURAL NOTE

Find the word *outfox* in ¶3. The prefix *out-* means ***more than*** or ***better than;*** the second part of the word is the animal *fox.* In English-speaking cultures, the fox is an animal that represents clever deception. In folk stories, smooth-talking foxes deceive stupid chickens and ducks, who end up as dinner on the fox family's table. In the reading, "hoping that they can outfox the deceiver" means "hoping that they can deceive him even more than he is deceiving them."

Vocabulary

SPECIALIZED BUSINESS VOCABULARY

If you're planning to go into business, you may be interested in the specialized business terminology to be found in Reading Four. There are several ways of categorizing these words. See if you can fill them in on this list (some words may be used in more than one place):

- persons (5 words): ________________ ________________
  ________________ ________________ ________________
- companies (3 words): ________________ ________________
  ____
- money (1 word): ________________
- business relations (2 words): ________________ ________________

- legal terms often used in business (2 words): ________________

____

- something you want to happen (2 words): ________________

____

- something you don't want to happen (2 words): ________________

____

VOCABULARY IN CONTEXT

1. Close your eyes and make a mental picture of a comb with very fine teeth. Then look in ¶3 and find the sentence that mentions this object. What do you think that sentence means? Is it talking about a real comb?
2. In ¶5, find the word *burned.* What do you think it means to *be burned?* What words in the same sentence help to explain the meaning?

KEYWORDS

1. honesty (title)
2. honesty pays ¶1
3. moral ¶1
4. profit* ¶1
5. reputation* ¶2
6. client ¶2
7. assumption ¶3
8. take it in stride ¶3
9. greed ¶3
10. win over ¶3
11. be sued ¶4
12. victim* ¶4
13. track record ¶5
14. dealings ¶5

KEYWORD EXERCISE

1. Each of these sentences appears in the reading above. Give an example of how each can be true.

   Honesty pays. (¶1)
   Dishonesty pays. (¶3)
   Crime pays. (¶5)

2. A *moral* story is a story with a lesson in it. Here's an example:

   A shepherd boy got bored sitting on the hillside with his sheep, so he shouted, "Wolf! Wolf!" All the villagers came running, but they became very angry when there was no wolf. This was so much fun that the shepherd boy did it again. The villagers were even angrier the second time. Then a wolf really did appear. The boy shouted again, but this time no one came to help him, and the wolf killed one of his sheep.

   What's the *moral* of this story?

3. In Reading One ¶8, there is a word that is the antonym of *profit.* What is it?

   EXAMPLE: Sometimes businesses have to choose between honesty and dishonest *profit.*

4. Your *reputation* falls into which of the following categories?

   a fact   a thing   a belief   an event   an opinion

   EXAMPLE: Some firms have a *reputation* for honesty; some don't.

5. What is the difference between a *client* and a customer? (You can use your dictionary.)

   EXAMPLE: Lawyers have *clients;* stores have customers.

6. ***EXAMPLE:*** Businesspeople know that some dishonest people are going to come their way, and they just have to *take it in stride.*

   In the literal meaning, your *stride* is the way that you walk when you're relaxed and purposeful. What's the connection between this literal meaning and the meaning of the idiom *take something in stride?*

   When you go to live in a foreign culture, if you let everything bother you greatly, you'd be upset all the time and you'd probably decide to turn around and go back home. What's something that bothered you when you went to a new culture, but which you learned to *take in stride?*

7. What do you think this proverb means?—*Greedy* folks have long arms.

8. ***EXAMPLE:*** You can always find ways to lose your money if you want to take foolish risks with people who have bad *track records.*

   Were you able to find this phrase in your dictionary? If not, here's a definition: The *track record* of a person or a business is their record of good or bad performance. This term originally came not from business, but from another field of activity. Which of the following do you suppose it was?

   medicine   sports   music   education   science

9. *Matching:*

_____	**1.** *honest*	**a.** truthful
_____	**2.** *assumption*	**b.** business relations, trade
_____	**3.** *win over*	**c.** persuade someone to agree with you
_____	**4.** *be sued*	**d.** someone who has been wrongfully harmed
_____	**5.** *victim*	**e.** belief that something is true
_____	**6.** *dealings*	**f.** a kind of legal action taken against you

REVIEW

Now that you've studied the vocabulary, reread or reskim the passage.

Writing an Essay Test

Another common type of test question is the *essay* or *discussion* question. The purpose of this question is to find out how completely you understand a large concept or problem. Your professor may expect an answer that ranges from one well-developed paragraph to a full essay of several paragraphs.

For your essay in this chapter, choose one of the following questions:

1. Discuss some of the problems North American parents face in getting their children to tell the truth. Compare and contrast the way parents deal with this matter in your own culture.
2. Describe the kinds of behaviour that can give a lie away, and explain the risks of believing that you can "catch" a liar in this way.
3. Choose a specific business situation to use as an example for this question: Discuss the risks of trusting an unknown business that you have to deal with. How would you decide whether to trust them? What could you do to protect yourself?

Before you start writing your answer, find the paragraphs in the reading that give you information for each part of the question, and study them carefully for five minutes. You can highlight information and take notes if you like.

Now, without looking back at the reading or your notes, take out a piece of paper and write an answer. Your teacher will tell you how much time you can have. Use this format: Instead of repeating the question, your *very short* introduction should identify the topic (e.g., "Trusting an unknown firm can be risky business, but sometimes you have to do it"). Then continue, keeping one eye on the clock. Make sure that you can cover the entire topic in the time allowed. You'll lose points if your answer is incomplete. If possible, save yourself three to five minutes at the end to reread what you've written, making revisions and corrections.

LEARNING STRATEGY

Overcoming Limitations: Thinking in English helps you break the habit of translating.

Evaluating Learning Strategies

Look back over the learning strategies in this chapter. Were there any that weren't especially helpful for you? What wasn't helpful about them? Which ones did you find helpful? Think about times and ways that you can keep using them in your future reading.

Evaluating Your Learning

	Very little	*Quite a bit*	*A lot*
You learned to use some new vocabulary in your writing.	________	________	________
Your comprehension has improved.	________	________	________
You're getting better at paraphrasing in your own words.	________	________	________
You can identify issues in a reading passage.	________	________	________
You can answer several different types of test questions.	________	________	________
You learned about lies and honesty.	________	________	________

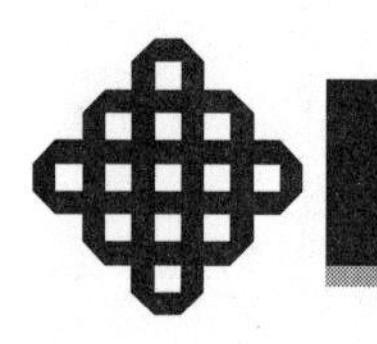

KEYWORDS FOR CHAPTER 6: LIES AND TRUTH

Verbs
accuse
apologize
attribute
backfire
convince
cover up
embellish
falsify
gain (2 meanings)
give someone away
harm
jeopardize
prevent
profit
prosper
refuse
sued, be
suffer
suspect
tell (distinguish)
trust
win over

Adjectives
genuine
guilty
justifiable
moral
profound
reliable
self-conscious
undetectable

Nouns
assumption
boundary
circumstances
client
dealings
deceit
deception
error
greed
honesty
intention
judgment
misbehaviour
morals
precaution
profit
reputation
stress
suspect
target
track record
trust
victim

Adverbs
intentionally
rarely
unfortunately

Introductory phrase
There is no question that

CHAPTER 7

Shapes and Sizes: Notions of Female Beauty

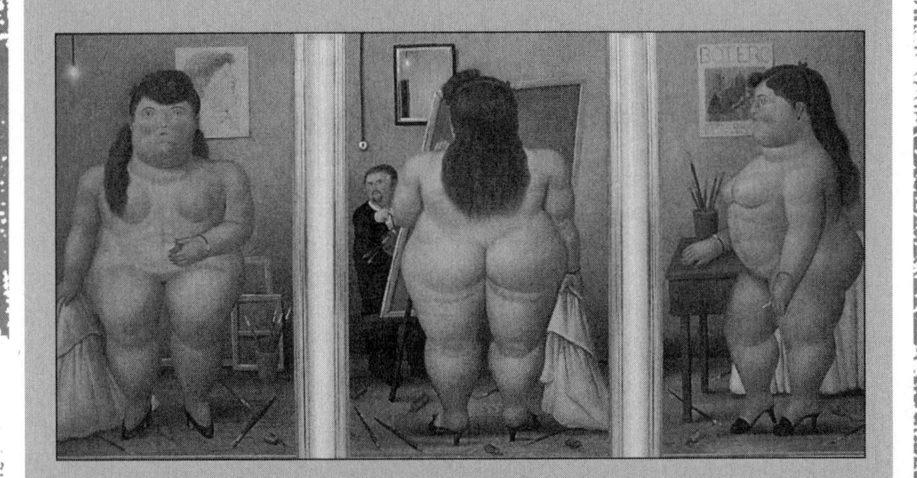

INTRODUCTION

PLANNING YOUR LEARNING

Review your overall goal statement. How much progress did you make toward it in the last chapter? Do you want to change it? Think about how you can work to meet your goal as you study this chapter.

- How many key words do you want to learn? (minimum 58, the number of keywords in the chapter)
- What grade would you like to make on the vocabulary section of the exam at the end of the chapter?
- What grade would you like to make on the reading comprehension section of the exam?
- What are you going to read outside of class?

PREVIEWING THE CHAPTER

- Look at the title of this chapter. What is a *notion*? Can you think of another word that has a similar meaning?
- Look in the Table of Contents at the titles of the four readings in this chapter. What are some of the things you expect to learn about? What are some things that you are curious about? What do you expect to find out?
- Which reading do you think has the most eye-catching title? What do you think it is about?
- Which reading do you think you'll be most interested in?

FREEWRITING

- What makes someone beautiful? Take a few minutes to write a description of a person whom you consider beautiful. This is *freewriting*. When you freewrite, you concentrate on content and on expressing yourself so that people can understand you, and you don't spend much time worrying about vocabulary or grammar. Try to write as much as you can in the time you have.
- After you finish writing, form a group with two or three classmates and tell each other what you wrote. Did your partners include any criteria of beauty that were different from yours?

LEARNING STRATEGY

Managing Your Learning: Sharing information with partners is a good way to get some idea of what to expect from a reading.

PREPARING TO READ: CONTENT

1. Draw or cut out from a magazine the picture of someone who you think is beautiful. Set it aside.
2. Working in small groups, use the information in your freewriting assignment and complete the following chart. For example, under Face you could write blue eyes.

THIS IS BEAUTIFUL!

Face	Body Shape	Height	Weight	Hair	Other

3. Take out your drawing or the picture you cut out, and compare it with the information in the chart. What conclusions can you make?

PREPARING TO READ: VOCABULARY

Here are a few words and concepts that you will encounter in the readings. Working with a partner, look them up in a dictionary. In the space provided, write down what they mean.

1. myth ______________________________

____

2. attractive ______________________________

____

3. narcissism ______________________________

____

4. allure ______________________________

____

5. beauty ______________________________

____

6. feminine ______________________________

____

7. Rubenesque ______________________________

____

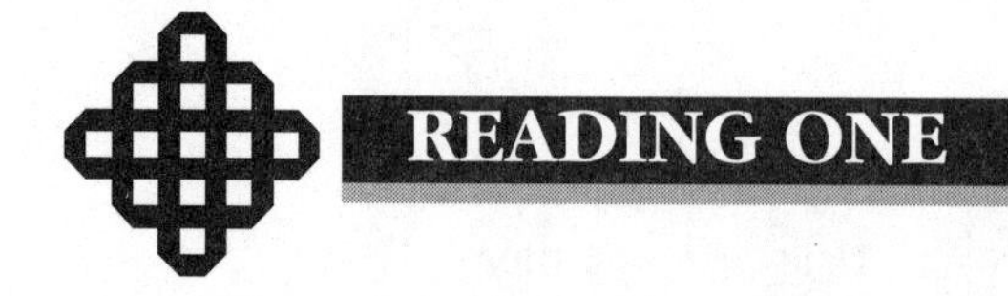

READING ONE

Reading Process: Your teacher will give you a few minutes to skim the five paragraphs in the following passage. After you've skimmed everything, read each paragraph at your own speed, marking vocabulary as usual. When you come to the end of each paragraph, review it and think about its main points.

WOMEN'S BEAUTY: PUT DOWN OR POWER SOURCE?

1 To be called beautiful is thought to name something essential to women's character and concerns. (In contrast to men, whose essence is to be strong, or effective, or competent.) It does not take someone in the throes[1] of advanced feminist[2] awareness to perceive that the way women are taught to be involved with beauty encourages narcissism, and reinforces[3] dependence and immaturity. Everybody (men and women) knows that. For it is "everybody," a whole society, that has identified being feminine with caring about how one *looks*. (In contrast to being masculine, which is identified with caring about what one *is* and *does* and only secondarily, if at all, about how one looks.) Given these stereotypes,[4] it is no wonder that beauty enjoys, at best, a mixed reputation.

2 It is not, of course, the desire to be beautiful that is wrong but the obligation to be—or to try. What is accepted by most women as a flattering idealization of their sex is a way of making women feel inferior[5] to what they actually are—or normally grow to be. For the ideal of beauty is administered as a form of self-oppression.[6] Women are taught to see their bodies in parts, and to evaluate each part separately. Breasts, feet, hips, waistline, neck, eyes, nose, complexion, hair, and so on—each in turn is submitted to an anxious, fretful, often despairing scrutiny. Even if some pass muster, some will always be found wanting. Nothing less than perfection will do.

3 In men, good looks is whole, something taken in at a glance.[7] It does not need to be confirmed by giving measurements of different regions of the body; nobody encourages a man to dissect his appearance, feature by feature. As for perfection, that is considered trivial[8] — almost unmanly. Indeed, in the ideally good-looking man a small imperfection or blemish is considered positively desirable. According to one movie critic (a woman) who is a declared Robert Redford fan, it is having that cluster[9] of skin-coloured moles on one cheek that saves Redford from being merely a "pretty face." Think of the depreciation[10] of women—as well as of beauty—that is implied in that judgment.

4 "The privileges of beauty are immense," said Cocteau.[a] To be sure, beauty is a form of power. And deservedly so. What is lamentable is that it is the only

form of power that most women are encouraged to seek. This power is always conceived in relation to men; it is not the power to do but to attract. It is a power that negates itself.[b] This power is not one that can be chosen freely—at least, not by women—or renounced without social censure.[11]

5 To preen,[12] for a woman, can never be just a pleasure. It is also a duty. It is her work. If a woman does real work—and even if she has clambered up to a leading position in politics, law, medicine, business, or whatever—she is always under pressure to confess that she still works at being attractive. But in so far as she is keeping up as one of the Fair Sex, she brings under suspicion her very capacity to be objective, professional, authoritative, thoughtful. Damned if they do—women are. And damned if they don't.

[a]*Jean Cocteau* (1889-1963): a well-known French author and film maker who worked in almost every artistic medium.

[b]*negates itself:* works against it.

The Giraffe Woman of Burma

After You Read

Identify the circled reference words.

COMPREHENSION QUESTIONS

1. According to the author, what characteristic do most people identify with being feminine? ______

   being masculine? ______

2. *Finish the sentence:*

   Society's view of beauty encourages ______ and reinforces ______.

3. How do women feel when they do not meet all of society's criteria for what is beautiful? ______

   ______

4. How are women taught to view their bodies?

   ______

5. How does society regard the following in men and women?

	Women	Men
perfection		
slight blemish		
good looks		

6. According to the author, what is the only kind of power women are encouraged to seek? ______
7. What additional pressure are women under even when they have become successful professionals? ______

   ______
8. What effect does this (answer to Question #6) have on the way society sees them? ______

LEARNING STRATEGY

Personalizing: You can get a better understanding of another person's actions if you try to identify yourself with his or her point of view.

FREEWRITING: VALUES AND POINTS OF VIEW

Susan Sontag is the author of "Women's Beauty: Put Down or Power Source?" Her *point of view* is the way she feels about society's attitude toward women's beauty. In your freewrite, try to answer this question: Does Susan Sontag think that women's beauty is a put down or a power source?

Sontag's point of view comes partly from her values—the ideas and actions that are important to her. You might also want to write answers to the following questions:

1. What message is society giving young girls about the importance of beauty?
2. How does this affect the way young women see themselves?

IDENTIFYING ISSUES AND TAKING POSITIONS

Working in a small group, identify three issues from the reading. Formulate them as questions.

1. ______________________________
2. ______________________________
3. ______________________________

LEARNING STRATEGY

Managing Your Learning: Look up only the most important words in the dictionary.

Vocabulary

KEYWORDS

1. throes ¶1
2. feminist ¶1
3. reinforces ¶1
4. stereotypes ¶1
5. inferior* ¶2
6. self-oppression ¶2
7. at a glance* ¶3
8. trivial* ¶3
9. cluster ¶3
10. depreciation ¶3
11. social censure ¶4
12. to preen ¶5

KEYWORD EXERCISE

1. *Finish the sentence:*

   When you are in the *throes* of passion with someone, you are ______________________________ with that person.

2. What is the dictionary definition of *feminist*?

   ____

   ____

   EXAMPLE: Greta considers herself a *feminist*.

3. To *reinforce* an idea is to ______________________________

   ____

   EXAMPLE: It is always a good idea to *reinforce* what children learn in school.

4. List two examples of common female *stereotypes* that many people have.

   a. ____________________ **b.** ____________________

5. What is the antonym of *inferior*? ________________________

   EXAMPLE: In the nineteenth century, women were generally considered to be *inferior* to men.

6. *Self* is a word that refers to your basic personality. In addition to the term *self-oppressed*, what other combinations of words using *self* can you think of:

   self-__________________ self-__________________

   self-__________________ self-__________________

   self-__________________ self-__________________

   EXAMPLE: It is a good idea for women to take a course in *self-defense* so that they can protect themselves against attackers.

7. Replace the phrase *at a glance* in the first line of ¶3: In men, good looks is a whole, something taken in ____.

8. List two things that you consider *trivial*.

   a. ____________________ **b.** ____________________

9. What word can you substitute for the word *cluster* in ¶3?

   ____

   EXAMPLE: A *cluster* of fans follows the actor Tom Cruise wherever he goes.

10. When you censure someone, you are criticizing that person. When the adjective "social" is used before censure as in ¶4, who is doing the criticizing? ______________________________________

11. List three things that can *depreciate in value*.

    a. __________________ **b.** __________________ **c.** __________________

12. *EXAMPLE:* Birds like to *preen*.

    Finish the sentence:

    When birds preen, they ____.

LEARNING STRATEGY

Remembering New Material: Making up paragraphs that contain several new words helps you remember them more easily.

READING TWO

NOTE: This reading is also on the tape.

IS BIGGER BETTER? NORTH AMERICAN SOCIETY IS BREAST-OBSESSED

1 Now more than ever, breasts—and particularly large ones—are prominent[1] not only in the adult-entertainment industry. They are used to sell everything from beer and chewing gum to clothes and cars. They have become so central to the clothing designer's craft that pictures in women's fashion magazines are sometimes hard to differentiate from those in so-called men's magazines. In the popular perception at least, breasts have become increasingly divorced from motherhood, and instead, are associated entirely with sexuality, youthfulness, femininity and self-confidence. North American culture has enshrined[2] a new ideal, very much like the ubiquitous Barbie doll—a flat stomach, slim hips and a big bust. Louise Whitney, 42, a Vancouver writer and actor who had silicone implants[3] following a mastectomy, recalled seeing a fashion editor on television who said that women should not feel self-conscious about being small-breasted. "That's so hypocritical,"[4] she declared. "It's those same editors who are responsible for filling the covers of magazines with great busty wenches."

2 Breasts have nearly always been an integral[5] part of feminine allure. And in the past, as now, many women took steps to accentuate their attributes—often at great personal expense. In the 19th century, a girl might start a process called tight-lacing by the time she was 8—and could still be wearing the binding corsets up to the seventh month of pregnancy. The result according to Donna Andrew, a social historian at Ontario's Guelph University, was that often an adult woman was unable to stand up without a corset because the muscles in the centre of the body had atrophied. With the increased popularity of high-heeled shoes in the 1950s, women's problems shifted to painful leg and lower-back muscles. But the shoes appealed—and still do—to both sexes by making the legs look longer and slimmer and by changing a woman's posture so that both the breasts and the buttocks were accentuated.[6]

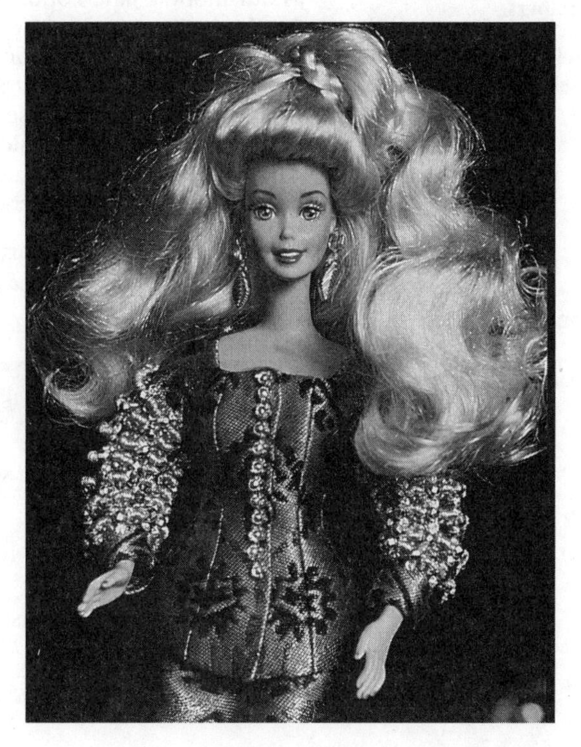

3 While the voluptuous[7] look of American actresses Marilyn Monroe and Jayne Mansfield gave way briefly in the 1960s to the boyish figure of British model Twiggy, the full-figured ideal has returned with a vengeance—although the fullness is confined to the bust line. Many models have breast augmentation[8] to conform to that ideal ... But breast implantation is not just the surgical procedure of the stars. Sometimes, a

woman may choose implants because her shape has changed after childbirth. Others ... just want their clothes to fit properly ...

4 But there are more complicated factors behind the quest for larger breasts. Marcella Tardif[a] ... maintains that one of the main factors is low self-esteem.[9] "Women have told me they do (it) for their husbands, for their boyfriends," she said. "You turn on the TV and your husband says, 'Oh, look at the shape on (her.') So what do I do?" That may help to weaken a woman's sense of self-worth. "Women are socialized to believe that you have to be romantically involved, to be in a relationship," said Greta Hoffman Nemiroff, joint chair of women's studies at the University of Ottawa and Carleton University. "I think that most people's notions of beauty are created by the media. And beauty in women is associated with getting love."

5 Plastic surgeons acknowledge the pervasive[10] influence of popular culture. "Society creates its own image of what is beautiful, is desirable, and everyone, in their heart of hearts, tries to live up to it," said Ian Curry, a plastic surgeon in Moncton. "And if you don't, it's a problem." Added Dale Birdsell, a Calgary plastic surgeon: "Our culture has put a value on this sort of ideal shape. It is a physical peculiarity to have a slim woman with large breasts, but that particular shape has become, from the movies and advertising, the desirable one."

6 ... [M]ass culture pointedly discourages women from going gently into middle age. "Our society has not had a very valued place for older women," said Gail Robinson, a psychiatrist and director of a women's mental health program at the Toronto Hospital. "Older men can be wise, they can be senior executives, they can have grey hair and still be handsome and date. But women's options seem to narrow as they get older." And the pressure to remain young-looking is increasing, even as the average age of the population grows. "There's even more the sense that as you age, you shouldn't age," added Robinson. "We have as our models Jane Fonda, Candice Bergen, Lauren Hutton—in their 40s and 50s, but still gorgeous. The image is, you really don't change."

7 Eventually, says Moncton's Curry, aging men and women may stop searching for the fountain of youth and accept a more relaxed model of beauty. In a perfect world, of course, even such optimistic predictions[11] would be unnecessary: people would simply value themselves for who they are, not for what shape they are. But until society broadens its definition of female beauty beyond bra size, the bigger-is-better ethic will remain a plastic surgeon's dream.

[a]Marcella Tardif runs a support group in Montréal called *Le Réseau Je Sais*/I Know Network for women who have had implants.

Threads

Woman ... cannot be content with health and agility: she must make exorbitant efforts to appear something that never could exist without a diligent perversion of nature.

Germaine Greer

To emphasize only the beautiful seems to me to be like a mathematical system that only concerns itself with positive numbers.

Paul Klee

After You Read

Identify the circled reference words.

COMPREHENSION QUESTIONS

1. In North America, breasts play a very significant role in three fields:

a. ____________________ **b.** ____________________ **c.** ____________________

2. According to the author, breasts used to be associated with motherhood. How has this changed?

____

3. According to the author, the North American ideal woman should look like a

____.

4. The ideal woman must possess these three physical characteristics:

a. ______________ **b.** ______________ **c.** ______________

5. In the nineteenth century, women wore corsets, which caused

____.

In the 1950s, they wore high heels which made their legs look

______________ and ______________ but also caused

____.

6. What are three reasons why many women go to plastic surgeons to have their breasts enlarged?

a. ____

b. ____

c. ____

7. What kind of social pressure do women face as they get older?

____

____

8. Do men and women have the same options as they age? (Y/N). Explain your answer.

____

____

IDENTIFYING THE ISSUES

The author has raised several issues in Reading Two. Can you identify some of them?

TAKING NOTES FROM YOUR READING

On a separate sheet of paper, take notes from the reading. Use the information in your comprehension questions to help you. Consider the organization of each paragraph as you decide how to present your notes in graphic form that makes it easy for you to see and understand the information.

LEARNING STRATEGY

Managing Your Learning: Look up only the most important words in the dictionary.

Vocabulary

VOCABULARY IN CONTEXT

1. Find the term *plastic surgeon* in ¶s 5 & 7. Based on what you have read, why do people go to plastic surgeons? What can she or he do for you that other doctors can't?
2. The phrase *fountain of youth* appears in ¶7. What do you think it means?
3. In ¶s 5 and 6, the author uses the adjectives "mass" and "popular" before the noun *culture*. Are these two adjectives similar in meaning? What do you think the author means by *mass culture* and by *popular culture*? What's the connection between the meanings of the parts and the meaning of the phrases?

KEYWORDS

1. prominent* ¶1
2. enshrined ¶1
3. implants ¶1
4. hypocritical ¶1
5. integral* ¶2
6. accentuated ¶2
7. voluptuous ¶3
8. augmentation ¶3
9. self-esteem* ¶4
10. pervasive ¶5
11. predictions* ¶7

KEYWORD EXERCISE

1. ***EXAMPLE:*** Dr. Villeneuve is a *prominent* plastic surgeon in Montréal.

   What does the word *prominent* tell you about Dr. Villeneuve's reputation?

   ____

   Can you name three *prominent* Canadian politicians?

   a. ______________________________

   b. ______________________________

   c. ______________________________

2. ***EXAMPLE:*** Our basic rights are *enshrined* in the Canadian Charter of Human Rights and Freedom.

   According to most dictionary definitions of *enshrined*, this means that our basic rights and freedom are ________________ and ________________.

3. ***EXAMPLE:*** To enlarge their bust size, many female movie stars have silicone *implants*.

   What other kinds of *implants* are possible?

   a. ________________ **c.** ________________

   b. ________________ **d.** ________________

4. Fill in the missing parts of the words in the following sentences:

   1. A person who pretends to share your ideas and beliefs about something is known as a h _ _ _ _ _ _ _ e.

   2. His or her behaviour can be described as

   h _ _ _ _ _ _ _ y or as h _ _ _ _ _ _ _ _ _ _ l.

   Can you trust this person? ________________________

5. ***EXAMPLE:*** A willingness to work hard is *integral* to success.

   Finish the sentence:

   ________________ and________________ are integral to a happy marriage.

6. ***EXAMPLE:*** She always *accentuated* her best qualities.

   In Reading Two, you learned that women *accentuated* their

   ________________ and________________ by wearing high heels.

7. ***EXAMPLE:*** The actress Marilyn Monroe was a very *voluptuous* woman.

   Name at least two obvious physical attributes of a *voluptuous* woman: ________________ and________________

8. ***EXAMPLE:*** My boss decided to *augment* my salary.

   List three synonyms for the word *augmentation*.

   a. ________________ **b.** ________________ **c.** ________________

9. ***EXAMPLE:*** Racist attitudes are *pervasive* in certain segments of our society.

   Finish the sentences:

   The Catholic church ____.

   An atmosphere of violence ____.

10. ***EXAMPLE:*** Many fortune tellers use crystal balls to *predict* the future.

Finish the sentences:

He predicted ____.

Predictably ____.

REVIEW

Now that you have studied the vocabulary, reread or reskim the passage.

LEARNING STRATEGY

Personalizing: Think of a way that you can benefit from each language learning task you do, either in class or outside of class.

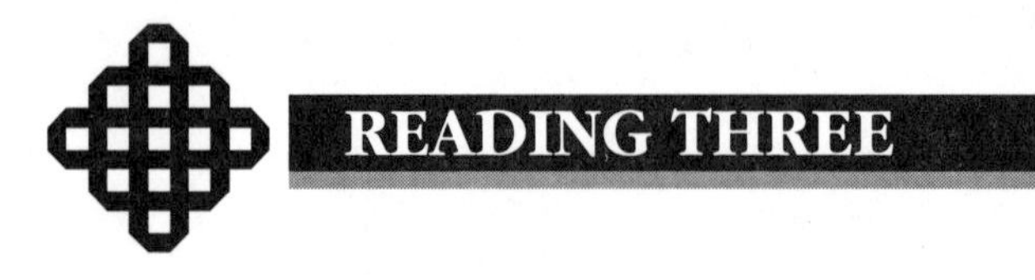

READING THREE

NOTE: This reading is also on the tape.

Threads

Beauty is only the promise of happiness.

—Stendhal

THE BEAUTY MYTH

1 According to one recent poll, nearly three-quarters of all North American women consider themselves to be fat. Skipping meals and searching for the perfect diet, they spend their youth struggling with the scales, an obsessive[1] battle that many researchers blame[2] on manipulative[3] images of the fashion industry. But a new study by psychologist Judith Anderson, a research associate at Simon Fraser University in Burnaby, British Columbia, suggests that standards of beauty in North America and elsewhere may be strongly linked[4] to biology, the environment and social factors.

2 Earlier studies had shown that body fat serves a number of important roles in females. "As well as storing calories and insulating the body core," says Anderson, "a minimum level of fat is required[5] for fertility." To determine whether cultural standards of beauty were set by biological needs for body fat, Anderson and her associates began a review of the anthropological[6] literature.

3 Combing through descriptions of physically attractive women from sixty-two cultures around the world—ancient Romans, precontact Maori and modern Vietnamese, for example—the researchers noted whether female beauty was associated with thinness or plumpness[7] in each society.

4 Compiling the data, Anderson and her team found that only 20 percent of the cultures preferred slim women, while 37 percent favoured moderate fatness in females, and 43 percent viewed plump women as physically attractive. More

interesting still, the concepts of beauty seemed strongly influenced by social and ecological[8] factors.[9] In cultures living in cool climates where food supplies were unreliable and males dominated, Rubenesque women were favoured. According to Anderson, such findings support her thesis[10] that fatter women are more likely to survive and reproduce despite food shortages and harsh climates.

5 In North America, she suggests, women may be following other biological[11] imperatives. "We found a link between fatness as a standard of beauty and the social stress associated with the onset of adolescent[12] sexuality," says Anderson. "Our culture is extremely[13] stressful for young girls. We say to them, 'Go out and spend a lot of time with boys, but if you get pregnant, there will be terrible consequences.' Obviously, it is not safe to ovulate, so perhaps girls are staying slim as an unconscious method of birth control."

6 While Anderson's study is a preliminary[14] one, it seriously undermines the theory that North American women are the slaves of fashion. "If we want to do something about our unhealthy dieting," she concludes, "then we should stop blaming the fashion industry and start looking at other areas such as the conflicting reproductive and economic pressures we as a society place on women."

Comprehension Questions

1. What did Judith Anderson and her team want to find out in their study?

____

____

2. What did these researchers find out?

____

____

3. What did the earlier studies on body fat in females show?

____

4. How many cultures did Anderson and her team examine?

____

5. _____ percent of the cultures examined preferred slim women, and _____ percent preferred moderately fat women. _____percent considered plump women to be physically attractive.

6. *Sending mixed messages* refers to speaking or writing in a way that lends itself to contradictory or incompatible interpretations. According to Anderson, what mixed messages is the North American culture sending to young girls?

____

____

TRUE–FALSE QUESTIONS

			¶ *number*
1. Anderson's study showed that North American women are slaves to fashion.	T	F	________
2. North American women are obsessed with their weight.	T	F	________

KEYWORDS

1. obsessive ¶1
2. blame ¶1
3. manipulative ¶1
4. linked*¶1
5. required*¶2
6. anthropological ¶2
7. plumpness ¶3
8. ecological ¶4
9. factors* ¶4
10. thesis ¶4
11. biological ¶5
12. adolescent ¶5
13. extremely ¶5
14. preliminary* ¶6

KEYWORD EXERCISE

1. *EXAMPLE:* His *obsessive* jealousy drove her crazy.

List three things that you think North American teenagers are *obsessive* about.

a. ____

b. ____

c. ____

2. *EXAMPLE:* Politicians have a considerable degree of *manipulative* skill.

The adjective *manipulative* comes from the verb *to manipulate.* You can use this verb in several different ways. See if you can complete the following sentences:

To *manipulate* election results is to ______________________________.

When children *manipulate* their parents, they ____________________.

3. *EXAMPLE:* Luck is a major *factor* in winning the lottery.

List two *factors* that can make you a successful student.

a. ________________ **b.** ________________

4. *EXAMPLE:* The chemical plant's problems cannot all be *blamed* on environmentalists.

Which of the following are elements of the word *blame*?
essential good bad genuine responsible

5. *EXAMPLE:* All citizens are *required* to pay taxes.

Finish the sentences:

Most students are required to ______________________________.

Most travellers abroad are required to ________________________.

Teachers ____.

Matching:

_____	**1.** *thesis*	**a.**	preparatory
_____	**2.** *anthropology*	**b.**	study of people, society, and culture
_____	**3.** *plumpness*	**c.**	synonym for main idea
_____	**4.** *linked*	**d.**	not yet an adult
_____	**5.** *ecological*	**e.**	related to the study of living things
_____	**6.** *adolescent*	**f.**	antonym for slenderness
_____	**7.** *preliminary*	**g.**	concerning the relationship between living things and their environment
_____	**8.** *biological*	**h.**	very
_____	**9.** *extremely*	**i.**	connected

REVIEW

Now that you have studied the vocabulary, reread or reskim the passage.

ANTICIPATING TEST QUESTIONS

Using Reading Two, write one of each of the following kinds of test question:
True–false Identification Multiple-choice essay Fill-in-the-blank

When you finish, get together with your classmates. Then find a partner and "test" each other orally.

TAKING NOTES FROM YOUR READING

On a separate sheet of paper, take notes from the reading. You should use the information in your comprehension questions to help you. Consider the organization of each paragraph as you decide to present your information in a graphic form that makes it easy for you to see and understand the information.

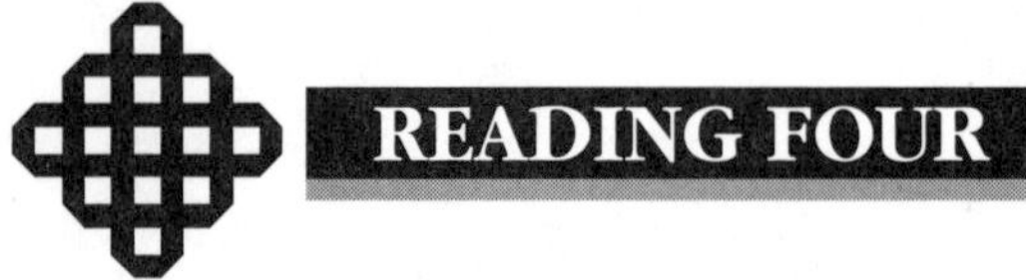

Personalizing: Try to find out how language learning works, and apply what you learn to your own situation.

READING FOUR

NOTIONS OF BEAUTY TRANSCEND CULTURE, NEW STUDY SUGGESTS

1 Beauty is not, as egalitarians[1] like to think, in the eyes of the beholder. Nor is it as strongly[2] influenced[3] by culture as many have long assumed. Rather, an accumulating body of evidence indicates that concepts of attractiveness may be universal and hard-wired into the human brain, whether that brain serves a Briton or a Japanese.

2 This "wiring," a built-in genetic tendency that evolved over milleniums[4] through natural selection, seems to prompt men to select as attractive those women whose facial characteristics are associated[5] with youth and good health, both of which are important to reproductive viability.

3 In the latest study, published in the current issue of the British journal *Nature,* both British and Japanese men and women ranked women's faces as most attractive when certain features associated with youthfulness, like large eyes, high cheekbones, and a narrow jaw, were exaggerated. Further, the study found, Caucasians gave top ranking to the same Japanese faces that the Japanese preferred, leading the researchers to conclude[6] in their report that there are "greater similarities than differences in cross-cultural judgments of facial attractiveness."

A Certain Geometry

4 "Clearly,[7] we have an innate[8] mechanism that sees a certain geometry of the face as beautiful and attributes to that face other characteristics seen as most fit," said Dr. Nancy L. Etcoff, a neuropsychologist at Massachusetts General Hospital who wrote a commentary[9] on the study.

5 Previous studies had shown that people rank[10] as more attractive a computer-derived composite face than the individual faces used to construct

the composite. This prompted researchers to conclude that an "average" face was more pleasing than faces with features that deviated[11] from average.[12] Sociologically, the findings made sense since people feel safest and most comfortable around others who appear familiar and similar to themselves.

6 In the animal world, however, researchers from Charles Darwin on have shown that averageness can be inadequate[13] in the competition for mates. Rather, natural selection has sometimes favoured those endowed with more extreme traits, like the peacock's stunning but physiologically impractical tail.

Improving on Beautiful

7 The new study, directed by Dr. David I. Perrett at the University of St. Andrews in Fife, Scotland, strongly suggests that, like peacocks, people with facial features that are exaggerations of ordinary attractiveness have by far the greatest appeal.

8 The researchers first had men and women rank in attractiveness 60 images[14] of women's faces. Then they used a computer to construct two composite faces: one the average of the 60 images and the other the average of the 15 images initially[15] ranked as most attractive. A third composite was derived from the highly[16] attractive composite by exaggerating the differences in shape between the average face and the highly average face, for example, by making the chin even narrower and the cheekbones higher.

9 A new group of men and women shown only the three composite faces clearly ranked the highly attractive composite over the average one and gave the highest ranking to the computer-derived caricature of the second composite. Furthermore, when Caucasian men and women were asked to select the most attractive faces similarly derived from images of Japanese women, they ranked as most attractive the same face, again with the exaggerated characteristics, chosen by Japanese men and women.

Threads

The ideal has many names, and beauty is but one of them.

W. Somerset Maugham

There is certainly no absolute standard of beauty. That precisely is what makes its pursuit so interesting.

John Kenneth Galbraith

Male Faces Ranked

9 In fact, the researchers reported, the facial characteristics that the computer-generated averages showed to be the most appealing[17] to Caucasians in Caucasian faces were also most appealing in Japanese faces to both the Japanese and the Caucasians.

10 The researchers also found a similar preference for composite male faces made from those ranked highest by participants. But they did not construct a caricature[18] of the most attractive male faces as they had done with the female faces, nor did they examine faces of Japanese men.

11 Dr. Etcoff said: "What this study shows is that there are two different faces of beauty. One is the 'average' face, comfortable and familiar, and the other a deviation from the average that is extremely attractive. Furthermore these choices are not arbitrary. They seemed tied in actuality to disease-resistance, fertility,[19] and youth." She cited as youthful and healthy looking those faces with full lips, large eyes, narrow jaw, and a lower face that is small in comparison to the upper face.

12 Dr. Perrett and his co-authors concluded that these "attractive facial features may signal sexual maturity and fertility, emotional expressiveness or a 'cuteness' generalized from parental protectiveness towards the young."

13 Dr. Judith Langlois, a psychologist at the University of Texas, has concluded from her own work that this tendency to pick out attractive faces is already

present in infancy rather than being learned through experiences like exposure to photography and films or the admiring comments of adults.

14 ... The Texas psychologist said her findings challenged current[20] thinking about the "origins of physical attractiveness preferences and stereotypes" and the "assumptions that preferences for physical attractiveness are culturally dependent."

15 Dr. Etcoff noted that although some qualities of beauty, like body weight and shape, may be culturally dependent and vary with time and place, others like facial characteristics "may be timeless and transcend[21] culture." In other words, the faces favoured by the ancient Greeks and Egyptians remain today what people worldwide still consider beautiful, a fact, she added, that helps to keep cosmetics companies and plastic surgeons in business.

After You Read

Identify the circled reference words.

COMPREHENSION QUESTIONS

1. Research shows that men are generally attracted to women whose faces reflect youth and good health. What explanation is given in the reading for this tendency?

___

___

2. What are two things researchers have discovered about notions of attractiveness?

___

___

3. What did Dr. David Perrett and his team discover as a result of their study?

___

___

4. To most people, an "average" face is ______________ and ______________.

5. According to Dr. Perrett, "attractive facial features may signal" ______________ and ______________.

6. Which groups of people did Dr. Perrett study?

___

7. What has Dr. Judith Langlois concluded from her work?

___

___

TAKING NOTES: SUMMARIZING AND PARAPHRASING

On a separate sheet of paper, take notes for Reading Four.

What did you learn from the reading? Write a one-paragraph summary in your own words, not more than 75 words long.

Now compare your notes for Reading Four with the ones you took for the previous reading in this chapter. What connections can you see?

Vocabulary

KEYWORDS

1. egalitarians ¶1
2. strongly ¶1
3. influenced ¶1
4. milleniums ¶2
5. associated*¶2
6. conclude* ¶3
7. clearly ¶4
8. innate ¶4
9. commentary ¶4
10. rank ¶5
11. deviated ¶5
12. average ¶5
13. inadequate ¶6
14. images ¶8
15. initially ¶8
16. highly ¶8
17. appealing ¶9
18. caricature ¶10
19. fertility ¶11
20. current ¶14
21. transcend ¶15

KEYWORD EXERCISE

1. ***EXAMPLE:*** *Egalitarians* are idealists.

   Egalitarians believe that all people are ___ and that all people should have ___.

   (Consult your dictionary for your answer.)

2. ***EXAMPLE:*** Teenagers are easily *influenced* by their peers.

   What *influence* do these people have on you? (a lot; some; none at all)

   parents ___

   friends ___

   teachers ___

schoolmates ______________________________

celebrities ______________________________

3. ***EXAMPLE:*** I *strongly* suggest that you review the lesson.

Rephrase the sentence in the example.

____

4. ***EXAMPLE:*** Parents like to tell their kids not to *associate* with troublemakers at school.

According to your dictionary, what other word can you use for the verb *associate?* ______________________________

5. ***EXAMPLE:*** The awesome vista of the Canadian Rockies has not changed for *millenniums*.

How many years are there in a

millennium? ______________

century? ______________

score? ______________

decade? ______________

6. ***EXAMPLE:*** How are you planning to *conclude* your speech?

A synonym for *conclude* is ______________________

An antonym for *conclude* is ______________________

7. ***EXAMPLE:*** Many people believe that intelligence is *innate.*

Finish the sentence:

Beethoven had an innate talent for ______________.

8. ***EXAMPLE:*** We usually listen to Andy Rooney's *commentaries* on the TV program *60 Minutes.*

My favourite TV *commentator* is ______________________.

My favourite radio *commentator* is ______________________.

9. ***EXAMPLE:*** Summer is *clearly* the best season of the year.

Finish the sentences:

Clearly ____.

Jack is clearly ______________________________________.

10. ***EXAMPLE:*** The *average* grade in my English class was very low.

Calculate the *average* age of the students in this class.

Average age: ____________

11. *EXAMPLE:* I was *ranked* first in my senior class.

Rank the following items from 1 to 5 in order of importance to you. (1 = least important; 5 = most important)

___family ___money ___friends ___education ___job

12. *EXAMPLE:* Jenny has not *deviated* from her position that abortion is a criminal act.

What does this sentence tell you about Jenny? ________________________

____

13. *EXAMPLE:* Many students eat *inadequate* meals.

What does the prefix *in-* tell you about the meaning of the word *inadequate*?

____

14. *EXAMPLE:* According to Dr. Etcoff, some qualities of beauty *transcend* time and culture.

What does this sentence mean? __________________________________

____

Matching:

_____	**1.** *images*	**a.** antonym: sterility
_____	**2.** *initially*	**b.** exaggerated drawing of someone
_____	**3.** *highly*	**c.** at the beginning
_____	**4.** *appealing*	**d.** appearances
_____	**5.** *caricature*	**e.** at present
_____	**6.** *fertility*	**f.** very
_____	**7.** *current*	**g.** attractive

REVIEW

Now that you've studied the vocabulary, reread or reskim the passage.

Writing a Longer Paper: A Cultural Survey

Imagine that the editor of your school paper has asked you to write a short report on what people really mean or understand by the word *beautiful*. The editor thinks that it would be interesting for you to compare the opinions and ideas of people of different ages and cultural backgrounds. You have read all the reading passages in this chapter, have taken notes, and have summarized most of the passages in your own words. At the beginning of the chapter, you shared your ideas on the topic of beauty with some members of the class. You are well-equipped to handle this assignment.

Start by rereading the freewrite you did at the beginning of this chapter. Go over any notes you might have made from your group discussion on the criteria of beauty. Review the information in your *This Is Beautiful!* chart. You might want to use the same chart for your survey. For your report, you will need to survey many more people than you did earlier in this chapter. You might ask your friends at school or from your neighbourhood, the students in your other classes, or your relatives to help you with this project.

After you have collected, organized, and studied your data, freewrite for about 15 minutes. Who participated in your study? What were their ages? What were their cultural backgrounds? What criteria for beauty did they use? What conclusions can you make?

Now review your notes and summaries (not the reading passages). Highlight the information that supports your conclusions.

How shall you organize your paper? Make a list of what you want to say first, then second, and so on—these are your main points. Then add the details that support each point. You can plan your paper any way you like: in a formal outline or an informal graphic presentation (similar to the format of your notes).

Now you're ready to write your first draft. Concentrate on clear content and organization. Don't worry about grammar and vocabulary at this point. Just try to get your ideas across. When you finish, exchange papers with a classmate and tell each other if your ideas are clear and well developed.

In your second draft, focus on grammar and vocabulary. What are your common problems in these areas? Try to find them and correct them. Use your dictionary. When you finish, work with a partner again—preferably not someone who speaks your native language, because you might miss each other's mistakes.

Finally, look for places where you have copied exact words from passages in this chapter. Change them as much as possible. If you cannot change them, you are permitted to use them if you put quotation marks around them—but don't put more than five *brief* quotations in your paper, and when you do, you must identify the original writer.

When you are satisfied that your report is as good as you can make it, give it to your teacher.

LEARNING STRATEGY

Personalizing: Find reading material in English that fits your personal interests to make reading in English easier and more enjoyable.

Evaluating Learning Strategies

Look back over the learning strategies in this chapter. Were there any that weren't especially helpful for you? What wasn't helpful about them? Which ones did you find helpful? Think about times and ways that you can keep using them in your future reading.

Evaluating Your Learning

	Very little	*Quite a bit*	*A lot*
Your vocabulary is larger.	______	______	______
You can comprehend unsimplified readings.	______	______	______
You can take good notes from your reading.	______	______	______
You write better than you used to.	______	______	______
You learned something about the different notions of beauty.	______	______	______

KEYWORDS FOR CHAPTER 7: SHAPES AND SIZES

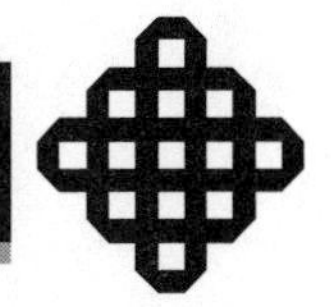

Verbs
accentuate
associate
blame
conclude
deviate
enshrine
influence
link
preen
rank
reinforce
require
transcend

Adverbs
clearly
extremely
highly
initially
strongly

Nouns
augmentation
caricature
commentary
cluster
depreciation
egalitarian
factor
feminist
fertility
images
implant
millenium
plumpness
prediction
self-esteem
self-oppression
social censure
stereotype
thesis
throes

Prepositional Phrase
at a glance

Adjectives
adolescent
anthropological
appealing
average
biological
current
ecological
hypocritical
inadequate
inferior
innate
integral
manipulative
obsessive
pervasive
preliminary
prominent
trivial
voluptuous

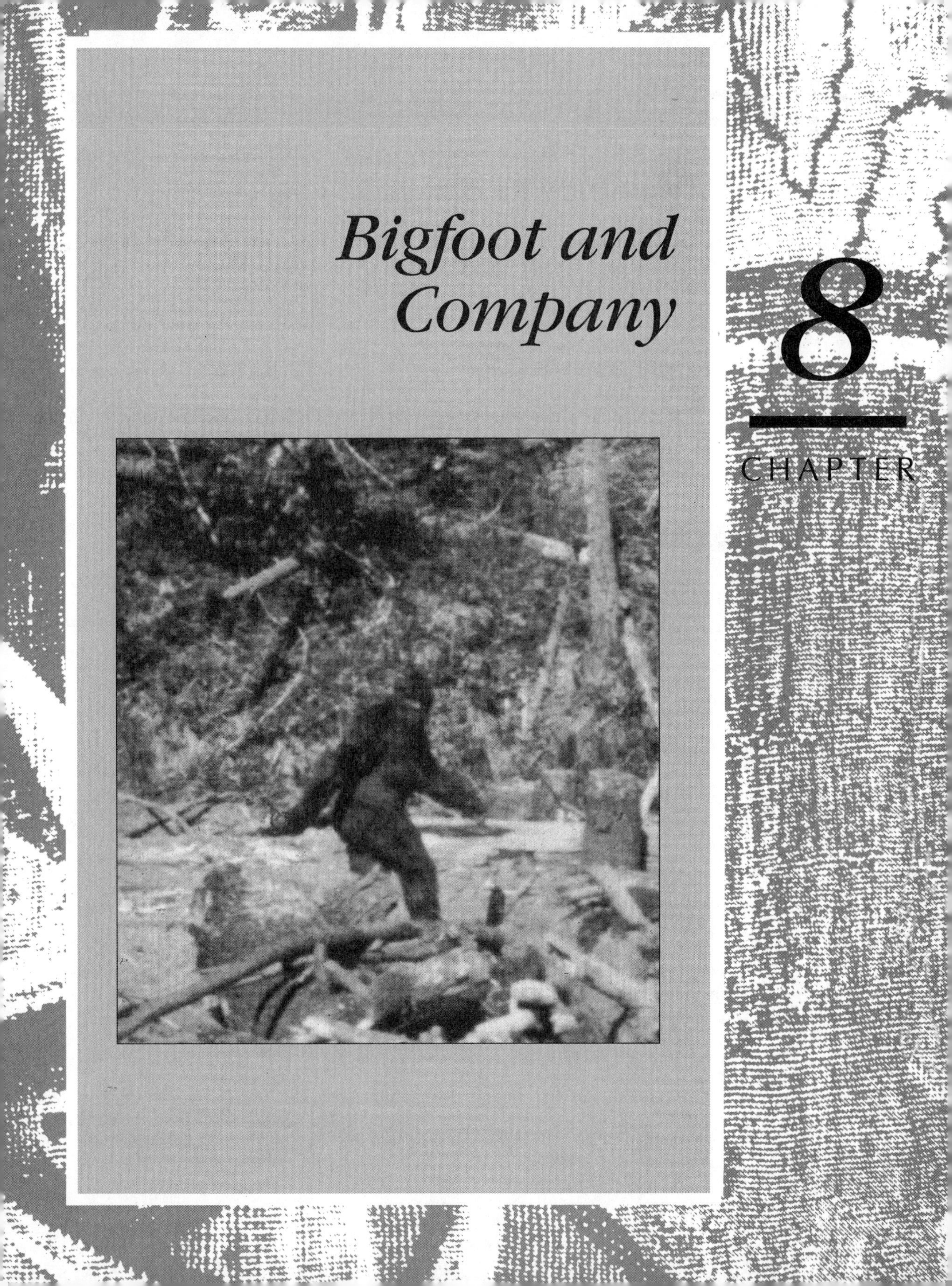

Bigfoot and Company

8

CHAPTER

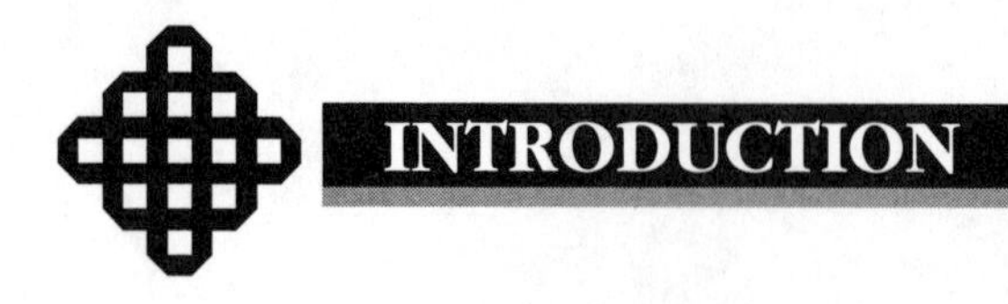

INTRODUCTION

PLANNING YOUR LEARNING

Review your overall goal statement. How much progress did you make toward it in the last chapter? Do you want to change it? Think about how you can work to meet your goal as you study this new chapter.

- How many words do you want to learn? (minimum 54, the number of keywords in the chapter)
- What grade would you like to make on the vocabulary section of the exam at the end of the chapter?
- What grade would you like to make on the reading comprehension section of the exam?
- What are you going to read outside of class?

LEARNING STRATEGY

Understanding and Using Emotions: Regular exercise, a healthy diet, and good rest periods improve your language learning ability.

PREVIEWING THE CHAPTER

- Think about the title of this chapter. What do you think "Bigfoot" refers to?
- Look through the chapter at the pictures and the map. What are some things you're curious about?
- What do you expect to find out?

PREVIEW ACTIVITY

For this activity you'll need a tape measure in centimetres and a scale that measures in kilograms. Take the following measurements of yourself:

- Your weight in kilograms: ______________________
- Your height in centimetres: ______________________
- Your foot length in centimetres: ______________________
- Your stride (the distance of one normal footstep): ______________________

PREPARING TO READ: CONTENT

From around the world come reports of peculiar animals that most people don't believe in because they have never seen them and because no one has ever captured one to show to the public. One of the most famous examples is the Loch Ness monster of Scotland. Can you name any others? If so, where do they live? Are there any in your home country?

Can you name such an animal that is reported to live in North America? Where does it live—if it really exists?

Cultural Survey: What Is "Bigfoot"?

Over the next week, interview several North Americans and ask them what they can tell you about "Bigfoot" or "Sasquatch." Find three people who can tell you something they've heard about it. Do they believe in it? Why or why not? Do they know any stories about it?

In about a week, you'll be asked to tell your classmates what you've learned from your survey and to write a brief summary of your findings.

PREPARING TO READ: VOCABULARY

Working alone or with a partner, write all the English words you know that are related to the following concepts. Feel free to use your dictionary and to ask your teacher questions. Try to think of three words for each.

animal ________ ________ ________

find ________ ________ ________

dangerous ________ ________ ________

proof ________ ________ ________

surprise ________ ________ ________

fear ________ ________ ________

not believe ________ ________ ________

false ________ ________ ________

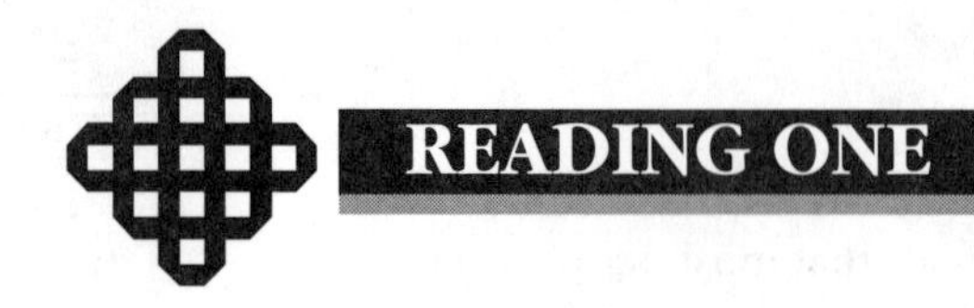

READING ONE

Reading process: Scan the passage for the following information. Your teacher will give you a time limit.

1. What drew the Sasquatch to the men working at the oil well?

___

2. How did the four men describe the Sasquatch?

Height? ___

Weight? ___

General features? ___

3. What other evidence was there to suggest the size of the Sasquatch?

___

4. How did the men describe its movements?

___

After you finish scanning and comparing your answers, read the passage carefully.

SASQUATCH WATCH: SIGHTINGS CLAIM SPARKS BIG DEAL OVER BIGFOOT

Category

1 The claim of a recent sighting of a large, hairy, human-like creature near Tumbler Ridge in Calgary, Alberta, has rekindled[1] fascination with the Sasquatch.

2 Since four Alberta men working at an oil well said they spotted the creature ... they've been deluged with phone calls from the curious and with requests for media interviews. Intrigued Sasquatch-followers have traced the men's steps to examine the evidence.

3 Myles Jack, 30, guessed the Sasquatch—if that's what it was— was drawn by[2] the noise of the machinery. "We were making so much noise out in the middle of nowhere," Jack said. "The thing was very curious to check us out."

It Moved Upright

4 He said he spotted the huge beast about 1 a.m. on March 14. It was watching the men from about 30 metres away. Jack estimated it stood about 2.5 metres [7 to 8 feet] tall and weighed about 150 kilograms [about 350 pounds]. "It was so much larger than an ordinary man. It sort of spooked us a bit."

5 He said the creature then ran across the road and through the bush, moving upright like a human with an extremely[3] long gait. He spotted the Sasquatch another four times during the next half hour. "Every time this thing saw us looking at it, it ran off. This thing could motor real good. He could move as quick as a deer." Jack said the experience was frightening. "We were hoping this thing wouldn't come out and try to attack us. It sent a chill up my spine."

6 Cochrane resident Danny Crowe, 27, said he first glimpsed the creature when his truck's headlights illuminated a stand of trees. "I just couldn't believe what I had seen. My first instinct was that it was a bear. Then again, I've never seen a Sasquatch."

7 When the men returned to the remote site the next day, oversized[4] tracks in the snow lent credibility to their story ... "From the description and the pictures, each leg was about a foot wide. The knees measured about three feet apart. A human can't get his knees three feet apart no matter how big [he is]," said Sasquatch-follower and reporter John Green ...

8 There have been about 3000 reported sightings of the beast along the western coasts of Canada and the United States and most accounts are remarkably similar, said University of Calgary archeology professor Vladimir Markotic, who has been gathering material on Sasquatches for years.

Evolved Separately

9 Wild exaggerations aside, the creatures apparently[5] stand more than 180 centimetres (6 feet) tall, weigh about 160 kilograms (350 pounds), and walk on two feet. They have round eyes and hairless faces and hands. What separates the Sasquatch so markedly from the ape is that its arms do not hang below its knees and they have even teeth whereas apes have huge canines.

10 Markotic said the Sasquatch probably results from some division in the hominid (humanlike) line that evolved separately to humans. He speculates Sasquatches are "more intelligent than apes ... and apes can be very intelligent. It's not surprising they avoid humans. If it exists, then it is a very, very important biological and anthropological discovery," Markotic said. "If it does not exist, then it's a very important part of Canadian folklore."

11 Plenty of people have tried to manufacture evidence of the Sasquatch's existence and Markotic's files are crammed with photographs of men in apelike suits posing as Sasquatches. But some evidence is more trustworthy, in particular 22 seconds of film shot by American Roger Paterson in northern California in 1967. "I knew Paterson. He was a highly intelligent man, and if he wanted to falsify it, he probably would have done better than 22 seconds," Markotic said.

12 In the film, the Sasquatch, which appears to be female, turns and looks briefly at the camera before walking calmly away. "If you want to falsify it, you could easily make a half-hour movie," Markotic said ...

"I Saw Those Tracks"

13 Markotic told of an anthropologist who while visiting California saw close to 1000 unexplainable[6] tracks. "So I asked him, 'What do you say?' And he told me, 'As an anthropologist, I know such things do not exist and cannot exist. But I saw those tracks, and I don't want to hear anything more about the whole thing.'"

14 Meanwhile, Jack said he has met with a lot of scepticism[7] in telling the story. "People agree, but don't quite believe you. But I know I saw something and so did three others." He said that prior to March 14, he would have told anyone

who had suggested there was such a thing as a Sasquatch that they were crazy. But now, he said, he is convinced the Sasquatch exists.

After You Read

COMPREHENSION QUESTIONS

1. What kind of passage is this?
   - encyclopedia entry
   - tabloid article
   - newspaper article
   - transcription of a personal, taped account
   - written report about someone else's experience

   Write the category under the title.
2. What do you think a Sasquatch is? Talk it over with a partner. Write a one- or two-sentence explanation.

   ____
3. What does archaeology professor Vladimir Markotic think a Sasquatch is?

   ____
4. Is Bigfoot another name for the Sasquatch? What clue are you given in the reading?

   ____

TRUE–FALSE QUESTIONS

			¶ number
1. According to the passage, there have been numerous reported Sasquatch sightings throughout Canada and the United States.	T	F	________
2. The Sasquatch is thought to be as intelligent as an ape.	T	F	________
3. From the description and the pictures, the creature appeared to be much larger than humans.	T	F	________
4. According to eyewitnesses, the creature was very swift and agile.	T	F	________
5. All the reports of the Sasquatch's existence are true.	T	F	________
6. The four Alberta oil men remained skeptical about the Sasquatch's existence.	T	F	________

Beginning a Chart of Information

Begin a chart of information about Bigfoot. Turn a piece of paper sideways, horizontally. Down the left side, from top to bottom, list the readings in this chapter: Readings One through Seven. Across the top from left to right, write categories of information about Bigfoot: Size, Colour, Features, Footprints, Method of Movement, Voice, Personality, Food, Habitat, Behaviour, Evidence, Human Reactions To, and Life Span.

Fill in the information that is contained in this article. Summarize it as briefly as you can. If there is no information for a particular category, just leave it blank. When you finish, compare your chart with a classmate's. (At the end of this chapter you may use the collected information on your chart to write a "profile" of Bigfoot.)

Freewriting: Can This Be True?

Do you believe this story? Do you think the author believes it? How could you find out if it is true?

Vocabulary

VOCABULARY IN CONTEXT

Look up the meaning of the word *spook* in your dictionary. Now look at how it is used in ¶4. Jack, describing the Sasquatch, said, "It was so much larger than an ordinary man. *It sort of spooked us a bit.*" What do you think the italicized sentence means?

KEYWORDS

1. rekindled ¶1
2. drawn by ¶3
3. extremely ¶5
4. oversized ¶7
5. apparently ¶9
6. unexplainable ¶13
7. scepticism ¶14

KEYWORD EXERCISE

1. ***EXAMPLE:*** Interest in the Sasquatch has been *rekindled* by recent sightings of the creature.

   Break the word *rekindled* down into its parts and define them.

____

____

____

What part of speech is it? ____________________

What's the connection between the meanings of the parts and the meaning of the whole word?

____

2. *EXAMPLE:* The Sasquatch was *drawn by* the noise of the machinery.

   In the context of this sentence, which of the following meanings of *drawn* is most appropriate?

   extracted attracted pulled inhaled stretched out

   ____

3. What part of speech is *extremely?* ____________________

   What does "extremely long gait" tell you about the Sasquatch?

   ____

   ____

   EXAMPLE: The Sasquatch moved with an *extremely* long gait.

4. Name three different things that you can describe as being *oversized.*

   a. ____________ **b.** ____________

   c. ____________

   EXAMPLE: The Sasquatch left *oversized* tracks in the snow.

5. *Apparently* is the adverb form of the verb *appear.* From the list below, circle the synonyms for *apparently* and underline the antonyms.

   dubiously evidently obviously ambiguously clearly

   EXAMPLE: The Sasquatch is *apparently* more intelligent than an ape.

6. Break the word *unexplainable* down into parts and define them.

   ____

   ____

   ____

   Now put all the parts together and answer this question: when something is *unexplainable,* that means

   ____

   What part of speech is it? ____________________

EXAMPLE: There are many *unexplainable* phenomena in the universe.

7. Can you think of one reason why many people listened to Jack's story with obvious *scepticism*?

____

Do you consider yourself a *sceptic*?

____

EXAMPLE: The police listened to his story about alien spaceships with *scepticism*.

REVIEW

Now that you have studied the vocabulary, reread or reskim the passage.

READING TWO

As you read the two passages below, try to decide whether the authors want you to believe in or to doubt the existence of Bigfoot. At the end of each reading you'll be asked how the author's use of language makes you believe or doubt.

BIGFOOT

Category

1 Bigfoot is a humanlike creature said to live in the Pacific Northwest. Bigfoot has been reported most often in the mountains of California, Oregon, Washington, and British Columbia. Canadians call it *Sasquatch*. Bigfoot stories resemble those about the Abominable Snowman, a hairy beast said to live in the Himalaya and other mountainous areas of central and northeastern Asia ...

2 Hundreds of people have reported seeing the bigfoot or its footprints. They describe the creature as standing from 2 to 3 metres (7 to 10 feet) tall and weighing more than 230 kilograms (500 pounds). Like an ape, it has thick fur, long arms, powerful shoulders, and a short neck. It supposedly[1] walks like a human being and leaves footprints that measure about 41 centimetres long (16 inches) and about 15 centimetres (6 inches) wide.

3 The evidence for the bigfoot's existence has so far not been sufficient[2] to convince most scientists. Many believe that some evidence, which includes footprints and photographs, has been faked.

Threads

There have been many reports of Yeti-like creatures in China, especially in Shennongjia area.

READING THREE

BIGFOOT

Category: ______________________________

1 Bigfoot is an apelike creature believed by some persons to exist in certain areas of the United States and Canada. It has been called *Sasquatch* by Canadian Indian tribes. Stories about it resemble those of the Abominable Snowman, or Yeti, of Asia.

2 Hundreds of persons since 1840 have reported sighting such a creature in wooded areas of the Pacific Northwest, California, New Jersey, Pennsylvania, Ohio, Illinois, and British Columbia, and one photographer took a brief movie sequence supposedly showing Bigfoot in northern California in 1967. Tracks measuring up to more than 43 centimetres [17 inches] long and 18 centimetres [7 inches] wide, and attributed to[3] Bigfoot, have also been found. However, no specimen[4] has ever been captured or photographed clearly.

3 Bigfoot is generally described as a primate resembling a man or ape 1.8 to 2.4 metres [6 to 8 feet] tall, standing erect[5] on two feet, with massive shoulders and a body covered with grey, black, or brown hair. It flees when approached, and generally makes no sound. Although most scientists do not recognize its existence, a few believe that it may be the descendant[6] of an extinct apelike creature, Gigantopithecus, that may have crossed the Bering land bridge from Asia to North America in prehistoric times. Indians of the Pacific Northwest and western Canada for generations have perpetuated legends[7] about Sasquatch and similar creatures with other names.

Threads

Gigantophithecus walked the earth from nine million to one million years ago, and was reportedly the largest primate that ever existed, at 3.3 metres [10 feet] tall.

After You Read

COMPREHENSION QUESTIONS

1. Under the title, write the category of these passages (they're both the same):
- ✓ encyclopedia entry
- tabloid article
- newspaper article
- transcription of a personal, taped account
- written report about someone else's experience

X **2.** In Reading Two, Bigfoot is described as a *humanlike* creature but as *apelike* in Reading Three. Look at Reading One. How is Bigfoot described? Which description is correct? ______________________________

x chart

✓ **3.** Did the authors present this information in a way that makes you believe in the existence of Bigfoot, or doubt it? How did their choice of words and their grammar tell you their position on this issue?

____

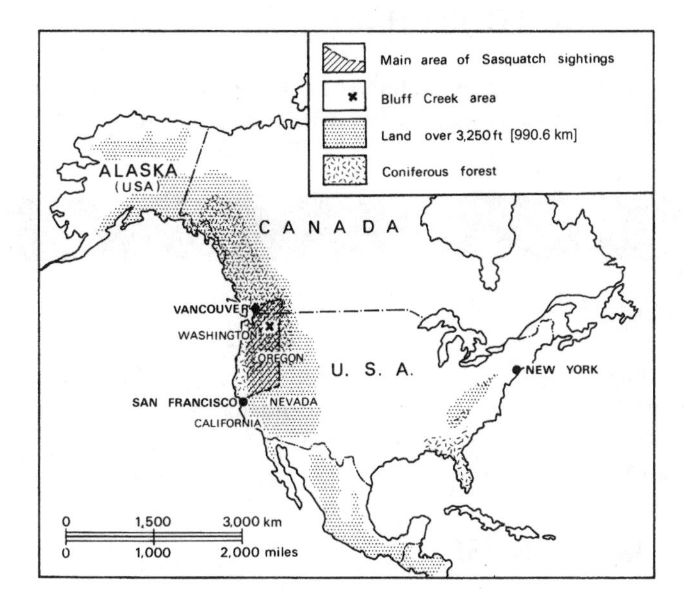

IN WHICH PARAGRAPH CAN YOU FIND ...

Question	*Reading Two*	*Reading Three*
1. Names for this animal	________	________
2. Comparison with the "Abominable Snowman"	________	________
3. Habits	________	________
4. Size	________	________
5. Habitat (location)	________	________
6. Evidence	________	________

TRUE–FALSE QUESTIONS

			Reading and ¶ number
1. Bigfoot supposedly lives in South America.	T	F	________
2. The Abominable Snowman is also known as the Yeti.	T	F	________
3. Most scientists doubt that Bigfoot really exists.	T	F	________
4. Bigfoot looks similar to an ape.	T	F	________
5. Sasquatch is another name for Bigfoot.	T	F	________

Threads

From southwestern Mongolia come reports of humanoid creatures who are called *Almas.* They are supposedly about the same height as the local humans and are often seen in family groups.

CONTINUING YOUR CHART

Continue your Bigfoot chart by adding the information contained in these two readings. When you finish, compare your work with a classmate's.

Vocabulary

KEYWORDS

1. supposedly ¶2
2. sufficient* ¶3
3. attributed to ¶2
4. specimen ¶2
5. erect ¶3
6. descendant ¶3
7. legend ¶3

KEYWORD EXERCISE

1. Compare the following two sentences:
   - The movie sequence *supposedly* shows Bigfoot in the Pacific Northwest.
   - The movie sequence shows Bigfoot in the Pacific Northwest.

   What's the difference in meaning? ______________________________

   What does the word *supposedly* contribute to the meaning of a sentence?

   ____

2. Think of the number of levels in the English program where you're now studying. In your opinion, what level of English is *sufficient* to prepare you for success in a college or university program? ______________________________

   Do your classmates and your teacher agree with you? ______________________________

   EXAMPLE: The evidence has not been *sufficient* to convince most scientists that Bigfoot exists.

3. ***EXAMPLE:*** Those large tracks were *attributed to* Bigfoot.

   Finish the sentences:
   The great amount of damage was *attributed* to ______________________________.
   Her success in the business world ______________________________.

4. Which of the following words is not a synonym for *specimen*?
   example factor case illustration instance sample

   EXAMPLE: No *specimen* has ever been captured or photographed clearly.

5. ***EXAMPLE:*** Bigfoot stands *erect* on two feet.

   What part of speech is this word? ______________________________

You'll find more than one meaning for *erect* in your dictionary. Which of the following sentences contains the same meaning as the sentence in the reading?

- We decided to erect a greenhouse in the garden behind our home.
- The soldiers stood erect as the general reviewed them.

6. Which of the following family terms are used to identify direct *descendants*?

   grandmother granddaughter nephew son cousin

   EXAMPLE: Bigfoot may be the *descendant* of Gigantopithecus, an extinct apelike creature.

7. Who is the original author of a *legend?* How old are *legends?*

   ____

   How did people originally learn about them—by reading them, or by hearing them? ______________________________

   Do you know many *legends* from your own culture? ______________

   EXAMPLE: There are many Native North American *legends* about Sasquatch.

REVIEW

Now that you have studied the vocabulary, reread or reskim the passage.

LEARNING STRATEGY

Managing Your Learning: Before an exam, make a schedule to review the material every day for a week.

READING FOUR

Reading process: Before you read the passage, scan it for information to add to your chart. Your teacher will give you a time limit. Then when you read carefully, you can make any necessary corrections.

[TITLE] ______________________________

Category: ______________________________

1 Man or beast, or both? Whatever it was that sent John Bringsli of Nelson fleeing[1] in blind panic[2] from the head of Lemmon Creek, hurling his huckleberry pail into the bush and racing for home in his early-model car, it had

Sasquatch footprint

pulled a speedy disappearing act by the time he and a group of hunters returned to the scene.[3] Mr. Bringsli, woodsman, hunter, and fisherman in the Kootenay district for more than 35 years, swore on his reputation as an outdoorsman that it was "definitely[4] not a bear."

2 In an interview, Mr. Bringsli related[5] his experience with an "unknown creature" seen while on a huckleberry picking expedition alone near Six-Mile, and unashamedly told of his frantic race over 100 yards [91 metres] of stunted bush and dwarfed underbrush to his car. "I had just stopped my 1931 coupe on a deserted logging road a couple of weekends ago and walked about 100 yards [91 metres] into the bush. I was picking huckleberries. I had just started to pick berries and was moving slowly through the bush. I had only been there about 15 minutes. For no particular reason, I glanced up and that's when I saw this great beast. It was standing about 50 feet [15 metres] away on a slight[6] rise in the ground, staring[7] at me. The sight of this animal paralyzed[8] me. It was seven to nine feet [2 to 3 metres] tall with long legs and short, powerful arms, with hair covering its body. The first thing I thought was, 'What a strange-looking bear.' It had very wide shoulders, and a flat face with ears flat against the side of its head. It looked more like a big hairy ape. It just stood there staring at me. Arms of the animal were bent slightly[6] and most astounding was that it had hands, not claws. It was about 8 A.M. and I could see it clearly," Mr. Bringsli said. "The most peculiar[9] thing about it was the strange bluish-grey tinge of colour of its long hair. It had no neck. Its apelike head appeared to be fastened[10] directly to its wide shoulders."

Threads

More than 1000 Sasquatch sightings have been reported in the Pacific Northwest of North America.

3 Mr. Bringsli stood with mouth agape staring at the thing for about two minutes. Then it began to slowly walk, or rather shuffle, towards the paralysed huckleberry hunter. It was then that Mr. Bringsli decided it was time for him to find another berry-picking location. He sprinted the 100 yards [91 metres] to the car and drove recklessly[11] down the old logging road and home.

4 Mr. Bringsli returned to the scene next day with a group of friends armed with high-powered rifles and cameras but the strange beast did not reappear. They did find one track nearby. It was from 16 to 17 [41 to 43 centimetres] inches long. There were no claw marks but rather a "sharp toe" print as described by Mr. Bringsli.

> "They were beautiful," says Bond. "I remember them that way even though I had only a short glimpse of them before I started running away. No one should harm them; try to shoot them, or anything like that," he continued. "They made no move as if to harm me. I was simply startled and frightened."
>
> —*from a Bigfoot report*

Threads

No report has ever described Sasquatch as walking on all fours, as gorillas and chimps often do.

After You Read

Identify the circled reference word.

COMPREHENSION QUESTIONS

1. Write a good title for the passage.
2. Categorize the passage:
   - encyclopedia entry
   - tabloid article
   - newspaper article
   - transcription of a personal, taped account
   - written report about someone else's experience
3. What animal did Mr. Bringsli think the creature was at first? ______________________
4. What did the creature do? ______________________
5. What evidence was Mr. Bringsli able to show to his friends? ______________________
6. In your own words, summarize Mr. Bringsli's reaction to the creature. ______________________

TRUE–FALSE QUESTIONS

			¶ number
1. It was evening when this event happened, so the light was poor.	T	F	______
2. The Sasquatch had blue-grey fur.	T	F	______
3. It had a long, apelike neck.	T	F	______
4. It approached Mr. Bringsli.	T	F	______
5. The only evidence the next day was a single footprint.	T	F	______

CONTINUE YOUR CHART

Continue your Bigfoot chart by adding the information contained in this reading.

Vocabulary

VOCABULARY IN CONTEXT

1. Find the phrase *1931 coupe* in ¶2. What do you think this means? What clues in nearby sentences make you think so?
2. Find the verb *sprinted* in ¶3. What do you think it means? What clues make you think so?

KEYWORDS

1. flee ¶1
2. panic ¶1
3. scene ¶1
4. definitely* ¶1
5. relate (tell) ¶2
6. slight, slightly* ¶2
7. stare ¶2
8. paralyze ¶2
9. peculiar ¶2
10. fasten ¶2
11. recklessly ¶3

KEYWORD EXERCISE

1. Which of the following animals are most likely to *flee* from danger?
   a rabbit an elephant a cat a rhinoceros a leopard

   Grammar note: This verb is irregular: *flee, fled, fled*

   EXAMPLE: The Sasquatch sent Mr. Bringsli *fleeing* back to his car.

2. Which of the following are elements of *panic*?
   sudden anger a very strong feeling fear
   acting without thinking carefully

   EXAMPLE: Mr. Bringsli fled from the creature in blind *panic.*

3. ***EXAMPLE:*** Bringsli returned to the *scene* the next day with some of his friends.

   What part of speech is this word? ________________________________

   Which two of the following words are synonyms for it?
   victim resource attitude place location

4. Which of the following words is the weakest, and which is the strongest?
   definitely possibly probably maybe surely

   EXAMPLE: Bringsli said the creature was "*definitely* not a bear."

NOTE: *Definitely* is not the antonym for *indefinitely*. Review the definitions of the two words, and explain the difference to a classmate.

5. ***EXAMPLE:*** Mr. Bringsli *related* his experience to a newspaper reporter.

You'll find more than one meaning for this verb in your dictionary. Which of the following sentences contains the same meaning as the sentence in the reading?
- The sailor *related* his adventure to everyone in the bar.
- Children need to learn to *relate* properly to other family members.

6. Rank the following words and phrases from least to most.

somewhat a great deal quite a bit totally *slightly*

EXAMPLE: The animal's arms were bent *slightly.*

7. In your culture, is it considered rude to *stare* at a person who looks different from other people—for example a foreigner, a very old person, a very overweight person, a person in a wheelchair? ______________________

EXAMPLE: It just stood there *staring* at me.

8. What can't a *paralyzed* person do? ______________________

Name three things that can *paralyze* a person.

a. ______________________

b. ______________________

c. ______________________

EXAMPLE: At first Bringsli was *paralyzed* by the sight of the creature; then he turned and fled.

9. Why did Mr. Bringsli think the beast's colour was *peculiar?*

____

What would have been a less *peculiar* colour? ______________________

10. What is used to *fasten* the front of a shirt? ______________________

What is used to *fasten* a shoe? ______________________

What is used to *fasten* a door? ______________________

EXAMPLE: Its apelike head appeared to be *fastened* directly to its shoulders.

11. Mr. Bringsli drove *recklessly* down the old logging road and home. How would he have driven if he had driven in the opposite manner?

____

REVIEW

Now that you've studied the vocabulary, reread or reskim the passage.

Discussion and Freewriting: Report on Cultural Survey

Tell a small group of your classmates what you learned from three North Americans in the cultural survey that you took (from page 215). Then freewrite a brief summary of your findings.

LEARNING STRATEGY

Managing Your Learning: Control your time wisely by working on your most important tasks first.

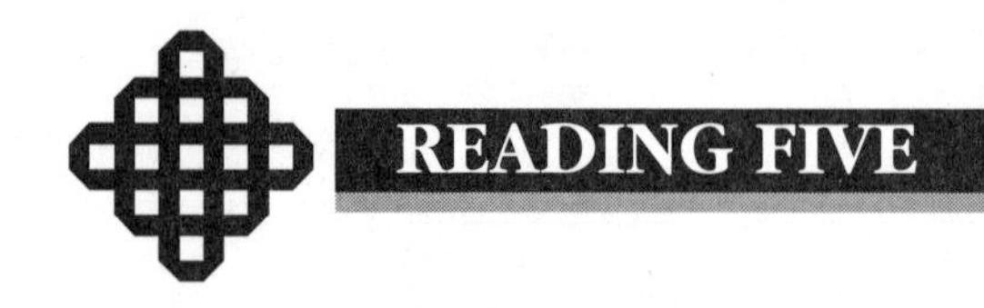

READING FIVE

Reading Process: You may find the following reading rather difficult. Focus on what you can comprehend, not on what you can't. First skim the passage; then go back through and highlight everything you can understand; then reread the highlighted parts from start to finish. How well do you understand the general idea? Use your dictionary only for the parts where you are totally lost, and then only if you think those words are really important to a comprehension of the whole.

MONSTERS OF THE WEST ...

[TITLE] ____

1 Monsters of one form or another seem to have titillated the human imagination[1] for untold years. Throughout recorded history, people have included super- or subhuman beings, giants, ogres, dragons, fanciful beasts of many descriptions, and frightening figures in widely variant forms among their cultural traditions. That all such people fervently believe in the literal[2] truth of these monsters certainly is open to dispute, but the fact that they told stories about such creatures definitely is not ...

2 It is, therefore, not at all unexpected that Canadians should have monster traditions,[3] as indeed they have had and still do. The "loup-garou," or werewolf, was a rather common figure in French-Canadian folklore; the bogey man in many forms has been and still is used to control Canadian children; some Newfoundlanders still believe in fairies of evil temperament; and Native peoples

once entertained various levels of beliefs in monsters such as Sedna, the hag whom the Inuit thought lived under the sea, and D'Sonoqua, the cannibal woman of the Pacific Northwest Coast ...

3 Sasquatch, a wild apeman of the woods, and Ogopogo, a lake serpent, are most commonly associated with British Columbia. There have, however, been accounts of them, or like forms, elsewhere in Canada and in the United States ... Sasquatch, in particular, is known in Washington, Oregon, and California, where he is commonly referred to as "Bigfoot" ...

4 More than three hundred eyewitness reports of Sasquatch/Bigfoot from Canada and the United States, as well as many other accounts, make it possible to create a composite[4] description of the creature. Accordingly,[5] Sasquatch (whose name is an anglicization of a Coast Salish word meaning roughly "wild man of the woods") is between 6 and 11 feet [1.8 and 3.4 metres], though most commonly 7 or 8 feet [2.1 or 2.4 metres] tall. Typically,[6] he is covered in reddish-brown or auburn hair, though other hair colours from black to silvery-white have been reported. On his head, this hair grows to 5 or 6 inches [13 or 15 centimetres] in length and hangs in a "bang" over the forehead. Female Sasquatches (less frequently reported on than the males) have hairy breasts, except immediately around the nipples. Other sexual characteristics are seldom remarked upon. The Sasquatch has broad shoulders (up to 4 feet [1.2 metres]), a barrel-chest, and no obvious neck, resulting in his hunched appearance. His face is monkey- or apelike with a backward sloping forehead, a flattened nose, and a slitlike, lipless mouth. Often he is said to have a cone-shaped head and a very prominent big toe. His footprints are between 12 and 22 inches [30 and 56 centimetres], though most commonly 14 to 18 inches [36 to 46 centimetres], long and usually seven inches [18 centimetres] wide. The Sasquatch has seldom been known to show any aggressive[7] behaviour and has most frequently been described as fleeing or standing immobile, staring expressionless, with his arms by his sides.

After You Read

COMPREHENSION QUESTIONS

1. Write a good title for the passage.
2. List some of the creatures that form the Canadian monster tradition.

   ____

3. The passage contains a lot of specific details about what the Sasquatch looks like. Where did these details come from?

   ____

   Which sentence in the passage tells you this?

   ____

4. What little do we know about female Sasquatches?

   ____

5. Why do we have so little information about them?

____

TRUE–FALSE QUESTIONS

			¶ number
1. The Sasquatch has humanlike features.	T	F	________
2. It is very aggressive and tends to attack humans.	T	F	________
3. The eye-witnesses all agree on the detailed description of the Sasquatch.	T	F	________
4. Monsters in all their variant forms exist universally.	T	F	________

CONTINUE YOUR CHART

Continue your Bigfoot chart by adding the information contained in this reading.

VOCABULARY

KEYWORDS

1. imagination ¶1
2. literal ¶1
3. traditions ¶2
4. composite ¶4
5. accordingly ¶4
6. typically ¶4
7. aggressive ¶4

KEYWORD EXERCISE

1. Complete the following sentences using the correct form of the word *imagination* and tell how it is used in the sentence.

He has a wonderful ____________.
(Used as a ____________.)

Children often create ____________ playmates.
(Used as an ____________.)

Try to ____________ a world without sunshine.
(Used as a ____________.)

EXAMPLE: "Use your *imagination*," my mother said.

2. What is one of the most interesting traditions in your family?

____

EXAMPLE: Celebrating Thanksgiving with our neighbours is a wonderful tradition.

3. *EXAMPLE:* Do you believe in the *literal* truth of vampires?

   What is the opposite of *literal?* ____________________

4. *EXAMPLE:* After interviewing many witnesses, the police came up with a *composite* description of the murderer.

   Find the sentence in the passage in which the word *composite* appears. What do you think it means in the sentence?

   ____

   ____

5. *EXAMPLE:* He read the instructions and assembled his computer *accordingly.*

   The second sentence of ¶4 begins with the word *accordingly.* What part of speech is it? ____________________

   Can you think of three other expressions that you can use in its place?

   a. ____________ **b.** ____________ **c.** ____________

   When you use the word *accordingly,* you are saying that something happened as a result of something else.

   Now look at the second sentence of ¶4 again and fill in the missing part of this equation:

   eyewitness reports = (result?) ____________________

6. *EXAMPLE:* He *typically* acts like a spoiled brat.

   Write down three things that you consider *typically* Canadian.

   a. ____________ **b.** ____________ **c.** ____________

7. *EXAMPLE:* Rottweilers are very *aggressive* dogs.

   What part of speech is this? ____________________

   In the passage, what evidence is given to show that the Sasquatch is not *aggressive* toward humans?

   ____

REVIEW

Now that you have studied the vocabulary, reread or reskim the passage.

READING SIX

 *NOTE:* This reading is also the on the tape.

[ALTERNATIVE TITLE] ______________________
SASQUATCH

Threads

Almost no one who has gone looking for Bigfoot has seen one. It generally appears by chance.

1 Many people swear they have seen a gigantic, hairy, apelike beast known as the Sasquatch in the wilderness of British Columbia, but an old logger by the name of Albert Ostman is the only one who claims[1] to have been kidnapped by a whole family of these creatures!

2 In 1924, Albert Ostman was vacationing near the B.C. coast, far to the north of Vancouver, in a place so isolated that he had hired an old Indian guide to take him there. The Indian had warned him about the Sasquatch giants lurking about in the woods, but Ostman thought nothing of it—that is, until one night when, as he says, "Things started to happen." Something was making nightly raids on his camping provisions. Since Ostman could tell it wasn't a bear or a porcupine, he decided to stay awake[2] one night to find out what it was. He kept his rifle in his sleeping bag next to him, just in case.

3 The next thing he knew, he was awake with a start. He was being carried along inside his sleeping bag! Unable to see anything or move a muscle, he listened carefully. Whatever was carrying him breathed heavily and sometimes coughed, especially when walking uphill. After what seemed like hours, Ostman was dropped to the ground. Slowly emerging from his sleeping bag, he saw in the early morning light four creatures he knew were Sasquatches. They were like a family, chattering away—an old man, an old woman, a boy, and a girl. The two young ones seemed afraid of the stranger and the old woman didn't appear too pleased with what the old man had dragged home.

4 "What do you fellows want with me?" Ostman asked, not really expecting an answer.

5 The old man appeared to be busy explaining to his family what he had done. Ostman looked around and saw that he was in a small valley with only one small opening. He realized too that the old man—who looked almost twice his own size—had no intention of letting him go. Fortunately for Ostman, his packsack had come along for the ride so he at least had some food and supplies. The boy and the girl became curious about his belongings,[3] and rather than give them his food, Ostman let them try his snuff, which they seemed to thoroughly enjoy.

6 For two days, Ostman thought long and hard about how to escape. Though he had his rifle with him, it was doubtful whether it would do much good against such huge creatures. Besides, they weren't mistreating[4] him or giving him any reason to kill them. It wasn't until he gave the old man a sample of snuff that he saw a way out.

7 One morning, after about a week of captivity,[5] Ostman was boiling up some coffee. The old man and the boy were drawn to the smell and squatted down beside him. As Ostman pulled out his box of snuff, the old man, who had developed a real taste for it, reached out for some too. But instead of taking a pinch,[6] he grabbed the whole box and swallowed the contents in one gulp. In no time at all, the creature's eyes rolled up into his head. In desperation, he

grabbed Ostman's coffee and drank it, grounds and all. He rolled on the ground bellowing like a wounded bear and then headed for the spring to get water. Ostman reacted immediately, snatching up his belongings and running for the opening, with the old woman in quick pursuit. He fired a shot over her head, and when he looked back, there was no one in sight.

8 The next day, Ostman staggered out of the bush[7] into a logging camp. When the startled loggers asked who he was, he just pretended to be a prospector who had got lost. Ostman eventually arrived back in Vancouver, but didn't tell anybody what had happened to him until more than thirty years later, when he swore his story under oath to a magistrate.

After You Read

Identify the circled reference words.

COMPREHENSION QUESTIONS

1. Write an alternative title for the passage. ____________________
2. How did the Sasquatch kidnap Albert Ostman? ____________________
____
3. How did the Sasquatch family treat the logger? ____________________
____
4. Was Albert Ostman afraid of the Sasquatches? ____________________
5. How did he manage to escape? ____________________
____
6. Why do you think it took him so long to tell his story?
____
7. Why did he swear an oath when he told his story?
____

TRUE–FALSE QUESTIONS

			¶ number
1. Ostman had no idea that Sasquatches existed.	T	F	________
2. Some of the Sasquatches seemed frightened of him.	T	F	________
3. The creatures really enjoyed snuff.	T	F	________
4. They were planning to free Ostman eventually.	T	F	________
5. He couldn't wait to tell people about his experience.	T	F	________

IN WHICH PARAGRAPH CAN YOU FIND ...

1. A description of the Sasquatch ____________________
2. How the Sasquatch family reacted to Albert Ostman ____________________
3. When and where the kidnapping happened ____________________
4. A description of how Ostman escaped ____________________

LEARNING STRATEGY

Remembering New Material: Putting new words into meaningful sentences helps you remember them.

Vocabulary

VOCABULARY IN CONTEXT

Locate the phrase *Things started to happen*. What do you think it means? What "things" was Ostman referring to?

KEYWORDS

1. claims ¶1
2. stay awake ¶2
3. belongings ¶5
4. mistreating ¶6
5. captivity ¶7
6. pinch ¶7
7. bush ¶8

KEYWORD EXERCISE

1. *EXAMPLE:* Albert Ostman *claims* that he was kidnapped by hairy, apelike creatures.

   When someone *claims* that something happened to him or to her, is he or she telling the truth? ____________________

   Do you think that Albert Ostman was telling the truth about his kidnapping? Give a reason for your answer.

   ____

   ____

2. *EXAMPLE:* Ben plans to *stay awake* all night to study for his exam.

   In other words, Ben is ______________________________

   What other compound words can you form with the verb *stay*?

   stay ________; stay ________; stay ________; stay ________

3. What *belongings* did Ostman have with him when he was kidnapped?

   ____

   EXAMPLE: He had very few *belongings.*

4. Look up the prefix *mis-* in your dictionary. What does it mean?

   ____

   Write two synonyms for *mistreat.*

   a. ______________________ **b.** ______________________

   EXAMPLE: The police arrested him for *mistreating* his dog.

5. *EXAMPLE:* Ostman spent about a week in *captivity.*

   What part of speech is this? ______________________________

   What is the verb form of this word? ______________________________

   Underline the synonyms and circle the antonyms of captivity:

   confinement, slavery, independence, imprisonment, liberty

6. *EXAMPLE:* All you need is a *pinch* of salt in the stew.

   How much salt should you put in the stew? ______________________________

   Here are several other expressions that use the word *pinch.* Write down the meanings of each of the expressions.

   a. He *pinched* my arm. ______________________________

   b. My new shoes *pinch* me. ______________________________

   c. He is *pinched for money.* ______________________________

   d. He *pinched the grocery money.* ______________________________

   e. Ginny will babysit *at a pinch*. ______________________________

7. Reread ¶1. Can you find a synonym for *bush* in this paragraph?

   ____

   When people talk about the *bush,* what kind of place are they talking about?

   ____

   EXAMPLE: It isn't very safe to go walking in the *bush* without a guide.

REVIEW

Now that you have studied the vocabulary, reread or reskim the passage.

Threads

Some of the "evidence" and reports of Bigfoot sightings are generally believed to have been faked.

Discussion: Arguing Both Sides of an Issue

In the following activity, each of you will argue your own position on the existence of Sasquatch. You will also receive a brief reading that will give you some additional information. Read it ahead of time and paraphrase it in the discussion.

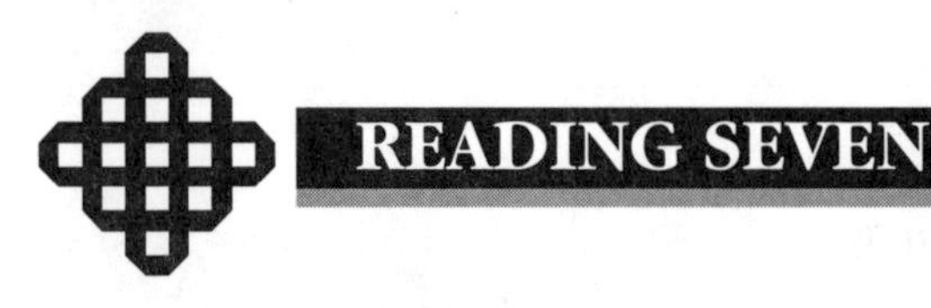

READING SEVEN

NOTE: This reading is also on the tape.

The following reading is written in conversational English. It contains some language that is a little different from "classroom" grammar and vocabulary. If you find any examples of this and want to ask your teacher about it, do so. You may also notice that the English is very informal.

Reading process: Read as far as you can in three minutes. Mark where you stop. Then start over and see if you can get farther in the next three minutes. Finally, read the whole passage.

The following story is told by a young man who was travelling with a friend when night fell. Rather than pay for a motel, they decided to camp out along a lonely forest road in their sleeping bags. Here's what happened to them after they settled down for the night:

[TITLE] ________________________________

CATEGORY: ________________________________

1 My friend started talking about different calls, you know. He said he was from Missouri, said he could make a black panther sound, like a woman's scream. So he did that, and I did a wolf call. About that time, after we completed our calls, we first noticed a big form on top of the hill ... To me it looked a good nine feet [3 metres] tall,[1] very very broad. I didn't get a good look at it ...

2 We thought we got a glimpse[2] of it coming down to the left of us and that was the last time we seen it for a while. About half an hour later it was coming

down the road. N—— shone the light on it. He started screaming "Look! Look! There it is!" and it was coming down the road and I turned around and saw it.

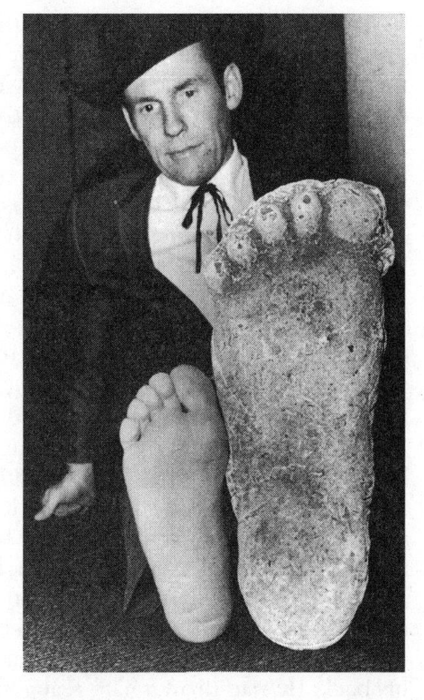

Roger Patterson comparing his foot with a plaster cast of a Bigfoot track.

3 He said he was going to stop it by blinding it in the eyes and it stopped cold and jumped behind the embankment, behind some bushes, and it looked like it was going to stalk us. We could see its hair and the outline[3] of it and the eyes. You know, like you'll shine another animal in the eyes, in the light they'll glow.[4]

4 I jumped in the car and accidentally locked the door on N—— and the thing got up and rushed us[5] and poor N—— couldn't get in because the door was locked. He started screaming and everything else so I got the door unlocked and he jumped in the car and all of a sudden that thing just hit the car and really made a ruckus.

5 It seemed to want to get in for some reason, or maybe it was trying to be friendly or curious. Whatever it was, we didn't like it. So then it went away and we decided, well, we're going to split, take off, but he couldn't find his keys. He figured he left them in the trunk. So we got out and sneak[6] around there and no keys.

6 Then we ... saw the thing so we think we better get back in the car, it would be safer'n out there, so we kept hearing this thing, kept seeing it and we decided well we've got to get out of here. We decided the keys have got to be around there, so we both got out and I took a pop bottle and I busted it as a weapon, but I busted it all to pieces so we stood there and here the thing came and we never got nothing ... had no chance of leaving 'cause we didn't have the keys and couldn't find them.

7 So the thing started rushing around ... just walking around us out of curiosity ... Well it didn't do any more damage after that, didn't attack the car and we just stayed there all night.

8 Next morning, it was about eight o'clock, we got out of the car and walked around to make sure the thing wasn't there. Actually we looked around first, we figured it wouldn't show in the daytime. We found the track, down in the cut we noticed these big tracks of this here particular thing, and they was good sized, they looked like a human's footprints.

> The most impressive thing about the big footprints is neither their size nor their shape, but the depth to which they are impressed in the ground ... False feet worn by a person would show the opposite effect, tending to sink in less than the normal amount, as with snowshoes.
>
> *—John Green, Sasquatch researcher*

9 We followed the tracks down the road for quite a ways and we lost them going into the brush. They went down towards a ravine. We could see some of the tracks and then we lost them. We searched around again for more tracks but they just all seemed to lead down that way.

10 The face was sort of a human-type face. It was pointed like on the top, it had a large pointed forehead on the top. A human's is sort of rounded off, his wasn't. It was dome[7] shaped. It wasn't really that it had a lot of hair on its face, except the side features, it had hair on that. And he had a nose. It resembled a human's nose except it was flatter and wider than a human's nose would be.

11 His mouth was somewhat like a human's except it was bare, but a larger mouth. And he had something like carnivorous teeth, like a dog's teeth, and his eyes were good sized, and like I said, they shone in the dark. Real bright, like whitish-yellow, very very glowing. He had a bull neck, didn't have an extremely long neck, in fact there wasn't hardly a neck there, it was a bull's.

12 His skin had a yellow tinge to it like it had been bleached in the sun, like leather would be, buckskin would be, sort of tanned like you get in a taxidermist's and stuff, that's what it looked like. His torso was very muscular.[8] I didn't get a good look at his hands because we didn't have the light actually on his body that much, you know, when we were trying to blind him in the eyes is when we actually shone the light on him outside. And he was bent over, stooped over. He had a pretty long stride[9] to him. His legs were long and muscular and his waist tapered. He did have actually a large waist. I didn't really get a good view of his back. He had brown hair, real good shape, wasn't ragged or nothing.

13 He was about nine feet [3 metres]. I'm six-two [2.3 metres], and he stood a good three feet [0.9 metres] taller than I was. Weight I'd say a thousand two hundred, something like that.

Threads

The average human stride is less than one metre long.

> For the first time I had a chance to appreciate the tremendous pressure with which the prints are made. Where they sank an inch deep in the sand my boots made only a heel print and a slightly flattened area in the center of the soles. To make a hole an inch [2.54 centimetres] deep I had to jump off a log about two feet high and land on one heel.
>
> *—John Green*

After You Read

Identify the circled reference words.

COMPREHENSION QUESTIONS

1. Write a good title for this passage.
2. Categorize the passage:
   - encyclopedia entry
   - tabloid article
   - newspaper article
   - transcription of a personal, taped account
   - written report about someone else's experience

3. What were the two people doing in ¶1? ______

4. In your own words, tell what happened in ¶4. ______

______

5. In your own words, tell what happened concerning a bottle in ¶6.

______

______

6. What was the creature's height in centimetres? (1 ft. = 12 in.; 1 in. = 2.54 cm)

______

What was its weight in kilograms? (1 lb =.4536 kg) ______

7. Have you ever slept out in the open as the two friends were planning to do?

After reading this account, would you want to? ______

CONTINUE YOUR CHART

Vocabulary

KEYWORDS

1. a good nine feet tall ¶1
2. glimpse ¶1
3. outline ¶3
4. glow ¶3
5. rush (someone) ¶4
6. sneak ¶5
7. dome ¶10
8. muscular ¶12
9. stride ¶12

The following words from the passage are very informal: *ruckus, split, busted,* … and *stuff*

KEYWORD EXERCISE

1. *EXAMPLE:* To me it looked *a good nine feet tall.*

Finish the sentences:
They stayed in Hawaii for a good ______.
I suppose my suitcase must weigh ______.

2. Which of the following are elements of the word *glimpse*?

hear see brief careful study

EXAMPLE: We thought we got a *glimpse* of it as it came down the hill.

3. Draw an *outline* of a classmate's profile (side view).

EXAMPLE: We could see its hair and the *outline* of it and the eyes.

4. Name three things that can *glow.*

   EXAMPLE: You know, like you'll shine another animal in the eyes, in the light they'll *glow.*

5. ***EXAMPLES:*** The thing got up and *rushed* us.
   The thing started *rushing* around.

   What's the main element of the verb *rush?*

6. ***EXAMPLE:*** We got out and *sneak* around there and no keys.

   (This verb is regular; most speakers would have said "sneaked.") Under what circumstances might a person *sneak*?

   What are some elements of the word *sneak*?

   quiet loud open secret

7. Name a world-famous *dome,* and tell where it is.

   EXAMPLE: His head was *dome* shaped.

8. ***EXAMPLE:*** His torso was very *muscular.*

   What part of speech is *muscular*?
   What's the noun form?
   Who's the most *muscular* person in your class?

9. Look at your measurements in the Preview Activity on page 214. Who has the longest *stride* in your class?
   How does it compare with a Bigfoot's *stride*? (Refer to your chart.)

REVIEW

Now that you've studied the vocabulary, reread or reskim the passage.

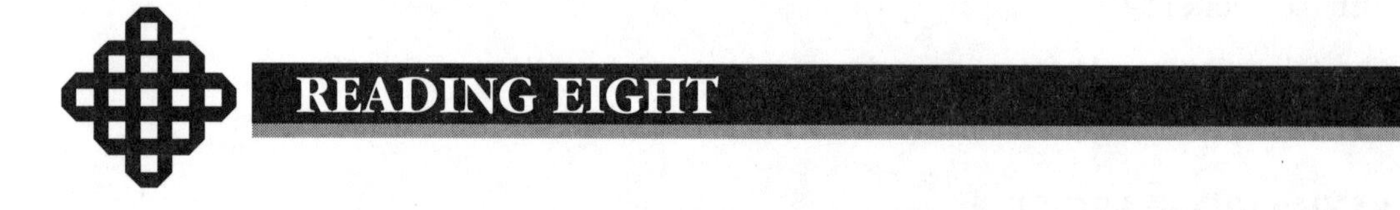

Reading process: Read the following passage as many times as you can in five minutes. Then try to answer the questions.

Threads

Sasquatches are very rarely seen together. Most reports are of a single animal only.

[TITLE] ____________________

On October 23 [1975], at 7:30 P.M., the police sergeant answered a call to a house where something had been heard pounding[1] on the back wall. The woman who lived there had gone next door to her son's house and there was no prowler to be found, but something had apparently torn some plastic that covered a back doorway, and there was a window broken. At 2:20 A.M. the same night something was again reported behind the house, and when the sergeant arrived, along with several other people, his spotlight quickly picked up what looked like a very large ape standing in the back yard. While someone else held the light on it the sergeant walked to within 35 feet [11 metres] of the animal, which made no attempt to run but crouched down[2] as he got near. There they stayed for "many minutes," while the sergeant wondered what to do next. He had a shotgun loaded[3] with buckshot but he was not sure if the thing was some kind of human, and if it wasn't, he didn't know how much buckshot it could take. He noted afterwards in his report that it was black in colour, would stand seven to eight feet [2.2 to 2.4 metres] tall and appeared to have no neck. It was covered with short hair, except on the face. He could see no ears. The eyes were small. It appeared to have four teeth larger than the others, two upper and two lower. Its nose was flat. He could see the nostrils. At the end there were seven people watching it, although only two others approached close to it. Then there were noises heard off in the dark at both sides, and the man with the spotlight swung it off to the right and called that there was "another one over there." At that point the sergeant decided to return to his patrol car.

After You Read

Identify the circled reference word.

COMPREHENSION QUESTIONS

1. Write a good title for the passage.
2. How many animals were seen? ______
3. Why didn't the policeman shoot? ______
4. Where was the owner of the house? ______
5. How helpful was the policeman to the homeowner? ______
6. Work with a partner. One of you play the part of the policeman, the other of the Bigfoot. Role play their behaviour as they confronted each other.

COMPLETING YOUR CHART

Add the information from this reading to your chart. Now it's complete. Compare it with two or three classmates' work, adding anything that you left out.

Vocabulary

KEYWORDS

1. pound
2. crouch down
3. load (a gun)

KEYWORD EXERCISE

1. ***EXAMPLE:*** The Bigfoot had been *pounding* on the back wall of a woman's house.

   To show that you understand this word, *pound* the wall or your desk. Which part of your body do you use if you *pound* something?

   ____

2. ***EXAMPLE:*** The animal *crouched down* as the policeman approached it.

   What is an antonym for *crouched down*? ______________

   Give two reasons why someone might *crouch down*.

   ______________ ______________

3. ***EXAMPLE:*** The policeman had *loaded* the shotgun with buckshot.

   Finish the sentences:
   We had forgotten to load ______________ with film.
   The movers ______________________________.

REVIEW

Now that you have studied the vocabulary, reread or reskim the passage.

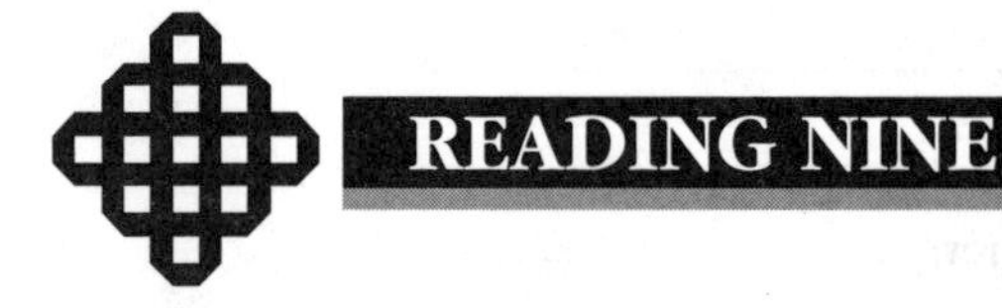

READING NINE

The following passage summarizes some of the important information about the Sasquatch that you learned from the previous readings in this chapter. It also presents several theories about the huge footprints many people have reported seeing.

[TITLE] ______________________________

1 Albert Ostman had been warned about the Sasquatch by his Indian guide for good reason. Legends told for centuries by the Indians of the Pacific Northwest have portrayed the creature as a kidnapper and even a cannibal.

2 Like the Ogopogo, however, the Sasquatch's image has changed over the years. According to hundreds of sightings[1] recorded in recent times, the Sasquatch flees instead of attacking, and seems to be more frightened of us humans than we are of him.

3 What are so many apparently sane people seeing? Like Bigfoot in the United States or the Yeti in the Himalayas, the Sasquatch is usually described as a hairy, smelly apelike animal that walks upright, is 2 to 2-½ metres [6½ to 8 feet] tall,

and weighs 300 to 400 kilograms [660 to 880 pounds]. People also report seeing footprints about half a metre [1.6 feet] long and almost ten centimetres [4 inches] deep, from which many plaster casts have been made.

4 Of course, there are many theories[2] to explain these footprints. One is that the Sasquatch is a subhuman primate that somehow survived the Ice Age. Another is that the footprints are just those of large bears. People who know bears disagree, saying that bears have smaller feet, with claws, not long toes, and do not walk long distances on two feet. And then there are those who believe that this is all the work of tricksters.[3]

5 Just the same, it's hard to imagine how so many footprints could be made so perfectly and so secretly all the way from Alaska to California.

After You Read

COMPREHENSION QUESTIONS

1. Write a good title for this passage.
2. How have Indian legends traditionally depicted the Sasquatch?

 ____

3. How has this image of the Sasquatch changed over the years?

 ____

4. How have various people tried to explain the gigantic footprints they saw?

 ____

VOCABULARY

KEYWORDS

1. sightings ¶2
2. theories ¶4
3. tricksters ¶4

KEYWORD EXERCISE

1. ***EXAMPLE:*** UFO *sightings* have been reported by many people not only in the United States but also in Canada.

 How is the word *sighting* used in this sentence? __________

2. ***EXAMPLE:*** *Theories* are ideas that try to explain something.

Do you have any *theories* about what happened to Albert Ostman?

____

____

Do you believe that he was really kidnapped by a family of Sasquatches?

____

3. *EXAMPLE:* Some people believe that the enormous footprints they found were created by *tricksters*.

   What do *tricksters* do? ______________________

4. Look at your measurements in the Preview Activity at the beginning of this chapter. How do the measurements compare with those of the Sasquatch? (Refer to your chart.)

ANTICIPATING TEST QUESTIONS

Write one of each for any of the readings in this chapter: multiple-choice, true-false, fill-in-the-blank, definition/identification, essay/discussion. Then work with a small group to "test" each other orally.

Threads

Which counts for more: The fact that no one can prove that Bigfoot exists, or the fact that no one can prove it doesn't?

Writing an Essay About Sasquatch

Choose one of the following alternatives:

1. *A Profile of Sasquatch*
   Using your chart for information, write a paper that is a *profile* of Sasquatch—that is, a composite of information about several of the categories you took notes on. You may use the name Sasquatch or Bigfoot, whichever you prefer.

2. *Argue For or Against the Existence of Sasquatch*
   Using the list that you helped put together of arguments for and against Bigfoot's existence, write a paper that explains your own position on this issue. Support your position with reasons and examples.

Writing process: First, freewrite about each category or argument. Then decide where to divide the information into paragraphs in the body of your paper. Next, write a first draft of the introduction, body paragraphs, and conclusion. At this point you should concentrate only on content and organization: try to develop your points well and clearly.

Trade papers with a partner (preferably someone who doesn't speak your native language). Encourage each other about the clear and interesting parts, and advise each other about points where the content and organization seem incomplete or confusing. Think carefully about what your partner says, and make your decisions about which advice to take. Then revise.

Now read your second draft carefully, paying attention to vocabulary, grammar, and punctuation. Think about your usual weaknesses when you write in English. Work with a partner again. Make decisions about which advice to take, and revise for a third draft. This is the one that you will hand in to your teacher.

If you ever see a Bigfoot or its tracks, take a photograph if you can. Write down everything you can about what happened, where, and when. Then contact the International Society of Cryptozoology, P.O. Box 43070, Tucson, Arizona 85733, U.S.A.

LEARNING STRATEGY

Personalizing: Using English outside the classroom improves your language skills.

Evaluating Learning Strategies

In this chapter you have been presented with several new learning strategies. Look back over them. Were there any that weren't especially helpful for you? What wasn't helpful about them? Which ones did you find especially helpful? Think about times and ways that you can keep using them in your future reading.

Evaluating Your Learning

	Very little	*Quite a bit*	*A lot*
You increased your vocabulary.	________	________	________
Your comprehension has improved.	________	________	________
You can identify different categories of writing.	________	________	________
You can argue both sides of an issue.	________	________	________
You can use a chart to compare information from different readings.	________	________	________
You learned what Bigfoot is (or is it?).	________	________	________

KEYWORDS FOR CHAPTER 8: BIGFOOT AND COMPANY

Verbs
claim
crouch
drawn by
fasten
flee
glow
load
mistreat
paralyze
pound
rekindle
relate
rush
sneak
stare
stay awake

Nouns
belongings
bush
captivity
composite
descendant
dome
glimpse
imagination
legend
outline
panic
pinch
scene
scepticism
sighting
specimen
stride
theory
tradition
trickster

Adverbs
accordingly
apparently
definitely
extremely
recklessly
slightly
typically
supposedly

Adjectives
aggressive
attributed to
erect
good & quantity
literal
muscular
oversized
peculiar
sufficient
unexplainable

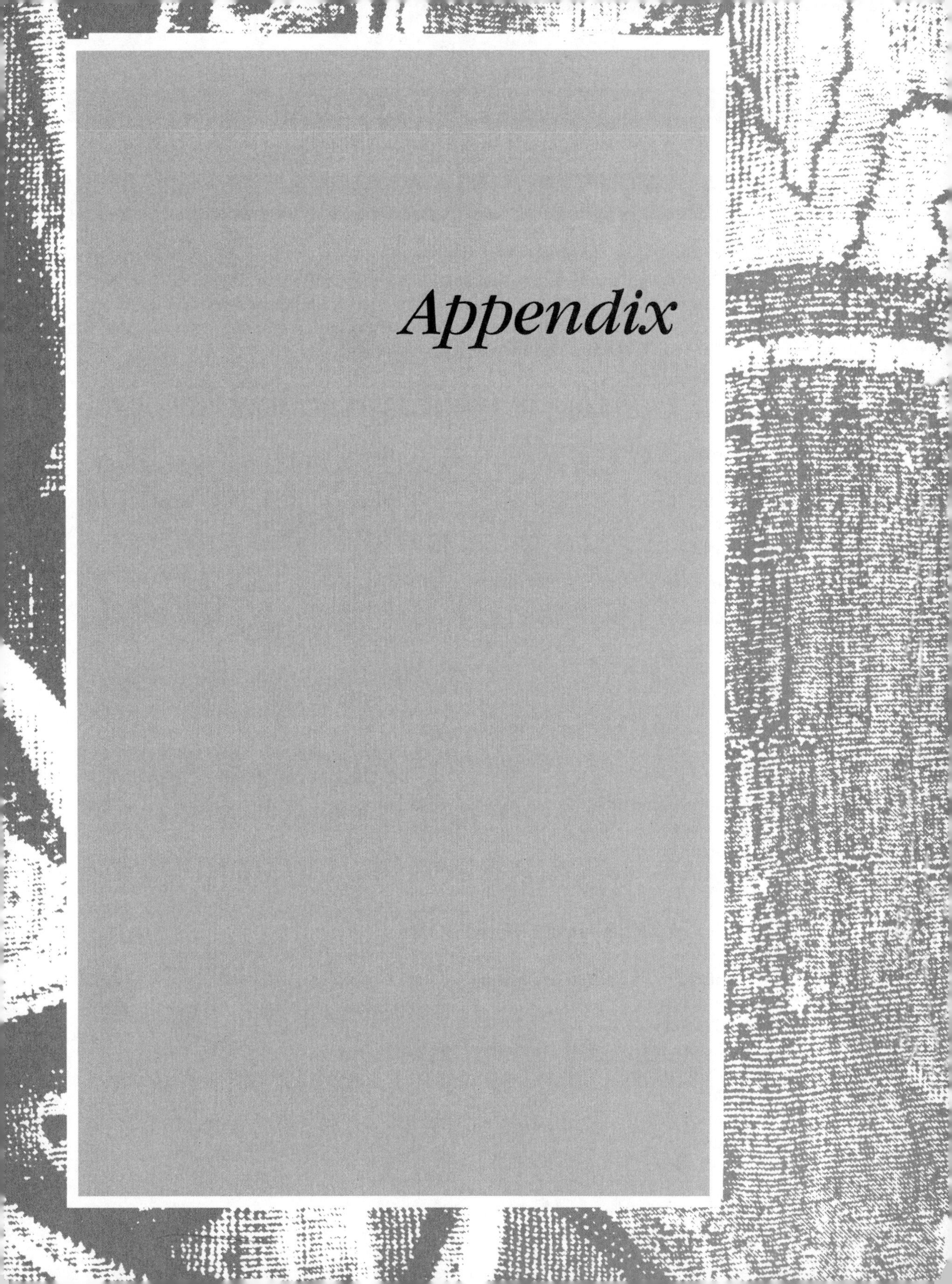

Appendix

ORGANIZATIONAL MARKERS

Chronological

Chronological is an adjective that means "by time." Chronological organization (also called "time order") means giving information in the order in which it happened. We use this organization when we are telling a story, giving historical facts, or describing a process. Here are some common *markers* or *signals* that will help you recognize chronological organization:

EVENTS IN A NARRATIVE, STEPS IN A PROCESS

to begin with	first	the first step is to	
second	next	then	
after that	after	afterward	later
finally	at last	the final step is to	
when			
in 1848	by 1830		
already	yet		
gradually			
eventually			

SIMULTANEOUS EVENTS

as
at the same time
during
simultaneously
while

OTHER TIME EXPRESSIONS

after	following
as long as	
as soon as	
before	prior to
by the time	
in	for
once	
until	
whenever	

ADDITIONAL INFORMATION

and additionally also as well furthermore moreover

Comparison, Contrast

COMPARISON

both
either/neither
in like manner
like
likewise
parallels
similarly

CONTRAST

although though even though while
but yet
in spite of the fact that despite the fact that regardless of the fact that
instead
in contrast
on the contrary
on the other hand
otherwise
still however nevertheless

Cause and Effect, Problem and Solution

as a result consequently therefore because of this thus so
because since as because of
be responsible for contribute to result in lead to
result from be a consequence of be due to be a result of
so much/many … that such … that

Listing Reasons, Examples, Characteristics, or Features

e.g. for example for instance such as
The reason is
The answer is
furthermore
additionally

Restatement or Equivalence

i.e.
to put it another way
in other words

PHOTO CREDITS

1, Deborah Davis/PhotoEdit; **11,** Gabrielle Roy/public domain; **21,** "Premiere Communion." Miyuki Tanobe, *Québec, Je T'Aime/I Love You*. (Montreal: Tundra Books of Montreal, 1976). Reprinted with permission of the author; **31,** Reprinted with permission of Bethune Memorial House; **35,** Reprinted with permission of the Banting Museum and Education Centre; **39,** Reprinted with permission of David Suzuki; **45,** Pierre Beaudoin/Ponopresse Internationale Inc.; **48,** chart of Native American housing and clothing. Excerpted from *The World Book Encyclopedia*. Copyright © 1994 World Book, Inc. By permission of the publisher; **50,** map of Native American tribes. From NATIVE AMERICAN TESTIMONY by Peter Nabokov. Copyright © 1978, 1979, 1991 by Peter Nabokov; Foreword copyright © 1991 by Vine Deloria, Jr. Used by permission of Viking Penguin, a division of Penguin Books USA Inc.; **68,** Trail of Tears map, from NATIVE AMERICAN TESTIMONY by Peter Nabokov. Copyright © 1978, 1979, 1991 by Peter Nabokov; Foreword copyright © 1991 by Vine Deloria, Jr. Used by permission of Viking Penguin, a division of Penguin Books USA Inc.; **74,** Gregoire/Schwartz/Ponopresse Internationale Inc.; **87,** McCarthy/Ponopresse Internationale Inc.; **97,** McCarthy/Ponopresse Internationale Inc.; **101,** Myrleen Ferguson Cate/PhotoEdit; **104,** Jeff Zaruba/The Stock Market; **110,** McCarthy/Ponopresse Internationale Inc.; **116,** McCarthy/Ponopresse Internationale Inc.; **123,** Alinari/Art Resource, NY; **125, 126, 127,** The Centennial Museum, The University of Texas at El Paso; **133, 137, 145** Reprinted from *Wolf-Children and Feral Man* by the Rev. J.A.L. Singh and Professor Robert M. Zingg © 1942. Reprinted in 1966 by Harper & Row, Inc.; **155,** John Neubauer; **187,** Botero/Ponopresse Internationale Inc.; **191,** Gamma/Ponopresse Internationale Inc.; **195,** Stills/Ponopresse Internationale Inc.; **201,** Camera Press/Ponopresse Internationale Inc.; **213,** Photo: Patterson/Gimlin. Copyright © Rene Dahinden/1967; **223,** Copyright © 1983 by Myra Shackley. Reprinted by generous permission of the author; **226,** Bigfoot track. Blue Creek Mountain, California. Copyright © Rene Dahinden/1967; **239,** AP/Wide World Photos. Reprinted by permission.

TEXT CREDITS

14–15, George Woodcock. "Gabrielle Roy: A Writer for Canada," *100 Great Canadians*. (Edmonton: Hurtig Publishers, 1980). Reprinted with permission.
20–22, Miyuki Tanobe, *Quebec, Je T'Aime/I Love You*. (Montreal: Tundra Books of Montreal, 1976). Reprinted with permission of the author.
25–27, Diane Thompson, "Canadian Women Over Four Centuries" Ministry of Skills, Training, and Labour (British Columbia), 1983. Reprinted with permission.
30–32, Michael Webb, "Norman Bethune: Doctor Under Fire." Reproduced with permission from Addison Wesley Longman Ltd.
34–36, George Woodcock. "Frederick Banting: Discoverer of Insulin," *100 Great Canadians*. (Edmonton: Hurtig Publishers, 1980). Reprinted with permission.
39–40, "David Suzuki: Canada's Popularizer of Science." Excerpted from *Current Biography Yearbook*. Copyright © 1995. Reprinted by special arrangement with The H.W. Wilson Company.
59–61, Beth Brandt, "Native Origins," *Mohawk Trail*. (Ithaca, N.Y.: Firebrand Books, 1984). Reprinted with permission.
63–63, Chief Dan George, "My Very Good Dear Friends." *The Only Good Indian: Essays by Canadian Indians*. Edited by Waubageshig (Toronto: New Press, 1970).
74-76, Carol Geddes, "Growing Up Native," *Homemakers Magazine,* October, 1990. Reprinted with permission of the author.
92–93, Excerpted from KEEPERS OF THE EARTH: NATIVE AMERICAN STORIES AND ENVIRONMENTAL ACTIVITIES FOR CHILDREN, copyright © 1988 by Michael J. Caduto and Joseph Bruchac. Reprinted by permission of Fulchram Publishing.
98–99, Adapted from THE WORLD BOOK ENCYCLOPEDIA. Copyright © 1993 World Book, Inc. By permission of the publisher.
110–111, Susan Semenak, "Stressing Teamwork in Schools: Quebec Tries Cooperative Education," *The Gazette* (Montreal), March 28, 1995. Reprinted with permission.
115–116, Robert Alex Moerman, "Special Education Program Makes the Grade," *The Ottawa Citizen,* May 10, 1994. Reprinted with permission of the author.

167–168, Arnold Rincover, "Parenting Trouble Lies in Childhood Deception," *The Ottawa Citizen,* June 9, 1995. Reprinted by permission of the author.
190–191, Susan Sontag, "Women's Beauty: Put Down or Power Source?" Copyright © Susan Sontag, 1975. Reprinted with the permission of The Wylie Agency, Inc.
195–196, Nora Underwood, John de Mont, Mary Nemeth, and Shaffin Shariff, "Is Bigger Better?: North American Society Is Breast-Obsessed." *Macleans*, March 9, 1992. Reprinted with permission.
200–201, Merilyn Simonds Mohr, "The Beauty Myth," *Equinox*, Nov-Dec. 1992.
204–206, Jane E. Brody, "Notions of Beauty Transcend Culture: New Study Suggests." Copyright © 1994 by The New York Times Co. Reprinted by permission.
216–218, "Captured Bigfoot Can Talk!" Copyright © by Rick Tracy, 1991. Reprinted by generous permission of WEEKLY WORLD NEWS.
221, From the *World Book Encyclopedia.* Copyright © 1994 World Book, Inc. By permission of the publisher.
222, From the *Encyclopedia Americana,* 1990 Edition. Copyright © 1990 by Grolier Incorporated. Reprinted by permission.
225–226, Reprinted by generous permission of Nelson (B.C.) *Daily News.*
230–231, M. Carole Henderson, "Monsters of the West: The Sasquatch and the Ogopogo." From *Folklore of Canada* (pp. 251-53) by Edith Fowke, 1976. Used by permission of McClelland & Stewart, Inc., Toronto, The Canadian Publishers.
234–235, "Sasquatch." *Legendary Creatures Souvenir Edition.* Reprinted courtesy of Canada Post Corporation.
238–240, "My Friend Started Talking ..." Copyright © 1980 by John Green, Cheam Publishing Ltd. Reprinted by generous permission of the editor.
242–243, "On October 23 ..." Copyright © 1980 by John Green, Cheam Publishing Ltd. Reprinted by generous permission of the author.
244–245, "Sasquatch." *Legendary Creatures Souvenir Edition.* Reprinted courtesy of Canada Post Corporation.

NOTES

NOTES

NOTES

Visit us on the Web at **http://www.nelson.com**
You can also send us your comments via e-mail at **college_arts_hum@nelson.com**

To the owner of this book

We hope that you have enjoyed *Thresholds in Reading,* and we would like to know as much about your experiences with this text as you would care to offer. Only through your comments and those of others can we learn how to make this a better text for future readers.

School _______________ Your instructor's name ______________________

Course __________ Was the text required? ______ Recommended? _____

1. What did you like the most about *Thresholds in Reading?*

____

____

____

2. How useful was this text for your course?

____

____

____

3. Do you have any recommendations for ways to improve the next edition of this text?

____

____

____

4. In the space below or in a separate letter, please write any other comments you have about the book. (For example, please feel free to comment on reading level, writing style, terminology, design features, and learning aids.)

____

____

____

____

Optional

Your name ____________________________ Date ______________

May Nelson Canada quote you, either in promotion for *Thresholds in Reading* or in future publishing ventures?

Yes ______ No ______

Thanks!

PLEASE TAPE SHUT. DO NOT STAPLE.
TAPE SHUT
TAPE SHUT
FOLD HERE
Nelson
MAIL POSTE
Canada Post Corporation
Société canadienne des postes
Postage paid
if mailed in Canada
Business Reply
Port payé
si posté au Canada
Réponse d'affaires
0066102399 01
0066102399-M1K5G4-BR01
ITP NELSON
MARKET AND PRODUCT DEVELOPMENT
PO BOX 60225 STN BRM B
TORONTO ON M7Y 2H1
TAPE SHUT
TAPE SHUT